D0060954

GALILEAN UPSTARTS

GALILEAN UPSTARTS

Jesus' First

Followers

According

to Q

LEIF E. VAAGE

TRINITY PRESS INTERNATIONAL
Valley Forge, Pennsylvania

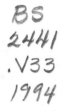

BS
2441
.V33
1994

Copyright © 1994 Leif E. Vaage

All rights reserved. No part of this book may be reproduced, stored in a
retrieval system, or transmitted, in any form or by any means, electronic,
mechanical, photocopying, recording, or otherwise, without the written
permission of the publisher.

Trinity Press International, P.O. Box 851, Valley Forge, PA 19482-0851

Library of Congress Cataloging-in-Publication Data

Vaage, Leif E.
    Galilean upstarts : Jesus' first followers according to Q / by
Leif E. Vaage. — 1st ed.
        p. cm.
    Includes bibliographical references and index.
    ISBN 1-56338-090-0
    1. Evangelists (Bible) 2. Jesus Christ—Friends and associates.
    3. Palestine—Social life and customs—To 70 A.D. 4. Q hypothesis
    (Synoptics criticism)   I. Title.
    BS2441.V33   1994
    226'.067—dc20   94-9100
                                                                            CIP

Printed in the United States of America

94   95   96   97   98   99   10   9   8   7   6   5   4   3   2   1

JESUIT - KRAUSS - McCORMICK - LIBRARY
1100 EAST 55th STREET
CHICAGO, ILLINOIS 60615

For Rivkah, Liv, and María
bendita trinidad

Contents

Preface and
Acknowledgments

D IRT ARCHEOLOGISTS are routinely encouraged to publish "preliminary reports" of their ongoing investigations. It is understood
that these initial efforts at interpretation are not the final word, but the
publication of such reports nonetheless serves the useful purpose of both
putting into general circulation as soon as possible what has been un-
covered as well as promoting wider discussion of the same material's
potential significance. It is as a preliminary report of this sort that I, too,
as a practicing "archeologist" of the New Testament synoptic tradition,
have sent the present book to the publisher, fully aware of the many
lines of inquiry in it yet to be developed. But sufficient evidence of the
specific social culture of Q's formative stratum has accumulated on my
desk to make me believe that an initial statement of its meaning might
be warranted.

The production of the book has its own archeology. Most relevant,
perhaps, to the tale of its successive occupations and preoccupations are
the years (1987–91) that my family and I lived and worked in Lima,
Peru. It was during this time that the substance of the book was first
conceived and roughed out. These years happened to coincide with
the incredible debacle of the APRA government under President Alán
García, the internal collapse and international isolation of the Peruvian economy, a drastic correlative deterioration of the country's social
infrastructure, and not surprisingly the increased success of the uncivil
war being waged by the "fundamentalist" Maoist insurrectionary movement, Sendero Luminoso, and the reactionary "forces of order" since the
"return" of electoral "democracy" to the land in 1980.

Many things were either not available to me during these years as a
scholar of Christian origins or possible as a human being in the midst
of an accelerating spiral of multiple shortages, general uncertainty, and

personal and political violence: a steady-state of interruption and *desequilibrio*. At the same time, other things became increasingly clear to me in this setting, both as a scholar of Christian origins and as a human being. Such contextual realities have undoubtedly left their mark on the following work. They are in large measure responsible for whatever strengths it may have, and account in part for certain of its weaknesses.

Before living in Peru, as a doctoral candidate in New Testament at the Claremont Graduate School, I began research in the area of "Q" under the tutelage of Prof. James M. Robinson, to whom I here express my deep gratitude for his many kindnesses. The dissertation written at that time under his supervision forms part of the substance of a number of the chapters of this book. I also wish to acknowledge the importance of numerous conversations enjoyed both as a graduate student and subsequently on diverse topics with Prof. Burton L. Mack. Finally, to Profs. Ronald F. Hock and Edward O'Neil and the "Hellenistic Text Seminar" that met biweekly under their leadership at the latter's home, I am indebted among many things for induction into the study of Greco-Roman Cynicism.

Since we returned to Canada from Peru, a number of other persons have also been extremely helpful in the final effort to prepare this book for publication. John Dominic Crossan read an earlier draft of the work, and his editorial suggestions, however hard for me to hear at the time, have all proven exceedingly apt. Wendy J. Cotter likewise reviewed the same version of the book and helped to identify both what was lacking in it and what did not need to be there. John S. Kloppenborg has been his usual collegial self and assisted me in too many ways to name. Thanks are also due to Alicia Batten, who helped out at the end.

There are, of course, still more people without whom I could do nothing. I will mention only three of them in conclusion, trusting that the rest will not mistake my silence at this point for lack of regard. One is my wife, Rivkah: *en todo tumulto te estimo mucho.* The other two are our daughters, Liv Johanna and María Siobháin, household upstarts whose chthonic ethos, strategies of domestic resistance, ad hoc ideologies of righteousness, and growing critique of parental authority daily reconfirm the creative value and destabilizing joy of a gentle anarchy. To them this book is dedicated.

Toronto, 30 August 1993
The Beheading of St. John the Baptist

Abbreviations

ANRW	*Aufstieg und Niedergang der römischen Welt*
APhilos	*L'Année philosophique*
ARW	*Archiv für Religionswissenschaft*
AssS	*Assemblées du Seigneur*
ASR	*American Sociological Review*
AU	*Der altsprachliche Unterricht*
B&O	*Bibbia e Oriente*
Bib	*Biblica*
BZ	*Biblische Zeitschrift*
CBQ	*Catholic Biblical Quarterly*
CHM	*Cahiers d'Histoire Mondiale*
CJ	*Classical Journal*
DHI	*Dictionary of the History of Ideas*
EClás	*Estudios clásicos*
ETL	*Ephemerides Theologicae Lovanienses*
EvT	*Evangelische Theologie*
Exp	*Expositor*
ExpTim	*Expository Times*
GTJ	*Grace Theological Journal*
HTR	*Harvard Theological Review*

IDBSup	*Interpreter's Dictionary of the Bible Supplement*
IJE	*International Journal of Ethics*
IQP	International Q Project
ITS	*Indian Theological Studies*
JAAR	*Journal of the American Academy of Religion*
JAC	*Jahrbuch für Antike und Christentum*
JBL	*Journal of Biblical Literature*
JHI	*Journal of the History of Ideas*
JSJ	*Journal for the Study of Judaism*
JSNT	*Journal for the Study of the New Testament*
JSS	*Journal of Semitic Studies*
JTS	*The Journal of Theological Studies*
JTSA	*Journal of Theology for South Africa*
KBW	*Katholisches Bibelwerk*
LCL	Loeb Classical Library
NJA	*Neue Jahrbücher für das classische Altertum*
NovT	*Novum Testamentum*
NTS	*New Testament Studies*
RB	*Revue biblique*
RE	*Real-Encyclopädie der classischen Altertumswissenschaft*
RevQ	*Revue de Qumran*
RGG	*Religion in Geschichte und Gegenwart*
RHPR	*Revue d'histoire et de philosophie religieuses*
RM	*Reinisches Museum*
RMM	*Revue de metaphysique et de morale*
RPh	*Revue de philologie, de literature, et d'histoire ancienne*
RSRev	*Religious Studies Review*
SBF	*Studii Biblici Franciscani Liber Annus*
SBLSP	*Society of Biblical Literature Seminar Papers*
ScEccl	*Sciences ecclésiastiques*

SF	*Sociological Focus*
SIFC	*Studi Italiani di Filologia Classica*
SNTW	*Studien zum Neuen Testament und seiner Welt*
ST	*Studia Theologica*
STr.-B.	Strack-Billerbeck
ThZ	*Theologische Zeitschrift*
TJT	*Toronto Journal of Theology*
TLZ	*Theologische Literaturzeitung*
TS	*Theological Studies*
TTZ	*Trierer theologische Zeitschrift*
USQR	*Union Seminary Quarterly Review*
ZNW	*Zeitschrift für die neutestamentliche Wissenschaft*
ZPE	*Zeitschrift für Papyrologie und Epigraphik*
ZTK	*Zeitschrift für Theologie und Kirche*
ZWT	*Zeitschrift für wissenschaftliche Theologie*

Social Identity, Historiography, Q, and Cynicism

T HIS BOOK seeks to sketch as concretely as possible a social profile of Jesus' first followers in Galilee, the earliest form of Christianity known to us, as attested by the initial literary stratum of Q, the "other" source-text used by Matthew and Luke besides Mark in the composition of their gospels.[1] The present work can be read from a number of different points of view: as an exercise in the discipline of historical reconstruction; as a more ambitious effort to describe the generative situation in life (*Sitz im Leben*) of a particular early Christian document; or, most happily, as a challenging contribution to modern New Testament scholarship's larger scientific mythology of Christian origins.

Given the fragmentary state of Q's preservation, the following portrait of "the first gospel's" initial tradents is necessarily composite, more akin to a series of snapshots than a complete photographic study.[2] Nevertheless, in my opinion, the various *aperçus* assembled here reveal enough of the specific character of Jesus' first disciples for a number of significant conclusions to be drawn about these "Galilean upstarts'" social identity.

Social Identity

For the purposes of this book, by "social identity" or profile I mean simply a coordinated (albeit partial) discussion of the original ethos of the persons whom Q's formative stratum represents (chapter one), their correlative elaboration of this ethos in the form of an ethics (chapter two), the production of an ideology (chapter three) and social critique (chapter four), as well as the developing memory tradition of the group's "founding fathers" (chapter five). Without purporting to suggest that these five features together constitute the essential elements of every social description, they have seemed sufficient in the present case, both in terms of the diversity of data that they provide and their mutual cohesiveness, to permit at least the outline of a well-rounded image to emerge. At the same time, excessive exaggeration of the significance of any one aspect of the document "Q" has not been allowed to skew perception.[3] Like Cubist painting, the resulting montage of distinct perspectives and competing distortions may occasionally beg for further clarification. But the overall effect will hopefully be as fulsome in its insights, and the final result comparable to the sense one has after viewing any object from a number of complementary points of view.[4]

Social anthropologists and their kin continue to debate among themselves what exactly the "main ingredients" are of social identity as such.[5] It seems certain, however, that the human subjects at the center of this open question are at least many things at once: what Renato Rosaldo, regarding the process of ritual, has called the "busy intersection" of changing social roles, variable bodily desires, acquired aspirations, loss, and conflict making up the concrete social self.[6] Any profile, therefore, of a group of persons like the Q people that aspires to some measure of descriptive integrity must not proceed by first trying to boil down their multifaceted collectivity to the working out of a few primary mechanisms, basic needs, or principal values. We should rather seek to incorporate as many of the variables as we can belonging to human "experience" as such, both in general and in particular, into our "historical" depiction of these "fictive" characters.[7] In this regard, the virtues of a good novel or story are finally more apropos the present project of social description than would be the methodologically reduced categories of so-called "social-scientific" explanation.[8]

No comprehensive theory of social identity is here assumed, though I admit to feeling a certain attraction for Claude Lévi-Strauss's "savage mind," especially his description of "bricolage" as the "science of the concrete."[9] Like the later authors in Eric Auerbach's survey of "realistic" fiction, I have tried to incorporate into the present work enough of the "stuff" of ordinary mundane existence to persuade a modern critical audience that the final version of the tale to be told corresponds more or less to what we otherwise may know of human life.[10] To make yet another comparison, like a Near Eastern dirt archeologist digging up a promising site, I have attempted in this book to discern in the fragile remains and mounded debris of Q's textual heap the specific shape of its fleeting formative culture.

I use, in fact, the figure of a dirt archeologist in some earnest. First, the stratigraphical analysis of any literary document like Q can be compared in more than one way to the excavation of a multilayered tell.[11] More importantly, the contemporary reader of every ancient text like Q, as a dirt archeologist, can develop only on the basis of the material markings displayed before him or her an account of the persons who once left these traces behind them. The opaque configurations of stone and ink, brick and letter are deciphered through a series of heuristic and conventional comparisons in the interests of producing as full a description as possible of the type of human social formation now preserved for us only in this fashion. The "meaning" of the text is thus the cultural world to which the artifact both once belonged and now is simultaneously made to recall.

I have purposefully not sought to derive this book's profile of Jesus' first followers in Galilee from among the structural options established by social historians of first-century B.C.E./C.E. Roman Syria/Palestine, locating the initial tradents of Q on the configured map wherever they might seem best to fit in. Not that I find such social histories unhelpful or irrelevant in any way. Quite the contrary! They establish the general parameters within which all social life at the eastern end of the ancient Mediterranean world occurred. But almost by definition, the same histories seldom succeed in painting more than a general picture of the specific cultural groups they ostensibly describe. The accounts produced typically focus on the "normal" patterns of ancient life and the so-called "average" person. Except as biography, social histories of this sort tend to exclude from serious consideration all particular or peculiar phenomena, necessarily understanding them as "anomalies" or "standard deviations." Such "glitches" in society "at large" are apparently unable to be seen as noteworthy, except insofar as they provide a possible point of departure for the discernment of new patterns.[12]

My interest, however, in this book is precisely to describe as specifically as possible the cultural contour of the particular group of persons whom the singular text of Q's formative literary stratum may be said to represent. If the resulting portrait must cohere to some degree with what we otherwise may know about the life of contiguous groups of persons in the same general social environment in antiquity, exactly what kind of people the initial tradents of Q were cannot be determined on these grounds alone or even primarily.[13]

Historiography

I spoke above of this book as a contribution to modern New Testament scholarship's "scientific mythology" of Christian origins. I should probably not have used such flamboyant language, given that I cannot develop here the view of history and historiography implied by such a reference to my general field of inquiry. And yet it is important in introducing the contents of this book to acknowledge my conviction that every effort at "reconstruction" of the past is first of all an instance of cultural construction in the present, a form of that mixture of story-telling and normative evaluation otherwise known as myth-making. Whatever the reality of the past may be, it remains "real" only to the extent that it has first been recalled and thus recreated in a particular time and place by specific persons for particular purposes: in the case of this book, by myself as, among other things, a member of the North American guild of professional biblical scholars for the various academic and non-academic constituencies that we serve and aim to please and influence.[14]

The writing of history as "history" is one of the ways in which "our" modern North Atlantic post-enlightenment cultures continue to practice the apparently inevitable, because necessary, habit of all known human communities of establishing a common identity for themselves through the narration of both their and others' experience. The idea itself of history describes not only the narrative framework within which "we" currently conduct a spate of specific technical investigations, but also purports to reveal to us the truth of our own modernity (or postmodernity); a notion which, if not unquestionable regarding both its accuracy and the value judgments that accompany it, nonetheless still marks most "educated" persons' self-understanding of their social situation in the world, i.e., their sense of who they are and how they got to be that way, doing thus exactly what myths are otherwise supposed to do in "underdeveloped" or more "traditional" parts of the globe, namely, provide the contours of a corporate social identity.[15]

Without purporting to resolve here the abiding question of what "myth" is, I should at least state my own understanding of the term. Myths, as I understand them, are essentially the stories that we tell each other about ourselves and/or others from the perspective of ourselves in order to situate ourselves and others in a particular time and place. If every story is potentially a myth, a myth itself may be more narrowly defined as that story or set of stories whose developed style of narration matters more to most of "us" at any given moment than other discursively similar productions in a specific cultural setting, due to the various paralinguistic acts of social exchange associated with its telling. Myths, in other words, are those stories in whose recounting, both when and how, there is plainly a "public" investment, versus, for example, the social significance of "literature" or "folk-tales," to whose enjoyment and utility a similar political value is not normally ascribed, whatever their specific cultural power and importance may be.[16]

To call the modern "historical" version of such mythic narration "scientific," as I did above, is simply to acknowledge the continuing importance of this particular "taste" of truth among ourselves as con-sumers of the histories we write: the role that certain modes of analysis and the attention paid to certain types of detail play in our assuming that the stories that we tell as "history" are finally realistic, responsible, verisimilar, and able to be proven or at least debated. Hence the need, for example, to document whatever can be attested in this fashion as a check on "pure" invention.[17]

At the same time, we acknowledge and even welcome the enduring possibility of writing "revisionist history," an example of which this book would gladly be. At stake in every such project is the ongoing constitution of a given social body's shared cultural memory. The peren-nial need to "update" previous accounts of the past makes clear how volatile this open-ended process of recurring recollection is, even in its most scientific mode. We might, in fact, compare it to the RAM in a computer.[18]

At one time, it was thought that "modern" historiography should es-chew the ruse of narrative. There is always more than one side to a story, more than one way to frame a sequence, more than one way to present the facts; each, moreover, bears in its train a set of ideological presup-positions and interests. Uncritical narratives naively, official narratives willfully, blur this consciousness with the implied necessity of their pro-gressive movement. Rightfully fearful of the lurking power to harm in all such master-plots, not a few scholars have therefore sought to "do his-tory" in non-narrative form, i.e., in a "more critical" fashion. A more creative response, in my opinion, would have been to develop instead a thoroughly self-critical style of narrative historiography, continuing to affirm thereby the myth-making function inherent in all such activity, but making of it as our own poetic practice a discourse permeated by internal — and interminable — debate.[19]

In this book, I am especially interested in the problem of charac-terization for such a project, both at the level of descriptive category formation and at the level of discursive performance.[20] How we depict, elaborate, and thus ascribe a specific value or "name" to a particular "text" (both utterance and writing), person, group, action, and setting (whether physical or temporal), determines deeply what we simultane-ously suppose that the story means in which these terms occur, i.e., the nature of its significance and the structure of our relation to it, both as a story and regarding the reality it relates. Indeed, if we may trust a certain twisting of Aristotle's poetics, after the framing of chronology or plot, characterization would be the second most important topic for the self-conscious myth-making historian to consider.[21] For it is charac-terization, more than anything else, that shapes the way in which we come to understand, disregard, remember, abuse, and respect the desig-nated "objects" under our attention, the nascent "subjects" established by our studious gaze, to wit, the social profile of the persons whom Q's formative stratum will soon be made to represent.[22]

New Testament Scholarship

With these remarks on historiography, I mean to recall the heated discussion that first greeted Rudolf Bultmann's early and influential essay on "The New Testament and Mythology," hopefully not to reopen that debate, but to reframe it.[23] What Bultmann principally meant to promote as "demythologizing" is essentially what I understand a self-critical historiography of Christian origins to entail, namely, the recognition and affirmation of a fundamental cultural distance between ourselves as so-called "modern" readers of the Bible and the so-called "ancient" texts that constitute the focus of our inquiry. Despite the fact that the actual context of the New Testament is always inevitably our own, given that the text as such does not exist anywhere other than where we, its readers, are, a "self-critical" or "demythologizing" reading of the New Testament takes as its basic methodological point of departure for all further commentary and elaboration the essential otherness of this text's ascribed originary context. We agree, in other words, to read the New Testament first as an alien writing.[24]

At the same time, by affirming that the early Christian histories we write as self-critical narrative are still a mode of myth-making, I disavow the tendency in Bultmann's program of demythologizing to imagine that there is somehow a kerygma, a message, a clarity of truth and persuasion — the object of Bultmann's mystical *Sachkritik* — that exists to be achieved beyond the epistemic murk of telling stories and asking questions about them.[25] The pertinent methodological issue is, therefore, not whether New Testament scholars should "mythologize," but how. The critical writing of early Christian histories should be engaged in precisely as "our" contemporary mode of myth-making, at whose heart recurring dissent and internal discrepancy are to be expected and indeed encouraged, at the same time that such programmatic "auto-alterity" self-consciously remains part of an ongoing effort at cultural construction that myth-making otherwise typically supports.[26]

Regarding once more the tradition of New Testament scholarship, it is important to underscore the documentary bias of this book over against certain previous habits of historical description that have dominated scholarly work in the area. I have in mind specifically the analytical practices of form-criticism and tradition-history, both of which purport to be able to say something about the shape and transmission of early Christian materials at an "oral" stage of circulation before the texts at our disposal were first written down and subsequently transformed redactionally as early Christian literature. Unlike scholars who read the New Testament in this fashion, I do not presume in this book to know anything "beyond" or "behind" the text of Q's formative stratum: neither who the historical Jesus was or what he might have said, nor the nature of the intervening period supposed to have extended between him and the first layer of Q, during which interval the different sayings assembled in the document were ostensibly passed on and developed.[27]

Both form-critical and tradition-historical analyses of the New Testament treat the individual "units" of these different writings as though such discursive "bits" could somehow still be seen "floating" unbound by their current contextual moorings on ever fluid "streams" of tradition. Even if this were a plausible theory of the way in which early Christian materials were first generated and enlarged, the same approach is finally impossible to apply as a concrete method of critical interpretation, insofar as its results cannot intelligibly be debated and/or persuasively demonstrated, being ultimately based upon either the institutionally enforced acceptance (or rejection) of the opinion of certain authoritative handbooks, or what the individual investigator and his or her like-minded colleagues "can imagine" as originally conceivable.[28] I have therefore preferred in this book to remain within the perhaps less adventuresome, but minimally assessable limits or "documentary bias" of a strictly source- and redaction-critical perspective.[29]

Q

Each chapter of the book revolves around interpretation of a discrete set of sayings from the "lost" sayings-gospel "Q." I obviously assume, therefore, that Q once existed and that, furthermore, the text of Q as used by Matthew and Luke in the composition of their gospels can still be recovered.[30] I also assume the basic validity of John S. Kloppenborg's recent work, *The Formation of Q*, in which, developing original insights by James M. Robinson and Helmut Koester, Kloppenborg distinguishes between two (in fact, three) distinct compositional strata in the document.[31] It is Q's formative layer that recalls Jesus' first followers in Galilee, the earliest embodiment of "Christianity" known to us.[32]

These assumptions are hardly self-evident. They admit debate and remain contested to various degrees by different New Testament scholars. But neither are they simply ad hoc statements of belief. They reflect instead the results of a series of specific developments within a particular tradition of New Testament scholarship. Full confidence in the validity of these assumptions will require at least familiarity with, if not a mastery of, the multiple analyses and competing observations now synthesized with deceptive ease in the symbol "Q" and recently elaborated in its stratigraphical description. At the same time, to dismiss, as it were, out of hand any investigation based upon these assumptions as being "too speculative," because "Q" is "hypothetical" and the delineation of its different strata doubly so, without disputing the validity of the foundational research on which such an investigation rests, would simply be irresponsible.

Recent work has demonstrated, to my mind convincingly, that Q was originally written in Greek.[33] A general consensus furthermore exists that Luke has largely preserved the sayings of Q in their original order.[34] For this reason, it is now conventional in North America, and will be the practice throughout this book, to refer to all Q sayings, whatever their original location in the document, using Lukan versification, sometimes preceded by the siglum "Q," sometimes not.[35]

Reconstruction of the original text of Q remains an incomplete task. Regarding the specific sayings discussed in this book, whenever possible I have used as the basis of my own translation into English the critical Greek text established by the International Q Project, always indicating and explaining where and why I am in occasional disagreement with its conclusions.[36] I am responsible for all other decisions made in this regard.[37]

The probable content and order of sayings in the final version of Q is as follows:[38]

Q/Luke	Matthew
3:7–9	3:7–10
3:16b–17	3:11–12
4:1–13	4:1–11
6:20b–23	5:3–12
6:27–36	5:38–48
6:37–38	7:1–2
6:39	15:14
6:40	10:24–25
6:41–42	7:3–5
6:43–45	7:16–20/12:33–35
6:46–49	7:21–27
7:1–10	8:5–13
7:18–28	11:2–11
16:16	11:12–13
7:31–35	11:16–19
9:57–60	8:19–22

10:2–12	9:37–38; 10:7–15
10:13–15	11:20–24
10:16	10:40
10:21–22	11:25–27
10:23–24	13:16–17
11:2–4	6:9–13
11:9–13	7:7–11
11:14–23	12:22–30/9:32–34
11:24–26	12:43–45
11:16, 29–32	12:38–42/16:1–2a, 4
11:33	5:14–15
11:34–36	6:22–23
11:39b–52	23:4, 13, 23–36
12:2–9	10:26–33
12:10	12:32
12:11–12	10:19
12:22–31	6:25–33
12:33–34	6:19–21
12:39–46	24:43–51
12:49–53	10:34–36
12:54–56	16:2–3
12:57–59	5:25–26
13:18–21	13:31–33
13:24–27	7:13–14, 22–23
13:28–30	8:11–12; 20:16
13:34–35	23:37–39
14:11; 18:14b	23:12
14:16–24	22:1–10
14:26–27; 17:33	10:37–39
14:34–35	5:13
15:4–7	18:12–13
16:13	6:24
16:17	5:18
16:18	5:32
17:1–2	18:6–7
17:3–4	18:15, 21–22
17:6	17:20b
17:23–30, 34–37	24:26–28, 38–41
19:12–26	25:14–30
22:28–30	19:28b

In my judgment, the formative stratum of Q contained the following sayings:[39]

>   6:20b–21, 27–49
>   7:24–26, 28a, 33–34
>   9:57–60
>   10:3–6, 9–11, 16
>   11:2–4, 9–13, 14–20, 24–26, 33–36, 39b–48, 52
>   12:2–7, 22–31, 33–34
>   13:18–21, 24
>   14:26–27
>   17:33

Cynicism

It will soon become apparent that the comparison of Q and Cynicism holds a certain pride of place in this book.[40] Not every New Testament scholar is immediately disposed to accept such a correlation. C. M. Tuckett's recent article "A Cynic Q?" is a case in point.[41] Given, however, that (a) virtually everything can be compared with (b) anything else, provided (c) it is clear in which respect the comparison is being made, the only criticism that might hold against the conjunction of Q and Cynicism would concern the way in which such a correlation has been made; not, however, whether the comparison should be made in the first place.

Such a perspective reflects the results of Jonathan Z. Smith's recent book, *Drudgery Divine: On the Comparison of Early Christianities and the Religions of Late Antiquity*, a devastating critique of the naive and disingenuous manner in which many New Testament scholars have set about the task of understanding the place of their texts and the social movements they represent in antiquity.[42] Of relevance here is especially Smith's second chapter on comparison itself.[43] Smith's principal conclusion quite simply stands on end the widespread habit among New Testament scholars of equating the attribution of parallel materials with a statement about origins or genealogical derivation. Smith contends that the purpose of comparison is not to determine the primordial character of anything, but simply a means — though, perhaps, the only means — whereby, on the basis of our own theoretical and practical interests, we may achieve a new appreciation — Smith's term is "disciplined exaggeration" — of some aspect of a given document or group of persons.[44] It is only the abiding conceptual confusion of comparison with genealogy, I suggest, that would still impede recognition of the strong degree of similarity that exists between the persons whom Q represents and the Cynics.

Regarding Cynicism itself, Tuckett is quite correct in his implied depiction of it as a still underdeveloped field of investigation.[45] Informed assessment especially regarding the specific social nature of this ancient philosophical tradition remains at best a loosely constituted area of study. Determining the precise relationship between Stoicism and Cynicism is just one of the many problems yet to be solved.[46]

It is now generally recognized, however, that the former habit among scholars of referring to different materials as "Cynic-Stoic" is clearly a misnomer, lumping together through the facile convenience of a hyphen two quite distinct moral-philosophical styles.[47] Indeed already in antiquity, Seneca had depicted well, albeit with his own evident bias, some of the pertinent differences between them:

> Inwardly [as Stoics], we ought to be different in all respects, but our exterior should conform to society [unlike the Cynics]. . . . it is quite contrary to nature [*pace* the Cynics from a Stoic point of view] to torture the body, to hate unlabored elegance, to be dirty on purpose, to eat food that is not only plain, but disgusting and forbidding. . . . [Stoic] Philosophy calls for plain living, but not for [Cynic] penance; and we may perfectly well be plain and neat at the same time. This is the mean of which I approve; our [Stoic] life should observe a happy medium between the ways of the sage and the ways of society at large; all persons should admire it, but they should understand it also [unlike the Cynic way of life].[48]

At the same time, both Stoic and Cynic shared a certain discourse, for example, that of "following nature," though, again, as Seneca reminds us, the same language was often understood and deployed in different ways. Nevertheless, in the absence of overt contradiction, it should come as no surprise that Stoic writers like Epictetus can occasionally serve as witnesses to ancient Cynic thought and practice, using Cynic speech and behavior as examples of the points they wished to make, so long as we remember that the source is "tainted" whence this testimony is derived and the fact, therefore, that it is typically unable to suffice as adequate evidence on its own of ancient Cynicism.[49]

The difficulty of using Stoic writers as sources of information about the Cynics belongs to the much larger problem of the highly biased character of all our ancient witnesses regarding Cynicism. By highly biased, I do not mean merely the partiality of perspective or a specific ideological tendency. By highly biased, I mean the polarized tendency when discussing the Cynics either to idealize or to vilify, mockingly to disparage or impossibly to praise them. For example, the pseudonymous Cynic epistles, or Book Six of Diogenes Laertius's *Lives, Teachings, and*

Sayings of Famous Philosophers, or the "wandering" orations of Dio Chrysostom, all are suspect for their general celebration of what was likely in reality a more motley and scurrilous set of performances. On the other hand, the scrupulous self-serving distinctions of Cicero and Seneca, the lampooning portraits of the Cynics painted looking down his nose by Lucian of Samosata, and the earnest defense of "true" Cynicism by Epictetus and Julian versus its all too real contemporary representatives, equally fail to allay doubt regarding their reliability, given the obvious desire in these authors either to debunk or to discern a hidden truth beyond the "dog's breakfast" before them. Every source we have, therefore, regarding ancient Cynicism is essentially untrustworthy, and our only means of knowing anything about these persons.[50]

Of equal, if not greater, importance for defining the nature of ancient Cynicism — and, in some respects, the flip-side of the preceding problem of strongly divergent testimony regarding it — is the question of the "very wide variety of thought [and action] permitted" among the Cynics themselves.[51] Tuckett is quite mistaken in asserting that I question "whether there is really as great a variety within genuine Cynicism as [Abraham J.] Malherbe claims."[52] Even a superficial reading of the Cynic lives in Diogenes Laertius's doxography or the different Cynic epistles makes clear that not all Cynics were cut from the same cloth. It is rather the meaning of this diversity that must be established and where, incidentally, I differ from Malherbe.[53]

It is precisely the division by Malherbe and other scholars of "genuine" Cynic difference into two "pure" breeds — rigorous/ascetic and milder/hedonistic — that I question.[54] Not that I assume that the alternative is simply to imagine as constitutive of Cynicism a momentary mongrel mating of whatever seemed good wherever. But too quickly to collapse the wide range of apropos pronouncement and public performance, equally labeled "Cynic" throughout Greco-Roman antiquity, into separate "schools" is to ignore the problem of how it is that all practitioners of this variable "dog's life" were nonetheless still generally identifiable as "Cynic."[55]

For the purposes of this book, the issue of dating the Cynic evidence becomes essentially irrelevant, once the practice of comparison as Smith defines it is understood to be not for the sake of producing "background" genealogical information, but, as already indicated, in order to facilitate as specific a characterization as possible of the persons whom Q's formative stratum represents.

The relatively late date, moreover, of many of the ancient texts regarding the Cynics does not erase the fact that Cynicism as a social phenomenon and living moral-philosophical tradition perdured throughout the Mediterranean basin for roughly a thousand years, from Antistheses and Diogenes in the fourth century B.C.E. to Sallustius in the sixth century C.E., with certain inevitable, if unpredictable, peaks and valleys in the general popularity of the movement and its notable embodiments.[56] In terms of Cynicism, the Q people — not to mention Jesus and the rest of early Christianity — emerge at the mid-point of this millennial trajectory. It hardly seems out of place, therefore, comparative methodology aside, to inquire how the document and its tradents might be related to what both preceded and followed their own brief existence in the ancient Mediterranean world.

The question of provenance is like that of dating. It matters only if we understand a statement of origin to be at stake in the comparative enterprise. Even so, Tuckett at this point betrays some erroneous habits of thought when he implies a certain fundamental opposition between socalled "Judaism" and the wider Hellenistic world. Only in this fashion can one avoid finding a non sequitur in his line of reasoning that begins with "the question of whether Cynicism permeated the society from which Q emanated," placed by most scholars "somewhere in Galilee or the environs," and then proceeds with the observation that "most would agree that the Christian group which preserved Q was in some kind of relationship (however hostile) with Judaism," to end with the question: "Is it then reasonable to think of Cynic preachers, and Cynic ideas, as present in such a situation?"[57]

Why would the assumption of a relationship between Q and one or more forms of early Judaisms in Galilee diminish in any way the likelihood of the Q people being simultaneously "Cynic" in some fashion? The implied unbridgeable gap between "Judaism" and "Cynicism" is meaningful — though thoroughly unverifiable — only when terms like "Judaism" function, as they have in the history of New Testament scholarship, according to J. Z. Smith, as part of a covert theological code for an exclusive (essentially Protestant) imagination of Christian origins. In fact, as is now increasingly clear, early "Judaisms" in their multiple forms belonged as much to the Hellenistic world as did "Cynicism" in its various guises.[58]

Who, then, were the Cynics? What was their social profile in antiquity? A question itself in need of book-length treatment, I offer here only the most cursory of sketches.[59] In modern terms, the Cynics might be called "contracultural" dissidents.[60] They were "popular" philosophers, unremittingly opposed to the dominant social values of the ancient Mediterranean world, explicitly rejecting the usual aristocratic "educated" means of achieving and enhancing human well-being (*eudaimonia*).[61] The Cynics made clear their basic disagreement with contemporary "commonsense" ideals of the "good" life by living, speaking, and acting in such a way that, however diverse in detail, their general comportment consistently cut against the grain of prevailing cultural assumptions regarding both prosperity and propriety.[62]

Not surprisingly, the Cynics consistently appear as marginal figures in the midst of ancient Mediterranean society.[63] Such a social location evidently suited their particular strategy of heterodox happiness. Being a Cynic meant, if nothing else in antiquity and whatever the concrete circumstances were under which such a decision was first made and subsequently ratified, to have opted for a stance of deliberate social marginality, believing that only in this fashion could one be assured of enjoying here and now, before a certain but unknown death, the fleeting experience of personal contentment.[64] The concrete particulars of every Cynic's self-defined regimen of training or "ascesis" toward this end, performed not infrequently with a certain flair for the dramatic and the impudent, would then determine the specific features of the variable social face that others in antiquity subsequently combined into the different characteristics of a "typical" Cynic.[65]

The Cynics did not all come from a single stratum of society, but counted among their numbers both the formerly rich and the no longer despairing poor, both slave and free, both men and women.[66] Beyond the fact that certain "Cynic" writings were eventually produced, there is no evidence that the Cynics themselves ever formed a special "school" of philosophy identified, as in other traditions of Greek wisdom, by association with a particular institutional setting.[67] The Cynics certainly never constituted a "community" like the Pythagoreans or the Epicureans.[68]

At the same time, it is clear that the Cynics shared a certain public "style," perhaps especially of speech, both in the form of wit and of effrontery, combined with a programmatic lack of most of the other "civilized" virtues, sufficient to permit a wide range of persons and behaviors continuously to be labeled and/or represented to the rest of ancient society throughout the Hellenistic and Roman imperial periods as being properly (or improperly) "Cynic." What exactly this style was, is, however, difficult to define in a phrase. Perhaps it was just that: an indefatigably ineffable "knee-jerk" resistance to conformity with the customary categories of ancient social placement, including those of total separation and retreat.

❧

By now, the reader has already noticed the numerous risks about to be run in the rest of this book, given the various open questions that inhabit its interior from the beginning. To summarize: I propose in the succeeding chapters to elaborate a social profile of Jesus' first followers in Galilee, according to the witness of Q's formative stratum, knowing that the constitutive elements of any group's social identity remain a matter of ongoing debate. A style of historiography is practiced here, whose theoretical aspects have yet to be fully developed. The sayings gospel, "Q," a number of whose texts form the primary basis of the book's discrete investigations, is no longer extant and must be reconstructed. I build, furthermore, upon a recent hypothesis by John S. Kloppenborg — whose widening acceptance among Q scholars does not diminish in any way its "hypothetical" character — distinguishing between two (or three) compositional strata in the document. I discuss only those texts ascribed by Kloppenborg (or by myself in occasional disagreement with Kloppenborg) to Q's formative stratum. Finally, a comparison is sustained throughout the book between Q and the Cynics, whose precise social nature in the context of the ancient Mediterranean world unfortunately remains inadequately clarified by scholarship to date.

This is plainly not a "safe" book, mainly because it does not want to be. I trust, nonetheless, that a close reading of the work will also find that it is at least clear and consistent in its procedure and never arbitrary in its judgments, at least not in an ad hoc fashion.

CHAPTER ONE

Ethos: "Like Sheep among Wolves"
The "Mission" Instructions (10:3–6, 9–11, 16)

I N HIS SEMINAL WORK *The First Urban Christians,* Wayne Meeks discusses the social history of the small ecclesial groups that constituted Pauline Christianity.[1] Not really a book about Paul, the investigations of Meeks concern instead the corporate experience of Paul's immediate followers, those "ordinary believers" at the start of what a few centuries later would become the official Roman imperial religion. After reading Meeks's book, one might ask: And what about the first followers of Jesus in Palestine, those even more obscure persons responsible for the gospel traditions deriving not from a converted tent-maker's civic wanderings and mix-ups west of Eden, but the result of developments at the eastern end of the Mediterranean basin in the cradle of Syrian Christianity? In terms of Q, we would be inquiring about the first Galilean Christians.[2]

A review of the history of scholarship on "the Q community" reveals the critical role played by the document's so-called "mission" instructions (10:2–16) in characterizing these persons.[3] Interpretation of this set of sayings has been determinative of conclusions reached about early Christianity in first-century C.E. Galilee and/or a major stumbling block to conceptions of it gained elsewhere. At the same time, reading the last two centuries of scholarly commentary on this text leaves one stunned by its overall futility. As I have tried to demonstrate elsewhere, modern New Testament scholarship since its inception has produced virtually nothing of lasting value regarding the meaning of these verses.[4] We are thus driven back to basic questions.

What do these instructions (10:3–6, 9–11, 16) mean in Q's formative stratum? Do they make any sense at all? What sort of persons are we to imagine as first having spoken and/or listened to such utterances? Who initially produced and/or employed a text consistently able in the last two centuries to leave "enlightened" Western academic commentators high and dry? What kind of social profile ought we to give to the men and women whom these sayings can be held to represent? At stake in this chapter is establishing the specific ethos or "lifestyle" that undergirded and provides the immediate social context in which the various other pronouncements — ethical, ideological, critical, commemorative — found in Q's formative stratum are to be understood. It is assumed hereby that the social "practice" of any human group provides the fundamental framework for determining the force and feeling of every discourse generated and deployed by its members. In other words, it is the concrete "situation in life" (*Sitz im Leben*) of text-and-tradent that must be established first, however provisionally and subject to later refinement and correction, before the precise significance of any particular statement can be proposed.

The text of Q 10:3–6, 9–11, 16, in English translation, is as follows:

10:3. Go. Look, I send you out like sheep among wolves. *10:4.* Take neither money nor bag nor sandals nor staff; greet no one. *10:5–6.* Whichever house you enter, say, "Peace to this house." And if a son of peace is there, let your peace come on him. If not, let it return to you. *10:9.* Treat the weak; say, "The kingdom of God has arrived." *10:10–11.* Whichever city you enter and they do not receive you, going out of that city, remove the dust from your feet. *10:16.* Whoever receives you, receives me. And whoever receives me, receives the one who sent me.[5]

The sayings in Q 10:3–6, 9–11, 16 form a series of "operational directives," akin perhaps to "marching orders." In the history of New Testament scholarship, these sayings have often been called "mission" instructions. But such terminology is deeply misleading, insofar as it continues to reflect more the modern colonial theological imagination of Christian origins than ancient socio-historical reality. It is now difficult to know what exactly one should call them, hence the quotation marks around "mission" instructions.

No obvious argument is pursued by the arrangement of 10:3–6, 9–11, 16. Nonetheless, a certain reasoned structure may be discerned in the progressive presentation of these sayings. The scene of operations within which the Q people are expected to wend their way is first established by the opening statement in 10:3. The context where they find themselves "like sheep among wolves" is plainly felt to be threatening in some way.

In 10:4, the Q people are then told in general but unambiguous terms how to dress and to behave in the midst of such a situation. The instructions given in this verse are apodictic in form and appear to promote a program of radical poverty.

In 10:5–6, the particular issue of "whichever house you enter" is next discussed. It is evidently assumed that at some point on any given day, the Q people would approach the homes of perfect strangers, for the purpose of 10:5–6 is to suggest how best to do so (saying "peace to this house") and with no guarantee of success (one apparently could not know ahead of time whether or not a "son of peace" would be there) what to do if the reception proved less than welcoming.

In the happy event of a favorable response, the Q people are then told in 10:9 what else to do.

If it should happen, however, that in a given locale all doors remained closed or were shut in their face, the Q people are subsequently instructed in 10:10–11 how to handle this extreme instance of rotund rejection. Such an occurrence was clearly not supposed to be the usual experience. Had such been the case, the preceding instructions would quickly have served for naught.

In 10:16, recalling both the "sending out" language in 10:3 as well as the suggestion in 10:9b of an accompanying superior presence, namely, the kingdom of God, a concluding rationale is finally given that explains rather bluntly why extending hospitality to the Q people was something worthwhile doing. With them, it is claimed, arrived a higher power.

10:3. Go. Look, I send you out like sheep among wolves.

Especially the first half of this saying ("Go. Look, I send you out") has regularly been misconstrued as the beginning of a "mission" discourse, mainly because of the use here of the verb *apostellein*.[6] Obviously, some sense of embassy is expressed, that those addressed in 10:3 were under a commission of one sort or another. But what kind of a sending is it: by whom to whom for what?

Intermediaries of every kind from errand boys to archangels circulated throughout the ancient world. They were the only available means of getting news and information from one place to another: from this side of town to the next, from the battlefield to those waiting at home, from heaven to earth. The obvious lack of electronic and other modern means of communication, not to mention a comparatively restricted postal service, made sending messages with whoever might be going "that way" the normal mode of staying in touch and making contact.

Everyone in antiquity with a message to deliver or an action to perform on someone else's behalf was thus on a "mission." Every messenger was a "missionary" in this sense. Even the Cynics occasionally described themselves as being "sent."

A favorite trope of Epictetus, for example, is precisely this one. Zeus, says the teacher from Nicopolis, has sent the Cynic into the world, whom the Cynic now serves.[7] The Cynic should know that he is both a messenger sent by God and his scout, as Diogenes had put it.[8] Indeed, in Epictetus's judgment, the Cynic deemed worthy of God's scepter and diadem can say:

> Behold, God has sent me to you as an example, that you may see
> O humans, that you are seeking happiness and serenity not where
> it is, but where it is not.[9]

With such speech, Epictetus seeks to sustain his conviction that the Cynic way of life was not merely one of "bumming around," as certain detractors had understandably suggested. Rather, it had a specific purpose, identified by Epictetus with enjoyment of the divine virtues of happiness and serenity. Likewise, the persons whom Q represents appear to have conceived of their indigent lifestyle in a similar fashion: their peculiar peregrinations were not simply due to down-and-out vagrancy, but registered instead the movement of divine messengers: that of scouts heralding a greater felicity.[10]

Not every scholar is willing to accept that what Epictetus says is comparable with 10:3. Consider, for example, Karl Heinrich Rengstorf's article on the verb *apostellō* in Gerhard Kittel's *Theological Dictionary of the New Testament*. Rengstorf begins his discussion with a few general affirmations, recognizing hereby that a certain similarity indeed exists between the discourse of ancient Cynicism and sayings like Luke 10:3 par. Once these opening statements have been made, however, Rengstorf then proceeds quickly to bury any insight that he might have had in this regard in a morass of surreptitious assumptions obviously intended to disqualify completely the initial comparison.

What does Rengstorf initially affirm?

> The use of ἀποστέλλειν in this sense [as authorized representative]
> is not in any way restricted to the legal sphere. On the contrary,
> it takes on its fullest sense when used, if we may put it thus, to
> express the impartation of full religious and ethical power. This
> takes place in the diatribe of the Cynics and Stoics, though in this
> respect it is simply following a common custom of philosophical
> religion.[11]

> Hence the Cynic as ἄγγελος is the messenger of Zeus who sends
> him and stands behind him. . . . If we want a term in which there is
> a material parallel to the NT use of ἀπόστολος, it is offered only
> by this word [κατάσκοπος, i.e., scout]. . . . We can at least say that
> the Cynic-Stoic sage in his role as κατάσκοπος is the figure of the
> period which we can set in closest proximity to the apostle.[12]

But, suddenly, we must be careful:

To the extent that in it [the notion of the scout] the Cynic himself is the acting subject and not God as in the case of ἄγγελος [though the Cynic too could be described in this way], this awareness is shown to be a consciousness of self rather than God.[13]

Rengstorf rejects the Cynic parallel because such a person "caused offense," supposedly required "religious assurance of his own authority beyond the mere fact of being sent," adopted "the formula θεῖος ἄνθρωπος as a self-description," recalling "with mystical echoes" the "language of the Mystery religions" with "no ultimate metaphysical foundation," approximating "the enthusiasm of the Greek prophets," giving "clear evidence of its origin in Pantheism, which finally entails the absorption of the divine in the ego."[14]

By contrast, Christianity had:

a consciousness of mission which manifests its theonomic character in the uniting of an unlimited claim in the name of the sending God with a renunciation of any significance of the man who is highly favored with this mission.[15]

For Rengstorf, the main problem with the Cynics and other groups like them is that:

At the decisive point, namely, at the moment when the ἄγγελος θεῶν becomes the κῆρυξ θεῶν, the accent is still laid on human initiative and human judgment. For, although the ἀπεσταλμένος belongs to the deity as ὑπηρέτης, he is never absolutely dependent on it as its δοῦλος; he rather stands alongside it as βασιλεὺς καὶ δεσπότης, and he is thus almost equal to it in rank and dignity (θεῖος ἄνθρωπος). Hence the relationship of the messenger to the deity never has the character of an unconditional appointment to which he is subject; it is more like an agreement between two partners. This is only possible, however, because in these circles there is no clear concept of God nor certainty of a definitive revelation of the will of God. But this is also the explanation why, for all its consciousness of mission and self-consciousness, the philosophical religion of the period never attains the claim to absoluteness which is the mark of all genuine religion and its messengers.[16]

One is simply overwhelmed by the "inevitability" of this reasoning, at the same time that it utterly fails to convince.

Not only Epictetus saw the Cynic as sent from God. Dio Chrysostom could also describe himself in these terms:

In my own case, for instance, I feel that I have chosen this role [of a popular philosopher], not by myself, but by the will of some deity.[17]

For you must not think that eagles and falcons foretell to humans what is required of them and that the counsel derived from such creatures is trustworthy because of its spontaneity and divine nature, but refuse to believe that a man who has come, as I have come, having no connection with you from any point of view, has come by divine guidance to address and counsel you.[18]

Certain of the pseudonymous Cynic epistles likewise share the same manner of speech:

For I am called heaven's dog, not earth's, since I liken myself to it, living as I do, not in conformity with popular opinion but according to nature, free under Zeus, and crediting the good to him and not to my neighbor.... the dog is under the protection of the gods and his clothing is God's invention.[19]

...I [Socrates] applied myself to the philosophic life at the command of God.[20]

Like the Cynics in these texts, the Q people also claimed to have been "sent." Why was it important and even necessary for such persons to speak in this way? In the case of Dio Chrysostom, he hoped thereby to gain a hearing: that his audience would not refuse to listen to him, as a man "come by divine guidance to address and counsel you." The first Cynic epistle uses such language to defend the "career" choice of its fictive author.[21] In every case, to say that one was "sent" responded to concerns about authority and authorization. It answered the implied question: And what gives you the right to say that? How is it that you can do this?[22]

Regarding Epictetus again, there is also a sense in which the Cynic as scout from God brings insight into the divine virtues of happiness and serenity. To receive such a messenger was thus, as 10:16 will shortly state, to receive the one who had sent him. Such a visit from God's own emissaries could only portend the highest of benefits.[23]

Of course, even divine messengers sometimes "got the shaft."[24] For those sent out in 10:3, fair weather and smooth sailing were not the immediate forecast. Rather, as the saying goes, "I send you out like sheep among wolves."

The unfriendly opposition between sheep and wolves was a proverbial contrast in ancient Greek literature, as well as, to a lesser extent, in certain Hebrew writings (e.g., Isa 11:6; 65:25). In Greek literature, the contrast serves to describe a state of chronic or irresoluble conflict (e.g., Homer, *Iliad* 22.262–64; Herodotus 4.149). An intriguing saying in the *Greek Anthology* (7.723) has the absence of the same familiar antagonism express lament that the old order of things has now been radically disturbed. Likewise Epictetus, wishing on one occasion to prove a point by referring to opposite extremes, invokes the contrary figures of sheep and wolf.[25]

In comparison with 10:3, especially interesting is the saying that Diogenes Laertius puts into the mouth of Crates of Thebes, the foremost disciple of Diogenes of Sinope. Crates is supposed to have said:

> Those found with flatterers [are] as defenseless as calves found among wolves.[26]

A situation of temptation — flattery — is here imagined. One must be prepared to resist it.[27]

The correspondence between 10:3 and Crates' dictum is not complete. In 10:3, for example, the persons whom Q represents appear to be sent precisely into the situation that the saying by Crates implies that its audience should avoid. Yet, it is clear that Crates assumes that flatterers already exist on every side, hence the need for the warning. At the same time, the statement in 10:3, "I send you out," hardly means what Crates has just advised against, namely, go forth and seek. The Q people are surely not dismissed as sheep in 10:3 in order to search for wolves to devour them.[28] Rather, those sent out in 10:3, like the Cynics, think of themselves as messenger-scouts, heralds of a better path to happiness. In this capacity, they are told to expect to have to face certain "wolves" along the way.

In 10:3, the reference to "sheep" is self-description. The Cynics did not typically refer to themselves as "sheep." Rather, according to Lucian:

> [the Cynics] collect tribute, going from house to house, or, as they themselves say it, they "shear the sheep."[29]

"Sheep" are here the "easy marks" of shyster beggars. Likewise for Epictetus, the same term, "sheep," is sometimes taken to represent precisely what this teacher thought his students ought not to become. Thus Epictetus insists:

> Well, when do we act like sheep? When we act for the sake of the belly, or of our sex-organs, or at random, or in a filthy fashion, or without due consideration, to what level have we degenerated? To the level of sheep.[30]

Epictetus nonetheless can turn around and use the very same metaphor of "sheep" to indicate precisely how he thinks his students ought to behave:

> And if talk about some theoretical matter should arise among laypeople, keep silence for the most part, for the danger is great that you will spew up immediately what you have not digested.

...For sheep, too, do not bring their fodder to the shepherds
and show them how much they have eaten, but they digest their
food within, and on the outside produce wool and milk. You, too,
therefore, make no show of theoretical matters to laypeople, but
let them see the results which come from these when they are
digested.[31]

The character of well-digesting sheep is then contrasted elsewhere by
Epictetus with the habits of wolves: persons whose character is "untrustworthy and contentious and foul-mouthed."[32] The same contrast is
drawn, moreover, by other moralists as well. Dio Chrysostom, for example, as at least one Cynic epistle, will likewise employ the figure of a
wolf to designate especially reprehensible or undesirable moral traits.[33]

In summary: Like the Cynics, the Q people styled themselves messengers of a sort: "Look, I send you out." Like sheep, the Q people
were told that they, too, could expect to meet certain persons along
the way best described as wolves. The contrast of sheep and wolf, beyond evoking the proverbial sense of conflict and obvious risk to the
sheep, serves to indicate contrary types of "personalities."[34] Face to face
with "untrustworthy, contentious and foul-mouthed" human beings, the
persons whom Q represents, like Epictetus's students, are instructed in
10:3 to conduct themselves with a "digested" demeanor, demonstrating through their personal comportment and general activity the greater
sense of virtue and felicity that they otherwise supposed themselves to
herald.[35]

**10:4. Take neither money nor bag nor sandals nor staff; greet
no one.**

New Testament scholars have been singularly unsuccessful at finding
anything with which to compare the saying in 10:4. Indeed, the usual
comment that is made simply remarks how unparalleled or impossible
to carry out in practice this set of instructions is.[36] As we shall shortly
see, however, a notable correspondence can be shown to exist between
what is said in 10:4 and the social habits of the Cynics.

One of the more striking features of the various instructions in 10:4
is their sheer mundaneness. The saying is a list of things not to do. Why
anyone would have made or repeated such an utterance, were it not that
what it says was, in Gerd Theissen's words, at one time taken "seriously
and literally," is difficult to imagine.[37] The saying has no obvious theological message to convey. Attempts have been made to give the different
directives in 10:4 a certain eschatological significance. But all such efforts finally fail to convince.[38] What 10:4 actually outlines is, instead, a
certain form of asceticism: the profile of a radically impoverished way of

life.[39] The "sheep" in 10:3, beyond the scourge of "wolves," are shorn in 10:4 of everything else they might have owned besides themselves.

Paul Hoffmann writes that all the prohibitions in 10:4 (except for the final injunction not to greet anyone) dispense with the typical equipment and provisions for a journey in antiquity.[40] Hoffmann then proceeds predictably to suggest that 10:4 advocates a wholly different way of moving from one place to another. But the fact that money, a bag, footwear, and a staff were regularly taken on ancient trips does not mean that, therefore, not taking them reveals a completely new mode of travel. For not only travelers used these things. Hoffmann is still influenced by the unnecessary assumption that the persons whom Q represents were on a preaching mission.[41]

The first thing in 10:4 to be prohibited is the use of money. There are many passages in ancient Cynic literature that likewise oppose the same practice. Archetypical of this perspective is perhaps the figure of Crates.[42] According to Diogenes Laertius:

> Diocles relates how Diogenes persuaded Crates to give up his property to sheep-pasture, and throw into the sea any money he had.[43]

Similarly Monimus, at one time "in the service of a certain Corinthian banker," after deciding to follow Diogenes:

> straight off pretended to be mad and was flinging away the small change and all the money on the banker's table, until his master dismissed him; and he immediately devoted himself to Diogenes.[44]

Julian was fond of saying that Diogenes had been:

> cityless, homeless, a man without a country, owning not an obol, not a drachma, not even a household slave.[45]

In one of Lucian's dialogues, the representative Cyniscus tells Charon, the underworld ferryman:

> I shan't be able to pay you your obol when we come to land, for I have nothing more than the wallet which you see, and this club here.[46]

Other notable parallels to the prohibition of money in 10:4 include the following statements:

> If all the gold, all the silver, all the copper should give out, I would not be injured in the least.[47]

> ... are you not afraid of the money? ... For by no means does money always profit those who have gotten it; but people have suffered many more injuries and more evils from money than from poverty, particularly when they lacked sense.[48]

The second item to be forbidden in 10:4 is a beggar's bag (*pēra*). This piece of equipment was one of the stereotypical trademarks of the ancient Cynic.[49] Its prohibition here would thus seem to register a deviation from the "normal" Cynic pattern in antiquity — a fact, in turn, predictably taken by not a few New Testament scholars as decisive proof against the possibility of any further comparison of Q and Cynicism![50]

But the stereotypical Cynic was just that: a stereotype. However much the standard image corresponded to reality, it hardly exhausted the potential variety of self-presentations by these incorrigible canine philosophers. Thus, Teles "the Cynic teacher" can write:

Actually, it is a great and noteworthy thing to take no heed even of a wallet, lupines, vegetables, water, but rather to be unkempt and uncompromising.[51]

By definition, the Cynics, advocating neglect of all social artifice, including the minimal use of most cultural artifacts, sought to get by with less and less:

Practice needing little, for this is nearest to God, while the opposite is farthest away.[52]

One day, observing a child drinking with his hands, [Diogenes] cast away the cup from his wallet saying, "A child has beaten me in plainness of living." He also threw away his bowl when in like manner he saw a child who had broken his plate taking up his lentils with the hollow part of a morsel of bread.[53]

Cynic use of the *pēra* was supposed to signal complete self-sufficiency. The followers of Diogenes were to rely only on what they could carry with them in a *pēra,* not requiring nor trusting in any other system of "social security":

To me life is so uncertain that I am not sure of lasting till I finish writing you this letter. But life has a sufficient store in a wallet. The equipment provided by those esteemed gods is greater than people think.[54]

The same bag is elsewhere called the "land and sea from which you are fed."[55] When Crates devotes a little poem (*paignia*) to the *pēra* as "a certain city," far from undertaking ancient urban planning, the Cynic is mocking the traditional city's pretension to provide for its citizens the necessary context of their total satisfaction. Instead, Crates claims, this could be achieved only through a thoroughly independent mode of provision.[56]

There is some evidence that in Syria under Roman rule the beggar's bag had paradoxically become a symbol of excess, an instrument of greed, just the opposite of what the Cynic's use of the *pēra* was supposed to represent. A monument erected at Kefr-Hauar by "a slave of the Syrian goddess" tells how he was "sent by the lady" to beg for her and boasts that "each journey brought in 70 bags" (*pērai*).[57] The Didaskalia later speaks of roving widows whose income made them "less widows [*chērai*], more wallets [*pērai*]."[58] In such a social environment, abnegation of the beggar's bag, as 10:4 recommends, would have meant exactly what the Cynics felt their alternate employment of the *pēra* otherwise demonstrated.[59]

Next in 10:4, one is told not to wear any sandals (*hypodēmata*). This prohibition of footwear has befuddled every previous attempt to explain it.[60] But the correspondence here between Q and the Cynics could hardly be more direct.[61] The following texts speak for themselves:

> For me, a Scythian cloak serves as my garment, the skin of my feet as my shoes, the whole earth as my resting place, milk, cheese and meat as my favorite meal, hunger as my main course.[62]

> Therefore, I am satisfied to have the plainest food and the same garment summer and winter, and I do not wear shoes at all, nor do I desire political fame except to the extent that it comes from being prudent and just.[63]

> But as for that barefoot Antisthenes, what else has he done than to make you [Simon the shoemaker] idle and without an income, since he persuades the youth and indeed all the Athenians to go barefoot?[64]

> [Diogenes] never protected his feet, either, because they were no more delicate, he said, than his eyes and face. For these parts, though by nature the weakest, endured the cold very well on account of their constant exposure; for people could not possibly walk around with their eyes tied up like their feet.[65]

> "What then shall I do?" [a man whose slave had left him] said, "for I have no other domestic slave." "Well, what will you do," said [Diogenes], "when you have no other shoes and those you have hurt and cut your feet? Will you not take them off as soon as possible and go barefoot? If, however, they fall off by themselves, do you tie them on again and pinch your feet? Why, sometimes people who are barefoot get around more easily than those who are badly shod; likewise, many live more easily and with less annoyance without domestic slaves than those who have many of them."[66]

...I [Micyllus] gladly flung away knife and leather (for I was working on a boot), sprang up at once, and followed her, barefoot and without even washing off the blacking...[67]

I hold it unnecessary to be a merchant or a farmer or a soldier or to follow a trade; instead I shout, go dirty, take cold baths, walk about barefoot in winter, wear a filthy cloak and like Momus carp at everything done by others.[68]

You there [the Cynic], why ever do you have a beard and long hair, but no shirt? Why do you expose your body and go barefoot, choosing this nomadic inhuman bestial life?[69]

Therefore my appearance is, as you see, to be dirty and unkempt with a worn cloak, long hair and bare feet.[70]

And now, you may witness a revolting and terrible sight, as he tosses back his filthy locks, a bold, insolent look in his eye, half naked in a ragged old cloak, with a little wallet hanging down, and holding in his hand a club made of wild-pear wood, barefoot, dirty, a man of no occupation, not recognizing the farm or us, his parents, but denying us, saying that all things are the work of nature and that birth is due, not to parents, but to the mixture of the elements.[71]

[Diogenes] used to make [the sons of Xeniades] crop their hair close and wear it unadorned, go lightly clad, barefoot, silent, not looking about them in the streets.[72]

Once again, the correspondence between Q and Cynicism is manifest. Comparison of the injunction in 10:4 against wearing any sandals and the preceding texts suggests, furthermore, that such behavior was not simply a matter of a personal quirk or inconsequential idiosyncrasy, but, rather, part of a specific social style. (This would be true, of course, also in the case of the other prohibitions.) Beyond inquiring why the Q people did not protect their feet (and abstained from other standard personal accouterments in antiquity), we ought to consider the extent to which, as with the Cynics, such comportment was but the tip of a larger countercultural iceberg. The refusal in 10:4 to put on any shoes is not just the expression of childish delight at going barefoot.

The fourth article proscribed in 10:4 is a staff.[73] Such a stick, like the beggar's bag, was again often included in the usual Cynic get-up.[74] Again, its non-use here would signify, as with the beggar's bag, a particular intensification (or contextualization) of the Cynic strategy of self-sufficiency.[75] Insofar, moreover, as the staff served as a weapon, not to carry one around would mean either defenseless self-exposure to the usual perils of ancient life or the clear demonstration of a certain fearlessness regarding whatever might happen.[76]

Not infrequently, the Cynics were targets of personal attacks and on occasion would assume a posture of defenselessness before them.[77] More significantly, in the face of such a threat, the Cynics promoted utter fearlessness. Dio Chrysostom, for example, has Diogenes of Sinope, the prototypical Cynic, explain his unprotected style in these words:

> "I, however," says [Diogenes], "go by night wherever I will and walk alone by day, and I am not afraid to go even through an army camp if need be, without the herald's staff, and amid brigands; for I have no enemy, public or private, who opposes me."[78]

The prohibition of a staff in 10:4 signals a similar stance.

The fifth and final directive in 10:4 demands full public silence: "greet no one." As with the prohibition of sandals, previous commentators on the verse have utterly failed to provide a plausible explanation for this command — despite, in one case, an entire book devoted to explaining it![79] The most famous practitioners of silence in antiquity were, of course, the Pythagoreans. The Cynics were better known for their noisome "barking."[80] But, again, this is the stereotype. The Cynics, too, knew how to say nothing, especially when their doing so would clearly contradict established codes of conduct. Thus, for example, Lucian has his designated "dog-philosopher" include precisely this behavior, namely, not greeting anyone, in a recital of Cynic ways:

> Seek out the most crowded places, and in these very spots try to be solitary and antisocial, greeting neither friend nor stranger; for to do so is to lose hegemony.[81]

The Cynic practice of occasional public silence sometimes had a more "positive" intent as well. When Diogenes was a slave in the service of Xeniades, entrusted with the task of educating his master's sons, part of the regimen he imposed on them included not to speak in public places: instead, they were to appear as already seen "lightly clad, barefoot, silent, not looking about them in the streets."[82] Likewise, Antisthenes equated ethical accomplishment with the assumption of a silent demeanor:

> Virtue is short of words, but wickedness interminable.[83]

In summary: Although ostensibly an "impossible" saying to understand as such, and furthermore lacking any notable parallel in ancient literature, many points of similarity have, in fact, been shown to exist between the specific instructions in 10:4 and the various traditions of ancient Cynicism. This correspondence is all the more remarkable, insofar as habits of conduct are here in view, not just shared figures of speech or common rhetorical forms, but similar social manners. While "identical" behavior may always harbor disparate intentions, unlike intentions such behavior cannot hide itself, being inevitably a bodily thing. On the basis of 10:4, it would have been extremely difficult to distinguish the persons whom Q represents from other Cynics elsewhere in the ancient Mediterranean world.

What, then, does the saying "mean"? 10:4 does not explain itself beyond articulating a certain social style. The Cynic parallels are doubtless a clue, especially if the other "mission" instructions in Q's formative stratum also lend themselves, as already 10:3, to the same comparison. In the case of the prohibition of sandals, it has already become clear that this particular trait belonged with the Cynics to a much broader strategy of cultural confrontation and resistance. Its specific "sense" would thus be derivative of that larger logic.

10:5–6. Whichever house you enter, say, "Peace to this house." And if a son of peace is there, let your peace come on him. If not, let it return to you.

More than the previous verses, the meaning of 10:5–6 depends heavily upon the particular "preunderstanding" that we bring to the task of interpreting this saying. What do we find especially "significant" about the specific instructions in 10:5–6? What exactly is "going on" here? Some scholars have paid especial attention to the fact that a *house* is explicitly mentioned in this context.[84] Others find the repeated language of *peace* the most noteworthy feature of the saying.[85] Yet other scholars have worried about what it might mean for this peace to be able to *come* and go (*return*),[86] while some investigators have especially wanted to identify the elusive *son of peace.*[87]

Each of these interpretations treats a particular aspect of the saying in 10:5–6. Each question is, moreover, obviously relevant to determining the saying's "full" meaning. But all equally skirt the main issue, which is: Why would anyone in the context of first-century c.e. Galilee repeatedly approach otherwise unfamiliar households in the first place?[88] Anachronistic notions of door-to-door evangelism or intensive neighborhood canvassing are clearly out of the question. If, however, we permit ourselves to imagine the Q people standing at the door of an ancient Galilean villager's home, poorly dressed and ill equipped as 10:4 has described them, the first thing those inside, looking out, are likely to have thought is that more vagrants had arrived: here, in other words, came another round of beggars, seeking a handout. Why not assume that this impression corresponded to reality?[89]

It is well-known that the Cynics begged.[90] Lucian has them "going from house to house" for this very reason.[91] Though not always welcomed with open arms, their sudden appearance at the door was neither inevitably rebuffed. Indeed, as Lucian describes the case of Demonax:

> Toward the end, when he was very old, he used to eat and sleep uninvited in whatever house he happened to be passing by, and those who lived there thought that it was almost a divine visitation, and that some good fortune had entered their house.[92]

Crates likewise "was called the 'Door-opener' — the one to whom all doors fly open — from his habit of entering every house and admonishing those within."[93]

How to deal with rejection — the absence of a "son of peace" — was also a concern of the Cynics. Like the Q people, the followers of Diogenes had learned that often the best thing to do with a hostile reception was simply take it on the chin and leave. They would let their initial advance — in Q, the standard greeting, "peace" — "return" to them. More than one text makes it clear that when refused, the Cynics did not immediately proceed to raise a ruckus or beat their head against closed doors.[94] In fact, sometimes they went to the opposite extreme:

> [Diogenes] once begged alms of a statue, and, when asked why he did so, replied, "To get practice in being refused."[95]

> Ask for bread even from the statues in the marketplace as you enter it. In a way, such a practice is good, for you will meet persons more unfeeling than statues. And whenever they give something to eunuchs and to the authors of obscenity rather than to you, do not be surprised. For each person pays honor to the one who is close to him and not someone far off. And it is eunuchs rather than the philosophers who pander to the masses.[96]

At the same time, Dio Chrysostom in his "Euboean discourse" speaks at length about the peaceable souls who, contrariwise, did receive and show hospitality to "shipwrecked travelers" and other such wanderers:

> And really, when I consider Euripides' words and reflect whether in fact the entertainment of strangers is so difficult for them that they can never welcome or attend to anyone in need, I find such a thing by no means to be true of their hospitality. Rather, they light a fire more promptly than the rich and guide one on the way without reluctance — indeed, in such matters a sense of honor would compel them — and often they share what they have more readily.[97]

In 10:5–6, a similar "entertainment of strangers" is imagined. The "son of peace" who would receive the persons whom Q represents was not a "sympathizer" of the group or local "party" member, but, rather, just another instance of the same bucolic hospitality that Dio

Chrysostom has eulogized (undoubtedly to excess, but equally true to experience).[98]

The Cynics did not beg from everyone. Criteria were proposed to determine from whom and how much one ought to seek as a handout.[99] Consider, for example, the following piece of advice:

> Do not beg the necessities of life from everyone, nor accept from everyone what is given to you (for it is not right for virtue to be supported by vice). Rather, beg only from those persons and accept gifts only from those who have been initiated into philosophy. Then it will be possible for you to demand back what belongs to you and not to appear to be begging what belongs to others.[100]

An interesting sort of beggary that does not want to "appear to be begging what belongs to others"! The opportunity to support God's canine colleagues (the Cynics) was to be given only to those who had already demonstrated their right to such a privilege.

In this regard, the reference in 10:6 to a "son of peace" would not only be a statement about generous hospitality, not only a question of acceptance versus rejection. Such a person would also represent a "worthy" donor to the cause.[101] The beggary of the Q people, like that of the Cynics, was not simply the result of a desperate search for physical survival at the bottom of the social heap, nor due to personal laziness or an unwillingness to work, but formed instead part of a broader strategy of social engagement: one that we might call a "militant mendicancy."[102]

I cite a final text, in part because it too discusses the subject of support from appropriate sources; but mainly because of the way in which the structure of its argument mirrors the sequence of topics in 10:3ff.

> And those following me often listened to me discussing patient endurance, and they often happened to be present as I actually exercised patient endurance or pursued that pattern of life. Because of this some gave me money, others things worth money, and many invited me to dinner. But I took from moderate people what was suitable to nature, but from the worthless I accepted nothing. And from those who felt gratitude toward me for accepting the first time, I accepted again as well; but never again from those who did not feel thankful. I scrutinized even the gifts of those who wished to present me barley meal, and accepted it from those who were being benefited. But from the others I took nothing, since I thought it improper to take something from a person who had themself not received anything. I did not dine with everyone, but only with those in need of therapy. These are the ones who imitate the kings of the Persians.[103]

Dependence of one text upon the other is hardly the point. Nevertheless, the similar line of reasoning both here and in Q 10:3ff is intriguing. "Those following me" would be like those whom "I send" in 10:3. "Patient endurance" describes well the situation of "sheep among wolves." The instructions given in 10:4 certainly recall the behavior of persons who "actually exercised patient endurance or pursued that pattern of life." "Moderate people" would be like the "son of peace" in 10:5. Finally, as in 10:5–6, we then read about support for those who lived this way.

In 10:5–6, the question is framed as a matter of self-presentation: "Say, 'Peace to this house.' And if a son of peace is there..." In the preceding text, the problem is rather stated as one of response: "some" and "many" wanted to give Diogenes money and similar goods, forcing him to decide from whom he ought to receive such things. In both passages, however, the underlying issue is essentially the same, namely, what constituted acceptable support.[104]

In summary: In 10:5–6, we learn that, like the Cynics, the Q people also begged. They did so, moreover, with a similar "sophistication," having likewise learned both to discriminate between possible donors to the cause ("if a son of peace is there") and to endure the pain of rejection without the inward crush of resentment and remorse ("let it return to you").

Lacking any guarantee of hospitality ("*if* a son of peace is there"), the Q people could nonetheless anticipate, if Dio Chrysostom is to be trusted, finding some warm souls disposed to "light a fire more promptly than the rich" and guide them on their way "without reluctance," sharing whatever meager provisions they might have.[105] Still, life must have remained a somewhat perilous existence for these homeless hounds of God. How could it not?

10:9. Treat the weak; say, "The kingdom of God has arrived."

Commentators on 10:9 have usually found in it simple confirmation of what they already knew about Christian origins. Nothing in the saying seems to strike them as the least peculiar. At most, the combination here of "miracle-working" and "preaching" (or their synonyms) is thought to be significant. This is noteworthy, however, only because of the traditional (Protestant) distinction between word and deed or the Word and Works. The historical Jesus is said not to have made such an opposition — key to the observation in the first place.

Heinz Schürmann, for example, writes as though it were simply obvious that what we have here is "the same as in the preaching of Jesus." Proclamation of the kingdom is "self-evidently (as for Jesus) accompanied by δυνάμεις"; for this reason, "then, also in the post-Easter mission."[106] Hoffmann remarks that the activity of Jesus:

> according to the witness of Q, held in close combination heal-
> ings and preaching.... Healings and the preaching of the kingdom
> fit, therefore, the other statements of Q. Both are named here [in
> 10:9] next to one another; the healings are understood eschatolog-
> ically in Q, as also the other passages make clear, as part of what
> happens at the end of time.[107]

Siegfried Schulz opines that not only *Wundermacht* is apparent, but:

> The marvelous healings of the sick are, according to the context of
> Q, nothing other than the full-powered accompanying manifesta-
> tions of the kingdom that is breaking in through the preaching of
> the messengers.[108]

In every case, interpretation of 10:9 maintains business as usual. But 10:9 is noteworthy for more than one reason. Despite everything at-tributed to the statement that "the kingdom of God has arrived," such a formulation is by no means widely attested in early Christian literature. In the New Testament, it borders, in fact, on being rare.

Although the phrase has been made famous by modern biblical schol-ars' use of Mark 1:14, Jesus never again says in Mark that "the kingdom of God has arrived." Its meaning in this gospel clearly belongs to the redactional design of the evangelist's overall narrative. Meanwhile else-where in the New Testament, excluding those texts dependent in one way or another on either Mark or Q, the same statement that "the king-dom of God has arrived" is found only in Q 10:9. If such speech in Mark is demonstrably at the service of an apocalyptic imagination, this is hardly self-evidently the case for Q.

The context of 10:9 itself suggests that in Q, reference to the arrival of God's kingdom was part of a general therapeutic practice. When the Q people used to "treat the weak," they were to tell them that the king-dom of God had come.[109] Just as in 6:20b the life of poverty is made a way of participating in divine aseity through association with "the kingdom of God," the same expression in 10:9 serves to characterize the experience of renewed health and well-being at the hands of those whom Q represents.[110]

Exactly what health and healing are, is, of course, anything but self-evident.[111] In the past, New Testament scholars have tended to call a "miracle" whatever did not conform, from their point of view, to more "orthodox" modes of medicine. Recently, some have advocated that we use the less mystical term of "magic" to describe the same ac-tivity.[112] Whatever we finally choose to name alternatives to "official" medical practice, there is not, in any case, much evidence otherwise of healing in Q.

Indeed, beyond the biblical pastiche in 7:22 that uses Isaianic phrases of physical recovery to answer affirmatively the christological inquiry of John whether or not Jesus is "the coming one," there are only two "other" accounts of actual "miracle-working" in the document, namely, 7:1–10 and 11:14–20.[113] It is noteworthy, therefore, that in the second of these passages (11:14–20) after the demon-possessed mute has been healed and the ensuing debate over "how'd he do that" draws to a close, the concluding statement is again that "the kingdom of God has appeared to you."[114] The logical sequence is identical to that of 10:9.

Many persons in antiquity of various persuasions treated the weak or healed the sick. Regarding Q, the evidence is too limited in scope to allow a judgment to be made about the meaning of this particular practice for the persons whom Q represents. In these terms alone, the people told in 10:9a to "treat the weak" would simply be one more example of ancient medical variety. The only thing that perhaps permits a more specific conclusion to be drawn is the striking connection already noted in both 10:9 and 11:14–20 between this "treatment" and the kingdom of God. Such a self-understanding of traffic in trauma and therapy is more distinctive.[115]

A first likeness to 10:9 may be found in Diogenes Laertius's account of the flamboyant Cynic Menedemus. Menedemus is said to have achieved such power in doing wonders (*terateia*) that he went about in the guise of a Fury, claiming he had come from Hades, the divine realm of the dead, to witness as an *episkopos* the sins being committed here, so that when he returned to the netherworld, he could report them to the powers below. Thus with Menedemus and his thaumaturgy arrived the kingdom of at least one god.[116]

A second parallel occurs in Lucian's less than unbiased account of the passing of Peregrinus, who was first a Cynic, then a Christian, then a Cynic once again. Lucian relates that before Peregrinus's self-ordained apotheosis by immolation, he had letters sent to most of the famous cities of antiquity via persons he called "messengers from the dead" (*nekraggeloi*) and "underworld couriers" (*nerterodromoi*) — essentially the same thing as Menedemus's claim to have come from Hades. Lucian also reports in a *vaticinium ex eventu* that after Peregrinus's death, "some will be found who say that they have been healed of quartan fevers by him." Thus associated with Peregrinus and his followers were both the experience of healing and a sense of the divine presence drawing near.[117]

How do these comparisons affect interpretation of 10:9?[118] Minimally, they underscore once again the correlation between Q and Cynicism, insofar as both Menedemus and Peregrinus were well-known

Cynics. The same parallels also make it clear that the experience of healing in antiquity and corresponding sense of the incursion of "God's kingdom" were not inevitably "a sign of the end-time."[119] They could be understood instead as simply among the effects of an uncommon wisdom.

To say in 10:9b that "the kingdom of God has arrived" accounts for the claim made by the persons whom Q represents to impart well-being, a "cure" from "illness," immediate access to that state of existence referred to elsewhere in the document as "happiness" or "blessedness" (6:20b–21) and "all these things" (12:31).[120] The "kingdom of God" identified with the Q people would describe the sudden sense of relief discovered by all persons healed from bodily distress under the tutelage of these divine messengers.

The kingdom of God in 10:9b explains the newly won ability dispensed by the Q people in 10:9a to enjoy freedom from debilitating woe in the midst of otherwise difficult circumstances, much as the Cynics promised *eudaimonia* to those who would join them in following the rule of "nature." The appeal of such persons, offering health as heavenly rule in a social context otherwise lacking modern medicine and under foreign occupation, is not hard to imagine. One might have risked a little hospitality to see if what they said were true.[121]

10:10–11. Whichever city you enter and they do not receive you, going out of that city, remove the dust from your feet.

I know of no parallels to the gesture depicted in this saying, beyond its repetition in later Christian literature.[122] One of the problems faced by previous interpreters of 10:10–11 has been the ludicrous figure cut, if one were actually to do what is here prescribed.[123] W. L. Knox, for example, is sure that the saying in 10:10–11 must refer to the removal of dust from one's shoes and not literally "from your feet" — although the relevant Greek term in 10:11 is clearly "feet" and sandals were expressly prohibited in 10:4 — because "it is hard to imagine a dramatic gesture for the latter," namely, dusting off your feet.[124] Paul Gächter says simply that the whole affair would be *lächerlich*.[125] Perhaps, however, a certain element of the ridiculous was not unintended.

The "symbolic" gesture depicted in 10:10–11 responds (negatively) to an entire community's unwillingness to receive the persons whom Q represents.[126] Like the act of healing in 10:9, this type of communication (by symbolic gesture) was not restricted to only one or two groups in antiquity. Many different persons might have recourse to such behavior in order to make public and poignant their case. The classical prophets of Israel, for example, often performed acts of this sort, as did triumphant Roman generals returning — or wishing to return — to the imperial city.

Most of these persons, however, did not try to look foolish in the process. But the Cynics often courted ridicule precisely in this fashion, making the point they wished to score in ways not unlike what we read in 10:10–11. Consider the following examples:

> One day [Diogenes] made his way with head half shaven into a party of young revellers, as Metrocles relates in his *Anecdotes*, and was beaten by them. Afterwards he wrote on a tablet the names of those who had struck him and went about with the tablet hung around his neck, till he had covered them with ridicule and brought universal blame and discredit upon them.[127]

> When someone dropped a loaf of bread and was ashamed to pick it up, Diogenes, wishing to admonish him, tied a rope to the neck of a wine-jar and dragged it through the Ceramicus.[128]

> [Diogenes] lit a lamp in broad daylight and went about, saying, "I am looking for a man."[129]

> Having exasperated the musician Nicodromus, [Crates] was struck by him on the face. So he stuck a plaster on his forehead and wrote on it, "Nicodromus' handiwork."[130]

At least two of these passages describe the response of Cynics to maltreatment at the hands of others, though none results directly from conflict with an entire city.[131] Eschatological judgment, in any case, is never the point.[132] As with the Cynics, a slightly wacky reply is the strategy of response recommended in 10:10–11 when faced with civic rejection: an I'll-show-you-how-foolish-all-this-is disparagement of those who refused to receive the Q people.[133] It is good to know that some early "Christians" could keep a sense of humor.

10:16. Whoever receives you receives me. And whoever receives me, receives the one who sent me.

Unlike the occasional rebuff anticipated in 10:10–11 (and 10:6), in 10:16 we learn what a positive reception of the Q people would finally mean.[134] Face to face since 10:3 with the threat of "wolves" and other mean-minded men and women, looking to be taken in by any peaceable soul (10:5) but also knowing complete rejection (10:10–11), just why these vagrant (10:4) "doctors" of a divine rule (10:9) ought to have been given better treatment seems a justifiable question. 10:16 provides the rationale for their irregular reception.[135]

At the same time, in 10:16 we return to where we began in 10:3 with the idea of being "sent." As every good *inclusio* will do, the saying in 10:16 recalls as it restates what was declared at the beginning of the "mission" speech.[136] The Q people are finally represented as divine messengers whose hospitable acceptance is equivalent to being visited by the superior power that first dispatched them.[137]

❧

Outlined in 10:3–6, 9–11, 16 is the daily "life-cycle" of the persons whom Q represents. A brief depiction of the social situation in which they found themselves is first given in 10:3, followed then by a minimal code of dress and manners in 10:4, a somewhat longer discussion of how the persons whom Q represents were to seek sustenance and to handle possible rejection in 10:5–6, 10–11, and a brief statement of their actual "work" in 10:9a along with a particular interpretation of its specific value in 10:9b. In 10:16, a transcendental warrant is lastly provided for what otherwise might easily have appeared to be a thoroughly mundane round of activities.

The sayings in 10:3–6, 9–11, 16 do not provide us with all the information we will need in order to paint a complete portrait of the persons whom Q represents. But enough is said here to begin at least the task of sketching their social profile. Like the Cynics, the persons whom Q represents embodied a thoroughgoing "radical" critique of local "Hellenistic" culture: the lake region of first-century C.E. lower Galilee. Styling themselves emissaries or scouts of a more satisfying life, the original Q people acted as agents of "God's kingdom," whose power they felt would grant all takers both the key to happiness in general and more particularly an effective treatment of "whatever ailed you" — much as the Cynics called their peculiar way of life a shortcut to felicity, believing that its demanding "program" of rigorous training (askēsis) would alone be able to cure the ills produced by what was otherwise falsely supposed to be the "good" life.[138]

The Cynics' determined self-dispossession of all "civilized" goods and services was meant to place them beyond the reach of the wider dominant culture's closely knit circles of dependency and obligation. The Cynics characterized their way of life as rather one of "following nature," although the idea of nature was never further developed by them. It simply provided analogies of opposition to reigning social norms.[139] In Q 10:4, we can see to what extent the Q people shared with the Cynics basic features of this so-called "primitivism."[140]

Wandering from town to town and house to house, the first Galilean Christians responsible for Q's formative stratum looked to other men and women of good will or "sons of peace" for signs of hospitality. In exchange, the Q people were prepared to trade the benefits of their uncommon wisdom. It was not an easy life, to be sure, made even harsher by the restrictions that these beggars imposed upon themselves, abstaining from all provision. Furthermore, they could count on meeting some hostility along the way, sufficient to warrant their own self-description as being "like sheep among wolves" and to require the creation of a strategy for exiting hostile hamlets in disgrace. Though we may find it hard to imagine contentment in such a form, the original disciples of Jesus in Galilee presumably thought that they were merely following the leader.[141]

CHAPTER TWO

Ethics: *"Love Your Enemies"*
Strategies of Resistance (6:27–35)

E VERY ETHOS rationalizes and reproduces itself by developing certain customs and conventions, codes, norms, and laws, whose articulation and problematization is the enterprise of ethics. Ethical discourse is, in this sense, always a second-order reflection on the embodied understanding of existence realized in the social practice of a group. Ethical discourse seeks to clarify this shared self-understanding either by resolving particular problems confronting its protagonists along life's way or by refining specific aspects of the same social style through considered elaboration.[1] A striking example of such reflection in Q's formative stratum is the well-known exhortation to "love your enemies" in 6:27–35 at the heart of Q's inaugural "sermon."[2]

Theissen regarding this text (6:27–35) has raised the pertinent question: What is the concrete *Sitz im Leben* that must be imagined for the ethical instruction given here, if taken at face value, not to register in practice merely an open invitation to repeated abuse by others and ultimately self-destruction?[3] I assume that the moral maxims gathered together in 6:27–35 were not initially proposed and subsequently appropriated by their first adherents simply to make life more miserable but, instead, to help these persons out by suggesting a better way of dealing with the various difficulties and displeasures facing them in life. In this regard, the language of the text has meaning only if and when it worked in practice. To state Theissen's question another way: What made the imperative to "love your enemies" and the related recommendations in 6:27–35 more than just "lousy" advice?

I bracket out at the beginning of this investigation every effort to define more precisely the exact meaning of the term "love" in "love your enemies." Obviously, the word's concrete significance must be considered at some point. But to presume at the outset a sufficient consensus as to the specific referent of the same four-letter expression in the face of abiding disputes regarding both the behavior and the sentiment it properly implies is hardly acceptable. Certainly, the paradoxical effect felt for centuries by commentators on this passage of the combination in it of "love" and "enemies" should alert us to the possibility that a certain rhetorical craft — and craftiness — is here expressed rather than self-evidently a high "altruistic" moral ideal.

The text of Q 6:27–35, in English translation, is likely as follows:

> *6:27.* Love your enemies. *6:28.* Pray for those who revile you. *6:29.* Offer the person slapping you on the cheek the other one as well, and let the person taking your cloak also have your tunic. *6:30.* Give to the person asking you for something, and do not ask back from the person borrowing from you. *6:31.* Treat people the same way that you want them to treat you. *6:32.* If you love only those who love you, so what? Even the tax-collectors do this. *6:33.* And if you only greet your brothers, so what? Even the Gentiles do the same. *6:35.* You be sons of God, because he makes his sun rise on the evil and the good.[4]

The sequence of sayings in 6:27–35 is not artless.[5] A certain argument subtends the series, just as later the same material was reworked by both Matthew and Luke in order to score the particular points that each evangelist wished to make.[6] There is no reason to assume, however, that the development of the discourse in 6:27–35 antedates the composition of Q's formative stratum.[7]

What is the logic of this speech? How do its different parts fit together? What kind of concrete strategy is here developed? How persuasive is it as an ethical posture? Are the claims it makes believable, both those implied and those explicit? What are the odds that it would work, if put into practice? What "objective conditions" must be in place for it to have a chance to succeed?

A complete answer to these questions will obviously require that each of the sayings in 6:27–35 be examined individually. Attention must also be paid, however, and indeed first to the line of reasoning that joins them all together in a single general statement.

Why "love your enemies"? At least two reasons are proposed at the end of the discourse in 6:32–35 for indulging in such unusual behavior. First, in the final verse it is suggested that thereby you will become sons of God, who also makes his sun rise on the evil and the good (6:35). The motivation is the same as in every other *imitatio Dei*.[8] It is assumed that you want to be like God.[9]

The other reason for loving your enemies is implied by the rhetorical questions asked in 6:32–33, namely, that you will be compensated for your efforts. Love that merely matches the behavior of most "ordinary" human beings (or worse) does nothing noteworthy. Only an outstanding performance in this regard will be recognized as meriting reward.[10]

It is not unusual for New Testament exegetes to argue that the imperative "love your enemies" in Q differs from similar statements by other persons in antiquity due to the purity of its, namely, Jesus' concern for the welfare of the enemy. At the same time, however, most scholars since Hans Haas would agree that the imperative itself, "love your enemies," cannot be said to be unique to early Christianity.[11] Instead, as William Klassen writes, "the focus of any comparative study must now be on the motivation, the scope, and the grounding of this commandment."[12] Such an approach, however, tends to exclude from further serious consideration every parallel text that might diminish in any way the unabated understanding of "love your enemies" as part of an elevated moral sensibility.

According to Q, to be a "son of God" and thus to stand out from the moral crowd was desirable not for its own sake, but because of the specific benefits it would deliver. Likewise, to "love your enemies" was advocated not for reasons of intrinsic merit, but in the hope that some other good might thereby be achieved. What "other good" was this? In Roman-dominated first-century c.e. Galilee — a simmering state of unresolved hostility and sporadic military repression, with personal enmity and the permanent threat of abuse as constant problems — it seems reasonable to assume that "liberation" of some sort from the menace of these things would be a basic goal.[13]

As already observed in chapter one, the main objective of the Q people, sent out "like sheep among wolves" into this rather intimidating social landscape, was to be able to enjoy in such a condition the highest degree possible of bodily happiness, to experience in the fullest available form the reign of blessedness, to attain a mode of existence in which the need constantly to defend oneself could be felt at last to have been overcome; despite the otherwise largely unhappy circumstances in which one still had to live, face to face with variable levels of socialized hatred and aggression, forced to manage a shifting cultural climate of mistrust and frequent disappointment.[14]

To be a son of God meant getting "one up" on surrounding evil and misfortune. It meant, to quote precisely what J. Piper dislikes about the ideal Cynic in Epictetus, being "sovereignly serene in adversity," getting "over" the reciprocity of anger and resentment, not being limited to only "those like us" for friendship and support.[15]

How, then, did you "love your enemies"? What constitutes "love" in this case? At least five specific acts are mentioned in 6:28–30. These are (1) prayer on behalf of those who verbally abuse you; (2) turning the other cheek when struck (to be struck again); (3) letting a second garment be taken (after the first one had been forcibly removed); (4) giving to whoever asks you for something; and (5) lending freely.

Are these different responses best understood as particular examples — "focal instances" — of how to "love your enemies," i.e., secondary attempts to clarify the opening imperative's otherwise "complex" meaning?[16] Or is the exhortation to "love your enemies" itself the secondary formulation: an effort to conceptualize in a more general way the diverse field of actions defined by the individual imperatives in 6:28–30?

The statement "love your enemies" is per se an oxymoron. Literally, it makes no sense. Furthermore, no actual behavior is described. No specific act is in view. This contrasts with the sayings in 6:28–30 where, however strange what is suggested there may seem, specific behaviors are stipulated. Again, these acts are: prayer for verbal abusers, exposing the other cheek, letting the tunic go as well, giving to whoever asks, and not asking back whatever may have been lent.

If Paul Ricoeur is correct that at the level of ethical choice, only specific acts — to be precise, the specific representations of ultimately unfulfilled acts — are in fact capable of generating or "motivating" concrete behavior,[17] then not only logically but practically the specific imperatives in 6:28–30 must have "preceded" the synthetic paradox of "love your enemies" in 6:27. At the level of the text, the pungent formulation "love your enemies" has been placed first for the sake of rhetorical effect, to be elaborated subsequently with more specific phrases. But in terms of actual performance, the latter are the former's originary matrix.

It is important to be clear about what exactly the term "priority" means here, if only because more than one analysis could be conducted in the name of "first" and "next," each leading to different results. A rhetorical analysis, for example, will once again find in 6:27 an especially apt point of departure for the kind of discourse that follows, according to the ancient rules and "agonies" of argument and persuasion.[18] The practice of persuasion, however, and a persuasive practice are not the same thing. What counts in the second instance is achievement, not agreement.

At least regarding 6:27, 28–30 and these sayings' general viability as a moral strategy, the critical question is where to "ground" the discourse. This is essentially what I mean by "priority" and why Ricoeur's reflections on the relationship between representation and action are relevant at this point. If the particular instructions given in 6:28–30 were ever actually useful to the persons whom Q represents, it is not because they first helped to understand and practically "apply" the literally quite impossible (as stated) opening commandment, "love your enemies." Rather, it was only through the occasional effort to realize in practice "the specific representations of ultimately unfulfilled acts" in 6:28–30 that their later "rationalization" in 6:27 could come into being.

The particular phrase "love your enemies" should not therefore be understood as ever having been itself the operative mainspring of the *modus vivendi* it now introduces. The opening exhortation in 6:27 is simply a secondary conceptualization of the specific acts referred to in 6:28–30. The statement "love your enemies" thematizes the content of these other sayings by attributing to their current conjunction in Q an underlying logic. Otherwise, not incorrectly, they might be seen as "just" a loose assortment of unlikely responses.

In Kantian terms, the leading oxymoron "love your enemies" establishes the domain of a certain ethical "objectivity": the intellectual space of "non-violent resistance." "Love your enemies" would be the constitutive antinomy creating the condition of the possibility that now permits the reader to imagine the heretofore "inconceivable" notion of overcoming evil with good, to use Paul's terms, or the defeat of enmity through different means than those of hatred and retaliation. The specific meaning of "love your enemies" is thus its discursive power to coordinate, as though they possessed some necessary relationship with one another, the various specific acts represented in 6:28–30. The initial imperative depends upon the "preexistence" of these other sayings in order to think itself.[19]

Are the specific gestures depicted in 6:28–30 at all "realistic," even if "ultimately unfulfilled"? Theissen thinks so, but finally only on the lips of his infamous *Wandercharismatiker*. Theissen writes:

> the original *Sitz im Leben* has great meaning for how we assess loving your enemies and non-violence. The sedentary Christian falls into ever greater dependence by giving way to his enemy. Indeed, he must reckon with the fact that he will meet him repeatedly again and again. Giving way often means in this case inviting continuation of the fact that one is taken advantage of and degraded. Non-resistance heightens the probability that infringements will repeat themselves. Nevertheless, the great command to love his enemy exists for him as well. The *Wandercharismatiker* can realize the command much more convincingly. He is truly free. He can abandon the site of his defeat and humiliation. He may reckon with the fact that he will not meet his enemy again. As long as he keeps moving on, he can maintain his independence and freedom. The price of this freedom is a rigorous asceticism: a life on the edge of the bare minimum for existence. But the profit is great.[20]

The best enemies to love are those you meet only once. The best way to assure such a situation is not to stay too long in any one place. Theissen insists, nonetheless, that sedentary Christians were equally obliged to love their enemies as well, though Theissen recognizes that "giving way in this case often means inviting continuation of the fact that one is taken advantage of and degraded." Theissen appears to assume that what is said in Q 6:27–35 already commanded canonical obedience from its original audience, despite the changing contexts in which the saying was initially heard, though, again, Theissen clearly knows that the same text in one life-situation (e.g., "itinerant radicalism") meant something entirely different in practice from what it would signify in another setting (e.g., established village life).

At the heart of 6:27–35, between the uncompromising imperatives of 6:27–30, on the one hand, and the demanding reasoning of 6:32–35, on the other, stands the widespread commonplace of ancient moral wisdom known as the "golden rule."[21] Perplexing for many readers has been the presence of this saying here at all.[22] One solution to the problem — followed by the evangelist Matthew — has therefore been simply to assume that it really ought not to be there. Thus Matthew moved it to a more "suitable" location elsewhere in the Sermon on the Mount.[23] But this is not the only possible interpretation.

The golden rule's self-evidence is relativized, if not indeed basically called into question, by its curious placement in Q 6:31. Given that enemies, revilers, pugilists, thieves, beggars, and borrowers, then as now, typically did not do what they did in the name of reciprocity, the standard code of mutuality among peers expressed in 6:31 was made in Q to undergird, at its own expense, the unusual commands in 6:27–30, insofar as the present location of the golden rule in 6:31 suggests that one should perform the preceding acts of acquiescence because, as someone else's enemy, that is how you would like them to respond to you. The dubious worth of the golden rule as a sufficient guide to moral action was then able to be evaluated explicitly and negatively in 6:32–33.[24]

6:27–28. Love your enemies. Pray for those who revile you.[25]

There is no reason to assume that the sayings in 6:27–28 do not mean what they say, however difficult they may be to understand. Words habitually opposed to one another as antonyms are here combined to form a single statement. Enemies are not generally those we love; those we love are not usually our enemies. Prayer for the persons who mistreat us is not likely the reaction they expected to elicit. To call these sayings paradoxical, however, explains nothing beyond the fact of their inversionary nature. Counsel is given here that cuts against the grain of customary wisdom.

Nowhere else in early Christian literature is the statement made as directly and in so unqualified a manner as in Q 6:27: "love your enemies."[26] An exception to this might seem to be 2 Clem 13:4, where God suggests that "it is to your credit if you love your enemies and those who hate you" versus simply "loving those who love you." According to 2 Clem 13:3, this tradition is "one of the great and beautiful sayings of God at which the heathen marvel." But the same writer immediately goes on to remark how "when they see that we not only do not love those that hate us, but not even those who love us, they laugh us to scorn, and the name is blasphemed." It seems that the intended readers of 2 Clement could hardly keep the peace at home, let alone exemplify how best to manage extramural conflict. The writer of the letter cites the "dominical" saying in 2 Clem 13:4, knowing full well that the actual behavior of his intended audience did not conform in any way to this "marvelous" proposal.

In other early Christian texts, it is always only prayer or benediction in the face of enmity and aggression that is mentioned: i.e., the second imperative in 6:28.[27] Paul writes, for example, in Rom 12:14: "Bless those who persecute you; bless and do not curse them," restating Rom 12:12: "Rejoice in your hope, be patient in tribulation, be constant in prayer." Such admonitions stand in a certain tension with the preceding explicit instructions about love in Rom 12:9–10: "Let love be genuine; hate what is evil, hold fast to what is good; love one another with brotherly affection; outdo one another in showing honor," where the practice of love is effectively reserved by Paul for the relationship between fellow believers. Regarding the rest of the inhabited world, a "put-up-with" attitude is essentially advised.

"Bless those who persecute you" amounts in Paul to the less than altruistic counsel: "You be nice to them, and some day they'll get what's coming to them." Thus, we read in Rom 12:17–21:

> Repay no one evil for evil, but take thought for what is noble in the sight of all. If possible, so far as it depends upon you, live peaceably with all. Beloved, never avenge yourselves, but leave it to the wrath of God; for it is written, "Vengeance is mine, I will repay, says the Lord." No, "if your enemy is hungry, feed him; if he is thirsty, give him drink; for by so doing you will heap burning coals upon his head." Do not be overcome by evil, but overcome evil with good.

Paul's main concern is simply to safeguard early Christian moral integrity under attack.

The saying preserved — as partly reconstructed — in *P.Oxy.* 1224 (fr. 2 recto col. i) counsels prudence:

> And] pray for your [enemies]. For he who is not [against you] is for you. [He who today is] far off will be [near you] tomorrow, and . . .[28]

A certain caution is here advised. The person presently opposed to you may soon prove useful to you as an ally. Don't burn your bridges before you have to. Indeed, build as many of them as you can by praying for your enemies.[29]

In Polycarp (*Phil.* 12:3) prayer is promoted for "those who persecute and hate you and for enemies of the Cross." These are part of the addenda to Polycarp's main concern: "Pray for all the saints" as well as for various emperors, potentates, and princes. The underlying purpose is not unlike that of Paul's above: "that your [moral] fruit may be manifest among all persons," being "noble in the sight of all" and "that you may be perfected in him."

In *Phil.* 12:2, Polycarp had already expressed the desire that his readers be built up "in faith and truth, and in all gentleness, and without wrath, and in patience, and in longsuffering, and endurance, and purity," having "lot and part" with the saints. The subsequent suggestion in *Phil.* 12:3 that the same persons pray for "those who persecute and hate you" is thus merely the acid test of these other virtues. Prayer "for enemies of the Cross" is the finest mark of sainthood. The logic is eminently martyrological.

Notable parallels to Q 6:27–28 may be found in Cynic literature.[30] Compare, for example, the imperative in 6:27 with the statement by Diogenes: "When asked [by someone] how to repulse an enemy, he replied, 'You be kind and good to him.' "[31] Regarding use of the word "repulse" here, it is important to remember that "love your enemies" in 6:27 does not mean (as, perhaps, it does in *P.Oxy.* 1224) that "your enemies" will thereby cease to be your *enemies*. The statement, "love your enemies," would lose all of its rhetorical force, if the activity of "love" in the imagined confrontation were somehow to eliminate or ignore the inimical character of the stated "enemy." In fact, the statement, "love your enemies," must signify in 6:27 precisely what Diogenes suggests above: a strategy for handling unfriendly opposition. "Love your enemies," in other words, and in this way take care of the "jerks."[32]

Consider in addition the following *bons mots* by Epictetus, commenting initially on the nature of "true" Cynicism:

> For this too is a very pleasant strand woven into the Cynic's way of life. He must be flogged like an ass and, while he is being flogged, love those who are flogging him as though he were the father or brother of them all.[33]

> To fancy we shall be contemptible in the sight of other persons if we do not employ every means to hurt the first enemies we meet is characteristic of extremely ignoble and ignorant persons. For while it is a common saying among us that the contemptible person is

recognized, among other things, by his inability to do harm, he is much better recognized by his inability to offer aid.[34]

Epictetus finds in the projected confrontation with hostile aggressors not simply another instance of Paul's concern to demonstrate moral integrity under attack but rather a useful opportunity for developing and refining the practice of virtue. A similar perspective was also held by Bion of Borysthenes:

> Bion said to his intimate friends that they might well think they were making progress when they could listen to their revilers as though they were saying: "Friend, since you have not the look of one who is base and unthinking, health and great joy be yours, and God grant that you ever may prosper."[35]

The Cynic parallels to 6:27–28 help us to appreciate the "agonistic" quality of these sayings. We are not here in the presence of an altruistic ethic of "selflessness" or even notable concern for the welfare of the other.[36] Indeed, quite the opposite. The counsel to "love your enemies" and to "pray for those who revile you" belongs in Q, as also in the different statements by Diogenes, Epictetus, and Bion cited above, to the formation and exercise of a certain social character. One of its more salient features was precisely this ability to handle hostility with notable restraint and calculated inversion. The same holds true for the following saying as well.

6:29. Offer the person slapping you on the cheek the other one as well, and let the person taking your cloak also have your tunic.

The next saying in 6:29 concerns assault, battery, and theft: whether plain and simple, as Luke has it, or legally, as in Matthew. What is said here has never been a welcome suggestion. Few Christians, early or late, have willingly passed the word along, and even fewer done what it says, if only because it is difficult to distinguish the advice given in this saying from a certain masochism.[37] The following words of admiration expressed by the Orthodox church father Gregory Nazianzus for the Cynic founder figure Antisthenes are therefore doubly interesting:

> How great a man was Antisthenes! When struck publicly by a certain daring and impudent person, he simply wrote on his forehead the name of the one who struck him, just as one writes the name of the artist on a statue — to accuse him more caustically in this way.[38]

A certain proactive strategy of passive resistance is here apparent. Like animals that "play dead" when threatened by danger, a forward pose of heightened vulnerability is struck at undeniable risk in the face of aggressive force. Not always successful, the same behavior may nonetheless frequently produce a "holding pattern," delayed attack, bewilderment, retreat, if not defeat on the part of the predator. Often, it is enough to turn what looked to be a fatal encounter into one less final in its ultimate results, if only for the time being.

Epictetus, of course, has a rationale for such behavior. The philosopher who knows his way around the world, says the limping teacher from Nicopolis, is not surprised at anything that happens to him:

> Does anything seem strange to him? Does he not expect worse and harsher treatment from the wicked than actually befalls him? Does he not count it as gain whenever they fail to go to the limit? "So-and-so reviled you." I am greatly obliged to him for not striking me. "But he also struck you." I am greatly obliged to him for not wounding me. "But he also wounded you." I am greatly obliged to him for not killing me.[39]

Lest you think that this is merely idle speculation:

> Practice, man, if you are arrogant, to submit when you are reviled; not to be disturbed when you are insulted. Then, you will make such progress that even if someone strikes you, you might say to yourself: "Imagine that you have thrown your arms around a statue."[40]

Or that you have been kissed on both cheeks.

> Now the Cynic must have such patient endurance that most people will think that he is insensate and a stone. Nobody reviles him; nobody beats him; nobody insults him. But his body he himself has given for anyone who wants to use it as they see fit.[41]

The same applies to material goods as well. Epictetus interprets the ancient moral philosopher's assumed adherence to "the law of God" reciprocally to imply a complete insensitivity on this person's part to the usual concerns of ownership and possession, much as these fixations were likewise opposed in 6:29b. The truly wise person knows, says Epictetus:

> [how] to use what is given and not to yearn for what has not been given. When something is taken away, to give it up readily and without delay, being grateful for the time in which one had use of it — all this, if you do not wish to be crying for your wet-nurse and your grandmother![42]

The Cynic poet Cercidas of Megalopolis makes it clear that this approach to property was not merely a matter of the Cynics' personal moral development. As in Q, it also formed part of their larger strategy for dealing with their enemies. Cercidas indicates in the following statement the kind of social posture that he himself hoped someday to embody:

> As for me, O Parnos, I would like to be self-sufficient and to be considered useful, to accomplish many things, and sometime to address my enemies: "It went as it came, unencumbered."[43]

Note the relationship implied here between the Cynic virtue of "self-sufficiency" and being able to "let it all go" in the face of ill-will and hostility. By not feeling the need to protect what they had, every material means of manipulating and imposing oneself on the ancient Cynic and first follower of Jesus in Galilee had been taken out of their enemies' hands.

As Robert Tannehill correctly notes, "no consideration is given [in 6:29–30] to whether this will be helpful to the other person.... the commands are not based upon prudential considerations as to what will result in the greatest good for the other."[44] Rather, at stake is the procurement of the maximum available good for those who otherwise stand in danger of personal assault and battery as well as uninvited theft. The imperatives in 6:29 — and 6:30, as we soon shall see — were originally prudential considerations provided for persons whose lives must wend their way through contexts of diverse insecurity. To turn the other cheek and give up both cloak and tunic were hardly expressions of "universal love," but just "smart moves" under the circumstances.

6:30. Give to the person who asks you for something, and do not ask back from the person borrowing from you.

Consider this saying (6:30) from the perspective of the following response made by Crates to the pointed inquiry why the person asking him the question should become a philosopher. Virtually the same point of view is expressed here as in 6:30. Crates said:

> You will be able to open your purse easily and to give away freely what you draw out with your hand: not as you do now, calculating, hesitant, trembling, as those with shaky hands. But you will regard a purse that is full as full and after you see that it is empty, you will not complain.[45]

The same "casual" approach to cash and collateral may be observed in the following sayings as well. All of them exemplify the Cynics' "subversive wisdom" regarding money and its proper (or improper) management:[46]

[Diogenes] also used to say that it is necessary to extend our hands to our friends without our fingers closed.[47]

When someone asked for his cloak back, Diogenes answered: "If you gave it to me, it's now mine; and if it was a loan, I'm still using it."[48]

When [Diogenes] needed money, he used to say not that he asked his friends for it, but that he asked for it back.[49]

Ideally, the Cynics did not require money (cf. Q 10:4). Of course, this does not mean that they never used it. But when the tokens passed through their hands, the Cynics sought to make it clear how little value they placed on the fact of having such a thing in their possession.

Indeed, the Cynics regularly made fun of the importance of owning anything at all, that is, of respecting the ownership by others of specific material goods. In full conformity to this carnivalesque *esprit d'abandon* is, again, the counsel given in Q 6:30 to give whatever one might have to the person begging from you and not to ask back whatever had been lent.

Except for 6:31, the only other statement in Q 6:27–35 with a parallel saying in the *Gospel of Thomas* is 6:30. The saying in question from the *Gospel of Thomas* (95) reads as follows:

[Jesus said:] "If you have money, do not lend it at interest. Rather, give [it] to someone from whom you will not get it back."[50]

The *Gospel of Thomas*'s specification of the issue at hand in terms of interest and profit (or loss) is consistent with the same writing's polemic elsewhere against tradesmen and merchants.[51] At the same time, the final imperative at the end of *GThom* 95 to give without expecting anything in return is of a piece with the similar statement in Q 6:30b. Both texts agree in recommending that material possessions should circulate freely with no thought given to gain or even to keeping a reserve.

The private ownership of property was plainly not a supreme value: neither for the Cynics nor for the *Gospel of Thomas* nor for Q. That the subject of possessions should arise in the midst of a discourse on enmity and abuse ought not to surprise us. After all, economic need and greed, the pain of want and the desire for wealth, have not infrequently been at the heart of human hatred and the forced expropriation of other people's goods. Significant deviation from the usual habits for handling such an issue (e.g., hanging on for dear life to whatever you've got and trying to make everything you own work as much as possible to your own advantage) belongs to the formative stratum of Q's general effort to upset the social order (or disorder) created by these patterns of both thought and action.

I am not suggesting, of course, that Q 6:30 corresponds in any proleptic fashion to the modern "socialist" critique of "bourgeois" capitalism, nor does 6:30 itself explicitly polemicize against the concept of personal possessions. Indeed, the saying assumes that on occasion you might actually have something someone else could need or want.

I will insist, however, that the transition in 6:30 from the focus in 6:29 on bodily violence and theft to matters of begging and borrowing, giving and lending, is not as notable or discontinuous a progression as some scholars have made it out to be.[52] In social situations like first-century C.E. Galilee, everything discussed in 6:29–30 can and should properly be seen as part of the regular daily grind of a subjugated people's struggle to survive.

In contexts of cultural disintegration and the correlative process of "restructuration" that accompanies it, personal violence and theft are as "normal" a part of everyday existence as the more "peaceable" exchange of goods and services. The fact, moreover, that no attempt is made in 6:29 to minimize loss — the saying rather encourages its original audience to abandon everything — anticipates well the equally "short-sighted" instructions in 6:30 to give to everyone who asks and lend without demanding back. In every instance, the governing strategy is one of thoroughgoing self-dispossession.[53]

6:32–33. If you love only those who love you, so what? Even the tax collectors do this. And if you only greet your brothers, so what? Even the Gentiles do the same.[54]

As already seen, a certain mockery is made here of the ancient convention of reciprocity among peers. If "tax-collectors" and "Gentiles" as the standard forms of "low-life" in Galilean antiquity were known to treat their counterparts with mutual care and respect, then merely doing what they did could hardly qualify as living in accordance with the highest virtue. Such a style of social relations only served to establish the lowest common denominator on a scale of ethical performance, one whose matched achievement amounted for the Q people to having done absolutely nothing worthy of note. Only by behaving in a patently different fashion from the "normal" patterns of typical collegiality would those addressed by Q's formative stratum be able to realize their distinctive virtue.[55]

6:35. You be sons of God, because he makes his sun rise on the evil and the good.

How to interpret the concluding statement in 6:35 is a problem insofar as the saying seems to suggest that God, the supreme ethical model to be imitated, does not himself observe the usual moral codes of antiquity. At least as a weatherman, God is clearly "beyond good and evil." On the other hand, it may be that the general superiority implied by the term "God" was evinced precisely in this very ability to ignore individual meanness and other signs of personal badness for the sake of sustaining a larger level of well-being.

6:35 is the only place in Q where anyone who wants to can become a son of God. The means of doing so, if not the end, are eminently ethical. By behaving as God does, treating evil people just like everyone else, a divine life through affiliation with God could be enjoyed, specifically by ignoring, like the heavenly Father, all customary moral categories of social justice and due recompense.

The fact that God's sun shines on all, regardless of comportment and accomplishment, means that no prevailing "standard" form of civic righteousness exists that God might ultimately validate. For better or for worse, God is here, like Nietzsche's *Übermensch*, a non-respecter of traditional wisdom, a dissident in the cultural house of established order.

The Roman senator Seneca speaks in strikingly similar fashion at one point in his treatise *On Benefits*. Actually, the worried patrician is quoting someone else with whom he begs to differ. The problem is that God's handling of the universe could be invoked as a rationale for behavior that was otherwise quite foreign to the ancient aristocrat's sense of proper moral judgment:

"If you are imitating the gods," one says, "then bestow benefits also on the ungrateful; for the sun rises also on the wicked, and the sea lies open also to pirates."[56]

Seneca does not agree with this conclusion, at least not in this form, but like the answer given to Job out of the whirlwind, the proffered rebuttal of the obvious leaves something to be desired.

Not infrequently, the Cynics in their unconventional wisdom claimed to be imitating God. We have already seen how Epictetus said that the true Cynic "must love those who are flogging him as though he were the father or brother of them all," believing that:

[the Cynic] has made all persons his children.... [I]n this way, he approaches them all and cares for them all.... It is as a father that he does it, as a brother and as a servant of Zeus, who is father of us all.[57]

J. Piper must begrudgingly admit that "there is at least a superficial parallel between the Cynic's acting as the servant and son of Zeus and the Christian's acting [in love towards his enemies] as his Father in heaven."[58] Likewise, Tuckett acknowledges that "Epictetus' description in III. xxiii. 53f. about the duties of a Cynic to love those who are beating him may provide a genuine parallel to the gospel tradition." But because "Diogenes is often portrayed as very far from exhibiting such a generous attitude to his 'enemies,'" Tuckett immediately concludes that "Epictetus' description is no more than an ideal which he (as a Stoic) would wish to see in Cynics. Many other Cynics were considerably less loving."[59]

That the Cynics were not doctrinaire passivists or early advocates of total non-violence goes without saying, just as the animals that "play dead" to protect themselves on one occasion will devour their own prey on another. Strategies are by definition not universal programs, principles, or postulates, but contextually determined and thereby limited probings of particular possibilities. The comparison of the exhortation to "love your enemies" in Q 6:27–35 with different habits of the ancient Cynics is hardly discounted by this recollection of the fact that the Cynics could also respond to hostility and personal confrontation in other ways as well. In this, they were again like many early followers of Jesus.

🐚

In this chapter I have tried to show how the general exhortation to "love your enemies" in Q 6:27–35 "resolves" a particular "problem" faced by the persons whom Q represents in living out the ethos sketched for them in chapter one. This problem was the experience of inimical opposition: the various predicaments provoked and suffered by the Q people as a consequence of their decided social marginality.

The different strategies of resistance developed by the Q people to deal with the various difficulties they encountered along life's way find their most notable expression in the series of what Ricoeur calls "specific representations of ultimately unfulfilled acts" in 6:28–30. The proactive passivity and programmatic self-dispossession advocated by these sayings was subsequently thematized in 6:27 with the oxymoronic imperative "love your enemies," which introduces the passage as a whole.

The "golden rule" slyly placed *in medias res* in 6:31, the blunt rhetorical questions that follow in 6:32–33, and the final unsettling example of God in 6:35 conclude the exhortation with a series of probing rationalizations, all of which sustain the earlier imperatives in 6:27–30 by calling into question the same standard behavior the former commands so plainly oppose. The result (Q 6:27–35) is a skillfully argued piece of "early Christian ethics," helping further to articulate in both word and deed as a moral posture the underlying ethos of the Q people — one frequently, it would appear, but not surprisingly under fire.

CHAPTER THREE

Ideology:
"The Kingdom of God Has Arrived"

Symbolic Subversion
(6:20B; 10:9; 11:2, 20; 12:31; 13:18–21)

L IKE ETHICS, ideology is also a "second-order" type of reflection. Ideology represents an effort to systematize or elaborate through the use of certain analytical (promotional) "categories" the different positions assumed by a particular socio-political persuasion under determinate circumstances. Unlike ethics, however, whose attention is directed especially at the resolution of concrete problems or specific "cases" as well as the further specification of an established (or developing) way of life, ideology is essentially the art of generalization, making of a given event, person, idea, term, and/or association the exemplary instance(s) of some other fundamental principle, truth, or conviction.[1] Regarding Q, the different "kingdom of God" sayings in the document's formative stratum would correspond to this sort of intellectual production.[2]

As with "love your enemies," I bracket out initially all proposals as to what the "kingdom of God" might otherwise have meant at the time that Q was written.[3] Obviously, the different uses of this term and other expressions related to it in early Christian and Jewish literature must be taken into account at some point.[4] But to presume at the outset a sufficient definition of the meaning of the term "kingdom of God" in the face of continuing scholarly disagreement about this topic is once again hardly acceptable. To affirm that the "kingdom of God" was originally a certain kind of symbol is merely to acknowledge, first, the fact that more than one or two ancient documents employ the term, and, second, the likelihood of the expression's original multivalency.[5] The repeated use of a specific symbol is, of course, hardly foreign to the rhetoric of ideology.

In the subtitle above, I suggest that the kingdom of God in Q's formative stratum is a type of "symbolic subversion." By the expression "symbolic subversion" I mean both the ideational resignification of the linguistic cipher "kingdom of God" and a form of social dissent in these terms. In the latter case, something is promised that may or may not have been actually or completely achieved in practice. As ideological rhetoric, its effectiveness remains the same.

Through repeated reference to another "order" of things called the kingdom of God, the Q people endeavored to imagine and construct an alternate reality to the dominant social institutions of their immediate context and its prevalent moral values. Just how entangled this project finally was in the same persons' own historical *Sitz im Leben* determines the degree to which we then should understand the same "talk" of the kingdom of God in Q's formative stratum as either a utopian ideal or merely a discursive instrument of ongoing socio-political destabilization.

In the case of Q's formative stratum, the latter option is, in my opinion, most likely true. But before a final decision can be made, each individual saying must be reviewed.

6:20b. Happy are the poor, for yours is the kingdom of God.[6]

The first kingdom-of-God saying in Q (6:20b) is the well-known beatitude that declares that the "poor" are happy. Notice, however, that the saying is not primarily about the kingdom of God but, rather, is a statement about the status (i.e., happiness) of the poor, just as the two subsequent sayings in 6:21ab address those who are hungry and weep. Reference to the kingdom of God in 6:20b explains how it is that the "poor," a term traditionally associated with hardship and sorrow, could nonetheless be thought of as content. It underscores the fact that, from one point of view, a life without political power or material prosperity was neither inevitably defeated nor depressed, but instead somehow "blessed." At issue is what poverty means.[7]

The theme of poverty is widespread in the moral literature of antiquity. Everyone knew that being poor made life more difficult. Most, therefore, considered poverty an evil. Not everyone, however, held this point of view. Beyond the standard invocation of the worries of the wealthy, it seems that some had already sensed the possibility that "less" might be "more."[8] We read, for example, in one of the Cynic epistles:

> Practice needing little, for this is nearest to God, while the opposite is farthest away.[9]

The same perspective is spelled out elsewhere in greater detail, arguing that a position of dominance could be achieved over life's vicissitudes and misfortunes precisely by assuming up-front the predictable and proverbial trials of an impoverished life and thereby approximating the unperturbed felicity characteristic of divine aseity:

> Get used to washing yourselves with cold water, to drinking water, to eating by the sweat of your brow, to wearing a coarse cloak, to being worn out on the ground; and the baths will never be closed to you nor shall the vineyards and flocks be fruitless and the delicatessens and bed-stores go bankrupt, as happens to those who have acquired the habit, for example, of washing themselves with hot water or drinking wine and eating though they do not toil and wearing purple and resting on a bed.[10]

The statement in 6:20b that the poor have God's kingdom registers a similar point of view. The poor are called happy because they share in God's reign. Beyond this assertion, however, no further information is provided about what exactly the specific attributes or identifying marks of such a rule might be. The only nuance to be added to the blunt equation in 6:20b between the poor and happiness would be perhaps the suggestion of the sayings in 6:21ab not to trust appearances.[11]

It is clear in 6:20b that a share in God's kingdom means not going along with the customary understanding of misery and bliss, if only because one is convinced that present tears and hunger will soon give way to laughter and satisfaction (6:21ab), just as Diogenes used to say that hunger was the best way to give food its fullest flavor.[12] In 6:20b, the kingdom of God is precisely this ability — call it wisdom, if you will — to incorporate adversity into the enjoyment of contentment. The dramatic "reversal" of the usual categories of judgment habitually discerned here by New Testament scholars is nothing more and nothing less than this: in Nietzsche's terms, an *Umwertung der Werte;* in those of Diogenes of Sinope, a "defacing the currency" of ancient beliefs about what made for the "good" life.[13]

10:9. Treat the weak; say, "The kingdom of God has arrived."

This saying was already discussed in chapter one.[14] The conjunction in it of a certain therapeutic practice with reference to the kingdom of God is more distinctive than the usual cursory paraphrases of the saying by scholars would suggest. To say in 10:9b that "the kingdom of God has arrived" accounts for the claim made by the persons whom Q represents that at their hands and through their ministrations a greater level of bodily well-being could be achieved, a certain "cure" from "illness," the experience of "total" satisfaction elsewhere described in Q as the state of happiness or "blessedness" (6:20b) and "all these things" (12:31). In the case of 10:9, the "kingdom of God" describes this newly won ability to find freedom from debilitating woe, thus overcoming obstacles to health, in the midst of otherwise difficult circumstances, much as the Cynics promised *eudaimonia* to all who would join them in their following the rule of "nature."[15]

11:2. Let your kingdom come.[16]

Many scholars still read the beginning of the "Lord's prayer" in Q (11:2), namely, "Father, let your name be honored, let your kingdom come," under the influence of the Jewish "Kaddish" prayer, which begins similarly.[17] But this comparison is fraught with numerous difficulties and, in my opinion, finally unconvincing.

According to Joachim Jeremias, a fervent champion of the comparison of the Lord's prayer and the Kaddish, the initial two "you" petitions would "correspond to the Kaddish, the holy prayer, an old Aramaic prayer, with which the worship of the synagogue ended and which was known to Jesus probably since the days of his childhood."[18] If the *Encyclopaedia Judaica* can be believed, however:

> The Kaddish prayer was not originally part of the synagogue service.... The Kaddish is mentioned as part of the prescribed synagogue daily prayers for the first time in tractate *Soferim* (c. sixth century C.E.).[19]

As far as I know, Jeremias never explicitly discusses the dating of the Kaddish. Only once does he suggest implicitly why he assumes that the "Lord's prayer" is best compared with this text. The Kaddish, writes Jeremias, is "one of the very few Aramaic prayers of Judaism."[20] Jeremias evidently assumes that the historical Jesus spoke in Aramaic and that the "Lord's prayer" was itself initially composed (by Jesus) in the same language.[21]

Leaving aside the problems connected with such assumptions, it is striking that Jeremias then goes on to indicate the real reason why the Kaddish was preserved in Aramaic: "it was prayed immediately after the sermon, which was delivered in Aramaic."[22] The language of the Kaddish thus reveals nothing about the prayer's original date, only its place in the liturgy: "after the sermon, which was in Aramaic."[23]

A second equally indefensible reason given by Jeremias for associating the "Lord's prayer" with the Kaddish is the following:

> A small stylistic consideration also suggests that Jesus is taking up the Kaddish. The two "thou" petitions of the Lord's prayer stand side by side in asyndeton, whereas the "we" petitions are joined

together by καί. This discrepancy can probably be explained from the fact that the two petitions of the Kaddish similarly stood side by side in asyndeton in the earliest tradition.[24]

The "original" text of the Kaddish is, however, far more fluid than Jeremias's tight grammatical analysis would imply. Moreover, according to Ismar Elbogen, the first part of the Kaddish — the section referred to by Jeremias — likely recalls the short prayer at the end of the sermon, which "may have had in the beginning no specific wording but depended on the preference of the speaker."[25]

Jeremias takes association of the "Lord's prayer" with the Kaddish as support for Jeremias's eschatological interpretation of the "Lord's prayer," though Jeremias never argues for the opening petitions of the Kaddish as themselves "eschatological." In his *New Testament Theology*, Jeremias appears to assume that the reference to God's manifestation as Lord and the so-called "enthronement" themes in the Kaddish are per se "eschatological." But the use of enthronement themes in the Kaddish need not indicate more than the general conservatism of most liturgical language, which continues to speak in terms of a socio-historical situation long since part of the past.[26]

Regarding the "Lord's prayer" in Q, there are good reasons to read the petition in 11:2 that "your kingdom come" together with the subsequent request in 11:3 for daily bread.[27] The kingdom here is a matter of bodily sustenance, just as in 6:20b having a share in "God's kingdom" means being happy and in 10:9 the experience of renewed health. For the persons whom Q represents, without a beggar's bag or any other visible means of support (10:4), depending on the hospitality of strangers (10:5–6), hoping that the good fortune of the ravens and the lilies would be theirs as well (12:22–31), regular meals could reasonably be called a kingdom come.[28] Moreover, just as in 12:22–31 the problem of what to eat and wear is ultimately resolved by the suggestion "Seek his kingdom, and these things shall be yours as well," so it is requested in 11:2 that "your kingdom come" in order to receive in 11:3 "our daily bread."

The correspondence between 11:2–3 and 12:22–31 can be extended even further. Just as in 12:30 it is "your father [who] knows you need these things," the same "father" is asked in 11:2 to supply them.[29] In addition, one interpretation of the much discussed *hapaxlegomenon* in 11:3, *epiousios*, is that it means not "daily" but "sufficient": just enough, in other words, to get by on.[30] Like the ravens in 12:24 without a barn to store up food from one day to the next, whom God feeds nonetheless, or the grass of the field in 12:28, suddenly alive with lilies, if only for today, life is lived in 11:2–3 one day at a time. The power to do so is, in both instances, the concrete benefit of seeking (and finding) God's coming kingdom.[31]

11:20. **But if by the finger of God I cast out demons, then the kingdom of God has appeared to you.**[32]

In Q 11:14, at the start of the "Beelzebul controversy," whose final statement is the kingdom-of-God saying in 11:20, we read that a mute with a demon began to speak and the crowd was amazed. Though richer in narrative detail than the bare imperative to "treat the weak" or heal the sick in 10:9, the act itself of healing in 11:14 is not elaborated any further. The basic elements of a standard "healing miracle" are simply mentioned.[33] What follows then in 11:15–20 is an extended argument about the significance of that fact.[34]

The objection stated in 11:15 to what 11:14 has described is quite specific. The person responsible for curing the mute is charged with practicing "black" magic. Apparently, the same charge had been made on a number of other occasions (11:17a).[35] A small display of logical reasoning in 11:17b–18 leads to the recognition in 11:19a that those who make the charge are themselves involved through their "sons" in the same activity.

Two conclusions can then be drawn (11:19b, *dia touto*). Either the accusers are equally guilty as charged and "they [i.e., your sons] will be your judges" or it is clear (11:20a, *de*) that the mute was healed not through black magic but "by the finger of God."[36] In the latter case, the result (*ara*) would be that "the kingdom of God has appeared to you" (11:20b).[37]

The claim in 11:20b that "then the kingdom of God has appeared to you" opposes the reference in 11:18b to "his kingdom," namely, Satan's.[38] One might think that here, at least, the "kingdom of God" is understood apocalyptically as a new aeon about to replace the old and evil one.[39] But the reference to "his kingdom" in 11:18b merely repeats in terms of the initial accusatory figure of Beelzebul=Satan the logical problem posed in 11:17.

The reference in 11:18b to Satan's kingdom is part of a rhetorical elaboration that recalls the defamatory language of the opening charge of casting out demons by the power of Beelzebul in the midst of refuting it. The fact observed in 11:19a that the "sons" of the accusers practice the same trade as the accused makes clear that the debate is finally not about two opposing realms of reality, but the exercise of a certain power and competing claims to its legitimate use.

Invocation of the "kingdom of God" at the end of this argument is merely a rhetorically effective way of underscoring the fact that it was not "Beelzebul, the prince of demons," but God whose power has been manifested in the healing of the mute. Technically, the statement in 11:20b that "the kingdom of God has appeared to you" is an illative (*ara*) conversion, marking the logical inversion of the initial accusation in 11:15 and thus constituting its ultimate disproof.[40]

The "kingdom of God" in 11:20b is a thoroughly "negative" category, used to negate the negation in 11:15 of the healing practice depicted in 11:14. Reference to the "kingdom of God" in 11:20b is thus simply another instance of the kind of discursive legerdemain otherwise typical of Socrates and the Cynics (not to mention Hegel and Kierkegaard).

12:31. But seek his kingdom, and these things shall be yours as well.[41]

The saying in Q 12:31 has not figured prominently in most discussions of the kingdom of God, perhaps because the kingdom here so clearly neither comes nor is bestowed on anyone, but represents the consequence of human inquiry and desire.[42] One must first *seek* the kingdom for its promise to be realized. Without struggling to achieve it, as 12:31 describes the situation, there is no way to enjoy the blessings of God's reign.[43]

The basic problem addressed by Q 12:22–31, whose final statement (12:31) as in Q 11:14–20 is the kingdom-of-God saying, is worry about what to eat and to wear: i.e., how to meet these needs. The extended reasoning of 12:22–31 works in Q as an elaboration of the cryptic equation in 6:20b that conjoins poverty and happiness, just as an extended defense is provided in 11:14–20 of what 10:9 so tersely links together. The poor are those who suffer most the insecurities addressed in 12:22 regarding food and clothing. The saying as a whole (12:22–31) argues for the possibility of a full and ultimately satisfying experience of life at the edge of subsistence.[44]

Juxtaposed in Q 12:22–31 are two distinct realms or kingdoms with their different rules and rulers. The animal kingdom, the realm of nature, the rule of God are set in opposition to the orders of human civilization, exemplified by Solomon in all his glory.[45] The carefree existence of the ravens and the lilies registers an alternative to the "normal" burdens of ancient society. Agriculture with its repeated obligations of sowing, reaping, and storing in barns stands in contrast to the sufficient nurture of God for the ill-favored but abiding ravens.[46] The resplendence of translucent blossoms in the midst of common grass remains unmatched by the highest excellence of human artisans, whose efforts simply cannot yield a comparable offering, though they spin clothes fit for a king. The quintessential monarch could not outshine a flower, nor was the learning for which he was so famous able in the end to add a cubit to anyone's allotted measure.

In 12:22–31, the cultural enterprise as such is called into question. We may be tempted to call the critique romantic and unrealistic. Instead of struggling to get more of what human society offers in the way of food and clothing, 12:31 flatly states: "Seek his kingdom, and these things shall be yours as well." To "seek his kingdom" means to seek the father who, in 12:30b, knows what you need, as demonstrated in the sufficient nurture of the ravens (12:24) and the lilies (12:27). The kingdom of God in 12:31 is not exactly equivalent to "nature." But the ravens and the lilies and, by extension, the rest of creation (see, further, Q 13:18–19, 20–21) are the best examples Q can find for how God's kingdom works.

We are very close in 12:31 to what the Cynics meant when they proposed as a shortcut to virtue and felicity their peculiar mode of life, which they deemed to be "in accordance with nature."[47] The line of reasoning pursued in 12:22–31 compares especially well to that of Dio Chrysostom in his tenth discourse, *On Servants*. Dio is arguing with a man whose slave has run away. The conversation quickly becomes a debate about what is needed for the good life:

> Are you not going to try to acquire first that which will enable you to profit from everything and to arrange all your affairs well, but instead of thinking smartly will you seek money or land or slaves or teams of horses or ships or houses? You will become their slave and suffer on account of them and do a great deal of useless labor, and spend your whole life worrying about them without getting any benefit whatsoever from them. Do you not see the beasts there and the birds, how much freer from sorrow they live than human beings and how much more happily also, how much healthier and stronger they are, how each of them lives the longest life possible, although they have neither hands nor human intelligence. But to counterbalance these and other limitations, they have one very great blessing—they own no property.[48]

Regarding specifically 12:31, an especially close parallel to this saying occurs in one of the moral epistles of Seneca. After opposing the false dreams and calculations of avarice, the wealthy Roman aristocrat writes:

> Let me go—give me back to the riches that are mine. I know the kingdom of wisdom, mighty and secure; thus, I have everything as they belong to all.[49]

Whether or not Seneca is the person best suited to advance this point of view, the perspective he promotes makes clear how the "kingdom of wisdom" was felt by some in antiquity to provide "everything" needed for a "mighty and secure" existence. One might even have said on occasion to those contemplating the pursuit of such a life: "Seek this kingdom, and everything else shall be yours as well."

13:18–19. What is the kingdom of God like, and to what shall I compare it? It is like a mustard seed that a man took and threw into his garden. And it grew and became a tree, and the birds of the air nested in its branches.[50]

An attempt is made in Q 13:18–19, 20–21 to explain what exactly the kingdom of God is. A term employed elsewhere in the document to shape perception of the surrounding world, the "kingdom of God" here becomes itself the object of reflection. We might imagine an early audience of the synoptic sayings source having muttered at some point, perhaps with irritation in their voice: "Kingdom of God, kingdom of God... you keep talking about the kingdom of God. What on earth is it?" To which our never daunted text would have replied: "It is like a mustard seed...."[51]

In any case, the kingdom-of-God sayings in Q 13:18–19, 20–21 unveil no new "parabolic" reality. They simply endeavor to define more precisely the meaning of this expression as it occurs elsewhere in the rest of the document.[52] Thus the happiness of the poor (6:20), the sense of healing that the "weak" receive from the persons whom Q represents (10:9; 11:20), the fulfilled desire for daily bread (11:2), and the lack of worry about what to eat and wear and "all these things" (12:31) are said in 13:18–19 to be "like a mustard seed" and in 13:20–21 "like leaven."

The first analogy of the mustard seed in 13:18–19, like the example of the ravens and the lilies in 12:24 and 12:27, is taken from the realm of "nature," again like the Cynics who looked to explain and elaborate their equally unconventional style of felicity through the trope of "following nature." In 13:18–19, however, no *imitatio sinapis* is proposed. Reference to the mustard seed does not invoke a model to be approximated, but simply serves instead to explain how it is that the particular point of view and marginal social practice of the Q people could be identified elsewhere in the formative stratum with the kingdom of God.

The meaning of 13:18–19 turns on the sequential triad of a mustard "seed" that "grew" into a "tree." It is a saying about the disproportion between start and finish, origin and destiny, appearance and reality. Only in this sense should it be called a parable of growth.[53]

At the time of planting, no seed is what it proves to be, perhaps especially a mustard seed.[54] The person who takes the little kernel and sows it in the ground confides not in the immediate evidence of his or her senses, which in the case of the mustard seed might suggest a worthless speck, but in a knowledge of potentialities: the possible "benefits" borne in the midst of present insignificance. The sower of the seed works with a conviction of reality not determined by the meager shape of how things currently appear or by their customary evaluation. In the same way, the poor in Q's formative stratum are considered happy, the weak find healing, and life lived from day to day is enjoyed as both sufficient and glorious.

A constant worry of scholars interpreting 13:18–19 has been whether or not anyone in ancient Palestine would ever actually have sown mustard seed in the ground, given its reputation as a sometime "weed," and the fact that no matter what kind of mustard seed it may have been, it could never literally become a tree.[55] Both concerns, however, fail to consider the possibility that a certain ironic playfulness inhabits the comparison at hand. Just as the Cynics toyed with other people's deprecating characterization of them as "dogs," seeking in one way or another to make this term of reproach work rather in their favor, so the Q people accounted for their questionable ethos as a manifestation of the kingdom of God in terms of mustard seed: a generally unwelcome but always tenacious plant that, once sown, i.e., taught, not only was extremely difficult to uproot, but promised threateningly to prosper.[56]

The reference at the end of 13:19 to the mustard seed as "a tree in whose branches the birds of the air nest," employing as it does the language of Israel's epic literature, is simultaneously a parody of the great tradition and of every effort at self-authorization in terms of it, just as the texts of Homer and other revered poets in Greco-Roman antiquity were often adroitly twisted by the Cynics to similar effect.[57]

13:20–21. To what shall I compare the kingdom of God? It is like leaven that a woman took and hid in three measures of flour until it leavened the whole thing.[58]

Like drinks, one parable leads to another.[59] In 13:20–21, a second comparison is made. The scene is taken from domestic life.[60] The kingdom of God is said to be like "leaven" taken by a woman and hidden in a lump of dough until it was all leavened. As before, size and growth are not the issue but rather the disproportion between initial appearance and eventual reality.[61] Indeed, the generative element in this case, namely, leaven, is, for all intents and purposes, essentially invisible, being hidden. Yet its ultimate effect could hardly be more plain to see: the whole lump becomes all leavened.

Likewise, the life of poverty and social marginality embodied by the persons whom Q represents, viewed by others as desperate and despicable, was identified in the document's formative stratum with the kingdom of God and said to be quite frankly happy, healthy, and sufficiently supplied. The kingdom of God, like leaven in a lump of dough, denotes the permeating power at work in such a social posture, whose source, once tapped, though hard to isolate, would soon reveal its practical truth.[62]

Once more, the fact that leaven, an element of uncertain social value in classical antiquity, is used here to describe the kingdom of God and, furthermore, that it is said to have been surreptitiously employed, i.e., "hidden" in the mass of rising dough, has led some scholars to find either shocking insouciance or an abiding patriarchal prejudice permeating the folds of the text.[63] Instead, I would argue that the dubious moral value of the substance in question is precisely germane to the comparison being made. For the kingdom of God as embodied by the persons whom Q represents appeared within their corner of the ancient Mediterranean world, exuding the same mixed virtue of fermenting decadence that leaven manifests in bread.[64]

In both cases, the final result of patently enlarged satisfaction would presumably be hard to counter. If some critics might have wished for purer means, the increase thereby in "abundant life" would nonetheless finally cover, or at least absorb, a multitude of sins.

The different kingdom-of-God sayings in Q's formative stratum (6:20b; 10:9; 11:2, 20; 12:31; 13:18–19, 20–21) represent the ideological reflection of this stage of the document's thoroughgoing transvaluation of local societal norms. A way of life that might have seemed to others to be poor and insignificant was here proposed as being instead quite satisfying, salutary, self-sufficient, free of worry, full of possibility.

An ascetic existence in need of little in order to be content (6:20b), the Q people claimed to have learned how to find freedom from debilitating "ills" and "weakness" in the midst of otherwise unfavorable circumstances (10:9). Astute at defending themselves under attack (11:15–20), the same persons sought to live one day at a time (11:2–3), like the ravens and the lilies without property. Theirs was a subversive view of society, insofar as the enterprise of human "civilization" was itself put into question through opposition to the "reign of God" (12:22–31). Like the mustard seed and the leaven, a form of political activity was implied up to more than met the eye (13:18–21).

At the same time, there is no indication that the persons identified with the kingdom of God at the formative stage of Q's composition ever imagined in this name the construction of a separate society, requiring for its realization either the destruction or forsaking of the present world. The kingdom of God in Q's formative stratum has not yet become a properly "utopian" symbol, projecting onto the screen of the beleaguered imagination a radical replacement for life as we know it. Instead, the kingdom of God acts in Q's formative stratum essentially as a discursive instrument, useful for placing in suspense, if not a quandary, the "self-evidence" of the current arrangement of things by the disclosure of another possible way of being in this time and place.

CHAPTER FOUR

Critique: "Woe to You..."

Appearance versus Reality (11:39–48, 52)

ORDS, WE KNOW, at best are only words. Semiotic science says that, in fact, they are simply empty signs we use as ciphers to demark positions of opposition and alliance. In less sophisticated terms, we chant as children: "Sticks and stones may break my bones, but names will never hurt me." Yet these words we use, at least as children, precisely to ward off the hurt we feel at the names that others call us. Neither is semiotic science naive in this regard. It too recognizes that the games of opposition and alliance that we play with empty signs are anything but innocent. The strong speech of certain early Christians against persons they perceived to be "opposing" them has certainly caused immeasurable injury in the centuries that followed. The legacy of anti-Semitism is a case in point.

Woes and other curses are precisely words whose point is to predicate harm.[1] At least, that is how they are often understood. In the case of early Christianity, there is no doubt that very soon in their transmission, if not right from the start, the woes attributed to Jesus in the synoptic tradition were deployed by his followers as lethal weapons.[2]

At the same time, it may be only because we know the ultimate results that we now "over-dramatize" these polemical pronouncements, excessively evaluating their import at the beginning of a soon nefarious trajectory. For the act of disagreement, dispute, criticism, and even the lampooning of another person or group's point of view and practice is not inevitably nascent genocide, though, to repeat, it clearly became so in the case of subsequent Christianity. Such behavior may simply be another form of the social debate and interactive conflict making up all cultural construction.[3] It would certainly be naive to think that the kind of social project depicted for the Q people in the preceding chapters of this book could have developed without some sort of accompanying social critique.

To what extent do the woes in Q's formative stratum (11:39–48, 52) represent such a discourse?[4] Were they always the violent speech that they so quickly became for succeeding generations? I am not implying with this question any sort of initial innocence for early Christian rhetoric in Galilee. I simply wonder whether the insights and discrepancies expounded by the movement's first protagonists were all that earth-shaking at the start.

Exactly what kind of critique did the woes in Q's formative stratum originally launch when first declaimed? Words put back in context often prove less inflammatory and, sometimes, less interesting than when wielded wildly, untamed by contextual constraints. On the other hand, the same placement may make their primary point all the more pungent.

The text of Q 11:39–48, 52, in English translation, is as follows:[5]

> *11:39–41.* Woe to you Pharisees, for you clean the outside of the cup and the dish, but the inside is full of rapacity and lack of self-control. Clean the inside.... [6] *11:42.* But woe to you Pharisees, for you tithe mint and dill and cummin, and neglect justice and the love of God.[7] *11:44.* Woe to you, for you are like unseen tombs, and the people walking over them do not know it. *11:46.* Woe to you Pharisees, for you load people with burdens hard to bear, and you yourselves do not move your finger. *11:47–48.* Woe to you, for you build the tombs of the prophets, but your fathers killed them. So you are witnesses and you consent to the deeds of your fathers; for they killed them, and you build. *11:52.* Woe to you Pharisees, for you have lifted the key of knowledge; you did not enter, nor did you permit those who were entering to go in.

The woes in Q (11:39–48, 52) belong to the writing of critical literature.[8] Modern book publishers would advertise the production of such rhetoric as "cultural criticism." For the woes in Q's formative stratum register a reading of the local culture in which their author(s) lived, making comments on it at the same time that the production of the woes is part of this target culture's own extended elaboration. The woes in Q constitute one side of the social debate they simultaneously represent for us as such.

When modern historians of early Christianity interpret the woes in Q, the doubled nature of criticism is again doubled, insofar as we now comment on criticism that was once itself critical commentary. We do this, moreover, always in the wake of additional commentary by previous scholars on the same set of sayings. Finally, as if this were not enough to impede any effort at unlocking "original intent," we must also recognize that the point of a critique is not inevitably equivalent to its exemplary matter. The critic will often argue one thing by describing another. Again, I refer both to the woes in Q and to their subsequent interpreters.

An example of the kind of difficulty to be faced when interpreting the woes in Q is the following. When in 11:39–41 umbrage is taken at cleansing the outside but not the inside of a cup, is the dispute here about proper *cleanliness,* i.e., good hygiene? Or is it rather a question of the *rules* about cleanliness, i.e., anxiety about purity, that animates the debate? Or is it, perhaps, the rules of a *particular group,* namely, the Pharisees, that is the point of contention? In this case, at issue would be divergent hermeneutical strategies for interpretation of the Torah. Or has the topic in question, namely, cleansing the outside but not the inside of a cup, been chosen primarily for the sake of making *another* broader *characterization* well-depicted by, but not coincident with, the concrete example?

When reading the woes in Q both individually and as a group, we must be careful not to become fixated, as though it were self-evident, on some particular aspect of their speech and assume, for whatever reason, that this feature is the key to their interpretation; in fact, the same feature may be no more than a standard component of the social context that was a particular saying's original setting in life. In this case, the erstwhile typicality of such an element would account for its elective use within the woe, at the same time that any attention paid to the phenomenon as such is not the specific point of the saying.

Interpretation of the woes in Q must be clear about the goal of interpretation itself. As historians and exegetes, do we first attempt to describe the particular point being made by these sayings? Or in a different sort of enterprise, are these sayings useful to us primarily as exemplary data for another kind of description, e.g., styles of purity and disputes about and between them as a social facet of early Christianity? Neither of the two inquiries is per se more valuable or interesting than the other. It is simply important to remember that both tend to operate under the same name of interpretation, but ought not to be confused.[9]

Much of the history of interpretation of the woes in Q is of the second type. Most interpreters have read them in the service of a larger agenda. The woes in Q have provided a useful opportunity for scholars to reconfirm certain basic (subliminal) assumptions about the nature of Christian origins, such as the importance of a radicalized understanding of Torah for the emergence of the Jesus-movement, its eventual separation from Judaism after a period of increasingly intense sibling rivalry, eventual persecution at the hands of unrepentant Jews as the cost of now being the new "true" Israel, the urgency and seriousness of all disputes about religious matters during this period due to the impending apocalypse of judgment and salvation proclaimed by Jesus and anticipated by his immediate followers, and so on.[10]

Read within the framework of this myth of Christian origins — the most recent one of wide dissemination produced by modern biblical scholarship — the woes in Q appear as oracular denunciations of a recalcitrant, devious, and ostentatious self-righteousness, still referred to sometimes (wrongly) as Pharisaism.[11] The imprecation "woe to you" becomes in this case a proleptic verdict of damnation, even though the sayings introduced by it are supposed to have been uttered as part of an erstwhile "mission" to Israel. I wish to propose a new interpretation.

What is the precise point of the woes in Q? Is it, again, just the fact that the Pharisees did not know how to get a cup completely clean, i.e., both inside and out (11:39); that they have somehow overlooked an important consideration, namely, justice, in their otherwise remarkably refined system of piety (11:43); that they show reverence for the prophets by building them monumental tombs (11:47); that they do not use or share more liberally their privilege of access to a certain experience of knowledge (11:52)? Is it, in other words, because they do not do to perfection the things they were supposed to do that they are chastised? Or is the problem, rather, that they do very well — indeed, all too well — precisely what they proposed to perform?

In the latter case, at issue is *not* what Matthew soon will slander, namely, a lack of moral integrity on the part of the Pharisees, that they were somehow social hypocrites and religious shysters.[12] At stake is rather the very notion of moral integrity itself so virtuously embodied by them. The Pharisees are made the object of Q's initial series of woes (11:39–48, 52) precisely because the Pharisees, better or more zealously than anyone else in their immediate social setting, promoted local society's conventional "convenanted" way of life. And it was precisely this belief in a normative ethos that the woes in Q (11:39–48, 52) set out to scrutinize.[13]

The woes in Q put into question basic practices of the socio-religious system represented by the Pharisees. The system itself was thereby prodded. Nothing is denounced as such. But by repeatedly poking at the system's self-evident correctness or righteousness, by pocking up its ideological armor and chipping away at its veneer of perfection and completeness, the cultural conglomerate of tradition and invention constituting every such arrangement was thus rendered more dubitable and, thereby, for its critics less imposing. The social world encompassing both the Pharisees and the Q people became in this way, at least for the authors of the woes, a more inhabitable region.

The woes in Q do not criticize the Pharisees in order to advance another social program. In this regard, we may wish to castigate the perpetrators of these sayings for being merely critics with no alternative to suggest. On the other hand, by recognizing the "purely" critical stance of the woes in Q, our interpretation of them can avoid pitting the persons whom they represent against the Pharisees in some sort of absolute contrast. We should cease to imagine on the basis of these sayings any kind of diametrical opposition between Jesus' first followers in Galilee and the different forms of early Judaism — not to mention other ancient Mediterranean "religions" — as well as the starker antagonism of Christian versus Jew.

Thoroughgoing social critique does not eschew ongoing participation in the society under criticism. The woes in Q do not signal a complete rejection or total condemnation of the Pharisees. Registered instead is merely a considerable depreciation of them. The woes in Q argue that the Pharisees are not everything they had been cracked up to be. Once this is seen and affirmed, it might be possible to live with them. Bursting the bubble of the Pharisees' desire for complete obedience and faithfulness created room for persons like the people whom Q represents, unattracted to such spiritual grandeur, to continue culturally cohabitating with them.[14]

11:39–41. Woe to you Pharisees, for you clean the outside of the cup and the dish, but the inside is full of rapacity and lack of self-control. Clean the inside...

The first woe in Q (11:39–41) plays explicitly with the quotidian dichotomy of in and out, distinguishing implicitly between the dictates of a cultural system of purity and the moral status of virtue.[15] The point appears to be that however complete one's treatment of "externals" might be, without a corresponding internal reality, the former is void of value.[16]

A certain burlesque exaggeration is evident in the example that is given — later taken literally and elaborated pedantically by Matthew — insofar as it suggests that the Pharisees would actually have meticulously cleansed the outside of a cup, only to leave the inside soiled and stained. The physical ridiculousness of such a prospect, however, makes plain how, at another level of human life, the assumption of ethical integrity based solely on the completion of certain customary rites without considering the overall status of the moral subject in question is equally laughable.

Compare what is said in 11:39–41 with the following sayings:[17]

1.1. Seeing someone perform religious purification, [Diogenes] said, "O unhappy one, don't you know that you cannot get rid of errors of conduct through sprinkling any more than you can mistakes in grammar?"[18]

1.2. But I do not mean by this that we ought to be shameless before all and do what ought not to be done; but whatever we refrain from and whatever we do let us do and refrain from, not because it seems to most somehow honorable or base, but because it is forbidden by reason and the god within us, that is, the mind.[19]

2.1. [Diogenes] was gathering figs, when he was told by the keeper that not long before a man had hanged himself on that very fig-tree. "Then," he said, "I will now cleanse it."[20]

2.2. When someone reproached him for going into unclean places, he replied, "The sun, too, visits cesspools, but is not defiled."[21]

2.3. When reproached for drinking in a tavern, "Well," he said, "I also get my hair cut in a barber's shop."[22]

2.4. And he saw no impropriety in taking anything from a temple or in eating the flesh of any animal; nor even anything impious in touching human flesh, as is clear from the customs of other peoples.[23]

3. Then the Savior said to [a Pharisaic chief priest], "Woe to you blind that see not! You have bathed yourself in water that is poured out, in which dogs and swine lie night and day and you have washed yourself and have chafed your outer skin, which prostitutes also and flute girls anoint, bathe, chafe, and rouge, in order to arouse desire in men, but within they are full of scorpions and of [bad]ness [of every kind]. But I and [my disciples], of whom you say that we have not im[mersed] ourselves, [have been im]mersed in the liv[ing . . .] water which comes down from [. . . .B]ut woe to them that. . . ."[24]

4. Jesus said, "Why are you washing the outside of the cup? Don't you know that the one who made the inside is the very same one who made the outside?"[25]

5. Purifications are for the purity of the soul, not of the body.[26]

The first two sayings listed above (1.1; 1.2), though distinct in many ways, agree — and therefore it is especially noteworthy — that the usual overt signs of ancient moral practice do not constitute true virtue. Rather, says Julian (1.2), the source of the latter is "the god within us, that is, the mind," thereby hypostasizing (apotheosizing) the style of critical reasoning typical of the Cynics.[27] The same holds true for Diogenes (1.1) when he exposed the non sequitur of contemporary ritual purification. Unlike Julian, however, Diogenes does not reify the means of his critique. Diogenes' remarks do not posit by way of response another interior version of what is criticized. Instead, they remain at the level of efficacy versus inefficacy.

From the perspective of these first two sayings (1.1; 1.2), the reference in 11:41 to cleaning the inside of a cup could be read as simply a positive restatement of the negative discrepancy already noted. No argument is made in 11:41 for true virtue's inner location. Indeed, a cup has no "within" in the sense of Julian's "god within us." The inside versus the outside of a cup is rather more like the relationship discussed by Diogenes between an act and its consequence(s), whereby one thing leads to another. If the attempt were made to purify a cup or one's behavior but the practice of purification did not extend beyond the most visible features of the vessel or one's personal comportment, the final result is as predictable as the initial action was ludicrous.

Like the saying by Diogenes (1.1) the critique made in 11:39–41 does not argue for true virtue as the "interiorization" of traditional religious rules and regulations, nor, as Julian would have it, as an inward principle. Instead, both Diogenes and the saying in 11:39–41 argue for true virtue as a limit concept, the unrealized ideal of specific cultural habits, seen most clearly in the local morality's internal contradictions.

The next group of sayings listed above (2.1–4) all exemplify the Cynic virtue of "shamelessness."[28] In this regard, they are typical of the dog-philosophers' thoroughgoing critique of ancient assumptions about purity and impurity. In an honor-shame culture like the ancient Mediterranean world, unrepentantly to call established moral conventions into question meant, because one did not honor them, that one was being simply "shameless."[29] The point of the different pronouncements is essentially this: that what was otherwise assumed to be impure, hardly is. The same, by extension, would apply to the idea of purity itself and/or how to achieve it, namely, purification.

The first saying of this second group (2.1) plays expressly with this theme. Notably, it does not resolve the issue beyond posing it in the form of a conundrum. One should not miss the very clever wit with which this is done. The business at hand, though profoundly penetrating, is not deadly serious.

The other three sayings (2.2–4) seek to rattle the foundations of current thinking about purity by contrasting certain acts generally thought to be impure with examples to the contrary. The point is to make the ruling assumptions less than self-evident without, however, erecting another ethical system in their place.

In the second saying (2.2), for example, nature itself in the form of the sun proves that it is possible to occupy a soiled environment without oneself becoming thereby (morally) stained. Obviously, the argument cannot finally be sustained as such. Human beings, including Diogenes, lack the material make-up of light permitting it to be both visibly present and untouched. Rhetorically, however, the saying does not operate at this level. Instead, it plays with the rigidity of a taboo, diminishing its absoluteness by demonstrating that, at least in one case, the imputed rationale does not hold true, namely, that one should not enter into "dirty" places because impurity cannot be avoided there. The saying is effective — it scores its point — because it makes the ancient audience stop and think, if only for a minute, about the moral prescript's lack of self-evidence.

In the next saying (2.3) the system of cultural values is questioned that would allow for certain bodily needs — a haircut — to be taken care of in a particular locale without the slightest hint of reproach, while the satisfaction of other bodily needs like cutting one's thirst was subject to a more searching and often negative evaluation. Why should the fulfillment of one need be considered somehow less morally correct than another?[30] Why should Diogenes not recover bodily fluids in a tavern, it being one place to do so, if no one objected to him taking care of other body-business like improving his appearance wherever possible, for example, in a barber shop?

Again, any number of mitigating factors make it clear that the argument cannot finally be sustained as such. But the saying is successful in raising the inquiry, "Well, why not?!" And that is precisely its point.

Notably, the comparison made here (2.3) does not invoke some aspect of nature, but instead refers to another feature of local society. The Cynic critique of conventional morality did not simply pit "natural" against "cultural" ways. Proposed was not one moral system in place of another. Under suspicion was, rather, the very notion of a moral system itself as represented by the conventions of pure versus impure. Hence not only nature but also human society could furnish, when convenient, the opposing evidence.[31]

The last saying of this group (2.4) is interesting mainly because of its reference to "the customs of other peoples." What is pure and impure is not constant from one culture to the next. Thus, the moral standards of a specific society cannot (or should not) make a claim to being the fulfillment of all righteousness.

The Cynics had integrated into their moral outlook certain aspects of the ethnological discoveries of the Hellenistic age.[32] To demonstrate the relativity of all ethical standards, Diogenes is said to have violated his own culture's longstanding conviction of the sanctity of temples, the dietary customs of his fellow citizens, even the prohibition of "touching" human flesh. Any abiding pretense in the direction of absolute virtue was here unmasked as so much self-deception.

The shared sense in all these sayings (2.1–4) of moral virtue's inadequate representation through prevailing "acceptable" social practices is also shared by the woe in Q 11:39–41. Unfortunately, Diogenes' wit is not as much in evidence here. The description in 11:39–41 of the cup's "inside" as "full of rapacity" is plainly less playful than Diogenes' reference to cleansing the hanging-tree by picking its fruit or his talk of the sun dipping undefiled into cesspools or the defense of tavern-hopping via the barber shop. By comparison, there is an edge to 11:39–41 suggestive of a certain choler. Exactly why remains unclear.[33] At the same time, there is no reason to assume that the suggestion in 11:41 to "clean the inside" of the cup is laden with greater meaning than Diogenes' retort, "I will now cleanse it." Both responses similarly imply that previously held presuppositions about purity simply lack validity.

P.Oxy. 840.2 (=3) is noteworthy, primarily for the following reason. On the one hand, it registers a more aggressive polemic than any of the antecedent statements made either in Q (11:39–41) or by Diogenes. On the other hand, it shares with these sayings the same perception of a strong incongruity between the lofty desire for moral purity and the bathos of circumstantial reality, which "you blind...see not."

The problem is this. The water used for bathing and cleansing is itself unclean. Calling it "water that is poured out" is not unlike the reference in 11:39–41 to washing the outside but not the inside of a cup. Physically ridiculous, the rhetorical exaggeration makes clear the underlying contradiction of the fact that purification is here being sought with less than pure means.[34]

The specific gestures of purification are, moreover, ultimately ineffective or ambiguous. Assiduous holiness is not the inevitable result of a rigorous routine of repeated bodily ablutions and self-laceration. For on the surface of things, prostitutes and flute-girls do exactly what the religious zealot also does, though "within they are full of scorpions and of badness of every kind," referring explicitly to the social reputation of these women and, by implication, just as easily to the latter *devotée*.

The next saying (*GThom* 89=4) is very similar to Luke's version of the Q woe (11:40), though there are certain differences.[35] In both sayings (*GThom* 89/Luke 11:40) the critique as stated focuses on the failure of the designated targets to realize that one and the same person, namely, God, is in fact responsible for the existence of both the inside and the outside of the cup. The object of concern has thereby ceased to be what it was in Q (11:39–41), namely, the human agent and his or her self-deception vis-à-vis true virtue.[36]

In summary: Observed in Q 11:39–41 is the basic incongruity between the Pharisees' ambition to attain a state of perfect holiness via a thoroughgoing system of personal purity and the fact that true virtue cannot finally be achieved in this fashion, given the enduring imperfection of reality, including both the instruments of purification and the agents who use them. Similar in many respects to a number of comparable pronouncements by the Cynics on the same sort of social practice, the saying in Q 11:39–41 is nonetheless notably less mischievous and playful in tone than are the Cynic statements (for reasons yet to be determined). Reference in 11:41 to the inside being clean does not mean that true virtue therefore has an inner location but merely belongs to the logic of the saying as the inversion of what precedes it.[37]

11:42. But woe to you Pharisees, for you tithe mint and dill and cummin, and neglect justice and the love of God.

The second woe in Q (11:42) essentially makes the same point as the first. Instead of using the pursuit of purity as its primary foil, however, the present saying takes piety's accomplished perfection (or imperfection) as its main example. The Pharisees' attempt to elaborate their faith's tradition to the utmost degree by dwelling on the smallest of daily details is called long on effort, but short on principle.[38] The forest has been lost amidst the trees. Fundamental legal values no longer enjoy their rightful place of prominence or directive profile by virtue of a stupefying specification, resulting in a certain trivialization. A similar perspective may be observed in the following sayings as well:

1.1. [Diogenes] was also moved to anger that persons should sacrifice to the gods to ensure health and in the midst of the sacrifice feast to the detriment of health.[39]

1.2. He would rebuke people in general regarding their prayers, declaring that they asked for those things that seemed good to them and not for what is truly good.[40]

1.3. Certain persons were sacrificing to the gods, that a son might be born to them. "But," said he, "you don't sacrifice to ensure the kind of man he shall turn out to be?"[41]

2. Once he saw the officials of a temple leading away someone who had stolen a bowl belonging to the treasurers, and said, "The big thieves are leading away the little one."[42]

3.1. Once he saw a woman kneeling before the gods in an unseemly fashion, and wishing to free her of superstition, according to Zoilus of Perga, came forward and said, "Are you not afraid, O woman, that a god may be standing behind you — for all things are full of his presence — and you might be put to shame?"[43]

3.2. When someone expressed astonishment at the votive offerings in Samothrace, he said, "There would be many more, if those who were not saved had set up offerings."[44]

4. Law is a good thing, but it is not superior to philosophy. For the former compels a person not to do wrong, but the latter teaches one not to do wrong. To the degree that doing something under compulsion is worse than doing it willingly, to that degree law is worse than philosophy. For this reason do philosophy and do not take part in government. For it is better to know the means by which persons are taught to do right than to know the means by which they are compelled not to do wrong.[45]

The first three sayings (1.1–3) by Diogenes argue against any easy fusion of religious practice with the pursuit of self-interest or the mere performance of certain rites apart from the embodiment of other more fundamental values. Thus prayer is criticized (1.2) when it represents not the desire for what is truly good, but is simply another means of satisfying personal wants: "those things that seemed good to them." Sacrifice (another form of ancient prayer) is chastised (1.3) when performed only for the existence of a child and not also for its future well-being: "to ensure the kind of man he shall turn out to be."

The attitude denounced here could lead to the most blatant of contradictions. Thus Diogenes condemns (1.1) the habit of sacrificing to the gods for health simply as an excuse for becoming ill: for making the sacrificial occasion, as was commonly done, the pretext for a party, at which one overindulged and for which one later paid the price, "feast[ing] to the detriment of health."

It was the lack of an intentional horizon beyond the "religious" act itself and/or the specific wish that first prompted it which calls forth Diogenes' repeated critique in these first three sayings (1.1–3), just as in Q 11:42 a similar reduction or restriction of "religious" life to the rigors of "totalized" tithing, though perceived by its proponents to be an extension and elaboration of their traditional faith, is said to result in a neglect of justice and other equally important things like what is truly good, the manner of man or woman one will be, or staying healthy.

The next saying (2) is by Diogenes again. It may be compared not only to 11:42, but also with a number of other statements in Q (e.g., 6:41–42). Regarding 11:42, the key question is one of "big" versus "small." The temple officials in this saying (2) insist on the legalities related to the theft of an insignificant vessel from their treasury, but — this is the implication of Diogenes' characterization of them as "big thieves" — the same persons are quite oblivious, if not simply devoted, to the ways in which they themselves rob others blind.

In 11:42, there is no explicit suggestion that the Pharisees actively prevent justice. Their neglect of it could simply be the lamentable consequence of an excessive preoccupation with other less weighty matters. But to reduce the degree of the Pharisees' "culpability" in this regard only underscores the basic problem that the woe addresses. Both the Pharisees and the temple officials denounced by Diogenes remain opaque to issues beyond the purview of a certain pettiness. Masters of the minor, both are incognizant of or duplicitous in what they avoid considering, namely, the graver matters of justice and its likely indictment of their own behavior. Both the saying in 11:42 and Diogenes work this gap, marking it off as one of irresponsible omission.

The third group of sayings listed above (3.1–2) mock different pious gestures, not so much because of their minor importance in comparison with higher causes, but due to their internal nonsense. Like 11:42 and the first group of statements already discussed (1.1–3), these sayings (3.1–2) remark the always less than perfect realization of religious devotion. Thus, a woman's contrite act of repentance or fervent supplication "kneeling before the gods" is mitigated by her bodily awkwardness, turning whatever the intention of her soul may have been into a physically "unseemly" posture (3.1). Likewise, the number of prayers answered for lives saved as symbolized by the votive offerings at Samothrace is a less impressive figure when one thinks about how many prayers for the same salvation went unanswered, given all who died (3.2).[46]

Comparison of the final saying (4) with 11:42 suggests that the second woe in Q may assume an underlying opposition between (for want of a better term) positive versus negative motivation. The Pharisees' rules and regulations for tithing would correspond to what ps-Crates calls "law," although at first glance tithing does not seem to compel anyone not to do wrong. In fact, however, it formed an integral part of the Pharisaic system of "preventative" piety: a style of faith constructed to defend the social identity it claimed to represent from perceived threats of erosion, the well-known "hedge around Torah," to guard the covenanted ethos from the changes to which it was apparently felt to be susceptible.[47]

Torah itself, of course, was not understood in negative terms. But the piety that protected it and guaranteed its "inviolate" state might be called "negative" insofar as its orientation was centripetal, seeking to assure that nothing would be done to alter what was now surrounded by a barrier of righteousness. In contrast, the search for justice would be rather more centrifugal, directed toward the creation of a different social arrangement constituted by changes in current customs and structures and, for this reason, understood as positive.[48]

These are dangerous contrasts. It must be understood that what I have just written has nothing to do with the traditional theological distinction between Judaism and Christianity, the Old and the New Testament, "law" and "gospel." I merely wish to explore the possibility that reflected in 11:42 is a point of view comparable to the contrast drawn by ps-Crates between law and philosophy. As such, the polemic of the second woe in Q would represent a purely intracultural debate waged among contemporary members of the same society.

From the perspective of 11:42, clearer ethical orientation was needed in the context of first-century C.E. Galilee under Roman imperial rule. Given the particular social situation of the times, one had no choice but to opt for a specific "response to the world." According to 11:42, it would have been better for both speaker and audience alike to develop together the means whereby their society and its "citizens" could deal more justly with one another, being "taught to do right," rather than continuing to codify the traditional order to minimize wrong.[49]

In 11:42, to summarize, preoccupation with the minutiae of a "religious" system, identified rightly or wrongly with the thoroughgoing detail-conscious piety of the Pharisees, is faulted for its failure to advance what ought to have been presumably the faith's ultimate aims and primary values. A certain nearsightedness is here observed on the part of the Pharisees, who are said not to have taken into account issues greater than those appearing within their narrow range of vision. An opposition may be assumed in 11:42 between negative and positive motivation for doing "good," the latter being seen as preferable.

11:44. Woe to you, for you are like unseen tombs, and the people walking over them do not know it.

In the third woe (11:44) the Pharisees are directly characterized — essentially an ad hominem critique — in contrast with the two previous profiles of them through analysis of their behavior. Specific social practices are here no longer the focus of attention. Instead, a certain metaphorical description has been applied. A comparison is made. The Pharisees are called a name. They are said to be like "unseen tombs." Why this name, whence it comes, and what the precise point of the analogy is, are questions yet unanswered. It is clear, however, that the purpose of the similitude was not to praise.[50]

11:46. Woe to you Pharisees, for you load people with burdens hard to bear, and you yourselves do not move your finger.

In terms of style of argument, the fourth woe belongs between the first two and the third. It seems to presuppose some type of concrete activity on the part of the Pharisees, but refers to it metaphorically as a matter of carrying cargo.[51] Again, a contrast has been observed between the official posture of the Pharisees as legislators and their human, all too human, inability or unwillingness to promote fulfillment of the laws they make. It is not clear, however, that the dichotomy addressed here is any more self-conscious or premeditated a split than those already discussed.

The same unthinking folly denounced in 11:46 occurred elsewhere in the ancient Mediterranean world as well:

1. And [Diogenes] used to wonder that the grammarians would investigate the ills of Odysseus, but be ignorant of their own. Or that the musicians would tune the strings of the lyre, but leave the dispositions of their souls discordant; that the mathematicians would gaze at the sun and the moon, but overlook matters at their feet; that the orators would make a fuss about justice in their speeches, but never practice it; or that the avaricious would cry out against money, but love it excessively.[52]

2. No good ruler ruins his subjects, nor does a good shepherd harm his sheep. But your whole land is empty of subjects and poorly managed by your officials....It would be better for you to be sparing of the people over whom you would have authority....[53]

The phrase in the first of these sayings (1) most pertinent to our interpretation of 11:46 is the statement referring to orators who "make a fuss about justice in their speeches, but never practice it." The point is plain enough. Such persons say one thing and do another. Expectations are raised and placed on people without those who raise and impose them ever helping to make sure that whatever has been required is brought to completion. Likewise in 11:46, the Pharisees are said to demand what they themselves do not fulfill and/or to whose fulfillment they do not contribute.

Why is this? On the basis of 11:46 alone, one might imagine as the reason for such a double standard any number of ulterior motives ranging from latent sadism to oppressive social-class structures. All of these would likely be hermeneutically more fruitful, if we were to pursue them, than the quizzical wit of Diogenes, who in a series of probing characterizations merely portrays as exemplary of human folly and its self-deceptions the internal contradictions of a series of selected "professionals."

Some people, it seems, in human society are always ready to "solve" everyone else's problems but their own. The same is true regarding the practice of responsibility and productivity. Likewise, the Pharisees are said in 11:46 to have created "burdens" that they imagine should be borne, but not by them. However irritating and unfair the inconsistency may be, it is difficult to make it more profound than that.

The second saying listed above (2) suggests, however, a somewhat more serious reading of the woe in 11:46, insofar as this saying (2) implies that the use and abuse of authority may be an additional factor to bear in mind regarding what is meant there. The folly described in 11:46 can perhaps be further specified. The indiscriminate exercise of power always ultimately works against itself. Instead of demonstrating the extent of one's strength, the result is rather diminished effectiveness and a reduced range of influence. Thus Tereus, the despot of Thrace, by virtue of his poor habits of government will shortly be left with nothing over which to rule.

The Pharisees are similarly said in 11:46 to run the same risk, insofar as their proliferation of laws and other "burdens hard to bear" lacks the balance and compassion that would likely be observed, if they too were held accountable or made themselves responsible for the same. It would be better, according to Q, for the Pharisees to be sparing of the people over whom they have authority or at least to share with them the difficulties caused by their interpretation of tradition, if only thereby to avoid the probable fate of soon being masters of a realm empty of subjects, marked only by the officiousness of its management.[54]

Once again, the Pharisees exemplify human folly. Speech and action — demands that have been made and the conditions necessary for their fulfillment — fail to coincide. If one wishes, as apparently the Pharisees do, to be the leader of a social group, the consequences of this sort of practice are finally detrimental to oneself.

11:47–48. Woe to you, for you build the tombs of the prophets, but your fathers killed them. So you are witnesses and you consent to the deeds of your fathers; for they killed them, and you build.

A sharp contradiction is decried in Q's fifth woe (11:47–48) at the heart of the reverential remembrance of the "prophets" by the descendants of those who earlier killed them.[55] It is the same sort of bitter incongruity that now attends the current recollection by the American people of Martin Luther King (or Malcolm X), presently accorded honor when only a generation or so ago he was denounced by many as a dangerous insurrectionist. The purpose of 11:47–48 is to expose how contemporary esteem typically masks a history of rejection, how the golden praise of modern-day memorials is founded on the slippery clay of past disdain, how current civic pride makes heroes out of ancient enemies, but not to set the record straight. What is ostensibly bestowing honor may really just be covering tracks.[56] Compare the case of Diogenes:

1.1. Hence, it is said, there arose a quarrel among [Diogenes'] disciples as to who would bury him: indeed, they even came to blows; but when their fathers and men of influence arrived, under their direction the man was buried beside the gate leading to the Isthmus. Over his grave they set up a pillar and on it a dog in Parian marble. Later his fellow-citizens honored him with bronze statues, on which they inscribed the following: "Time makes even bronze grow old: but thy glory, Diogenes, all eternity will never destroy. Since thou alone didst demonstrate to mortals the lesson of self-sufficiency and the easiest path of life." ... But some say that when dying he left instructions that they should throw him out unburied, that every wild beast might feed on him, or thrust him into a ditch and sprinkle a little dust over him. But according to others his instructions were that they should throw him into the Ilissus, in order that he might be useful to his brethren.[57]

1.2. He had commanded us beforehand that no care was to be bestowed on the body since it was worthless and no longer useful after the soul had left it. Nevertheless, as far as was possible, we disregarded the misfortune and misunderstood his words, and to the degree that we could we adorned him after we had washed him and put on his garments, and when we had buried him in a fitting manner, we went away.[58]

2. [A]s Stilpon says, neglecting the living because of the dead is the mark of a person who does not reason correctly.[59]

The swift post-mortem volte-face of society apparent in the first set of sayings (1.1–2) regarding Diogenes is the point of their comparison with the fifth woe in Q (11:47–48). When Diogenes was alive, his social ranking — the level of public esteem accorded him — like that of the prophets, was not very high, if only because of the things Diogenes himself said and did to ensure his own marginalization. Upon his death, however, and according to ps-Aeschines (1.2) against his own wishes, Diogenes was elevated through burial to a position of public honor. Indeed, if we can believe Diogenes Laertius (1.1) a tomb was built for the quintessential Cynic on government property in Corinth "beside the gate leading to the Isthmus."

Although Diogenes' prior habit of doing everything — "the works of Demeter and of Aphrodite alike" — in front of everyone had not incorrectly been interpreted as a sign of the Cynic's utter shamelessness,[60] the public display of Diogenes' body after death led to quite the opposite evaluation. He who while living did not respect local norms and customs, challenging their legitimacy and shirking their control, could finally be domesticated, once dead. It is this covert form of societal self-justification that 11:47–48 seeks to expose.

Both the sayings about Diogenes' death and the woe in 11:47–48 hold up for scrutiny the fact that tombs are built at all. In both instances — that of Diogenes and of the prophets — the social habit of erecting gravestones is seen primarily to serve the interests of the builders. That is, far from their ostensive purpose of recognizing and recalling the enduring worth of the person now enshrined in this fashion, entombment rather enshrouds and restricts by materially fixating the cultural memory of the buried man or woman and thus the form of his or her continuing presence. Remembrance by memorial thus proves to be really a means of forgetting.

In both accounts of Diogenes' burial, this is forthrightly admitted. In the one case (1.1) after giving all the details of the struggle and decision how properly to inter him, it is finally mentioned that when dying, Diogenes himself had rather different ideas about what should be done with his corpse. Moreover, these ideas were thoroughly in keeping with the Cynic's previous approach to life, which those who buried him plainly contradicted by acting out of their own personal preoccupations and care. In the words of ps-Aeschines (1.2) "as far as was possible, we disregarded the misfortune [of Diogenes' death] and misunderstood his words [regarding burial]."

In 11:47–48, the same insight is expressed, only here its mention is not placed on the lips of the participants themselves, but made by a "third-party" ·observer, namely, whoever is responsible for the fifth woe in Q (11:47–48). The stated contradiction is thus not confessed but charged. Perhaps for this reason, the contrast between past and present is also drawn more fiercely.

In 11:47–48, those who remember the prophets by building their tombs are said to forget the acts of murder that caused their death in the first place. Although these acts are not the precise point of the saying, which again concerns the ambivalence of tomb-building, it is clear nonetheless that a history of violence is here implied.

Forgotten violence tends to repeat itself. Recalling what the memorials do not mention is therefore not merely reveling in contradiction. The saying in 11:47–48 has an edge of anxiety to it. A warning is issued that such things should not continue to be done — certainly not as the result of ignorance and self-deception. Thus we read that "you are witnesses and participate in the deeds of your fathers."

It is not clear, however, that the statement "you participate in the deeds of your fathers" means that these persons, namely, the "children" of "your fathers" are now engaged in a similar form of slaughter. The meaning of the accusation in 11:48 may simply be that the descendants of the former group, precisely because they have inherited the fortunes of their killing ancestors, must also recognize and acknowledge an abiding responsibility on their part for the ill means by which such "goods" were achieved.

A modern example of this sort of thing would be the Vietnam Veterans' Memorial in Washington, D.C. The fact of its construction and the acts of homage accompanying its inauguration imply, among other things, an affirmation of the political-economic system and its representatives that sent the persons named on the memorial to their premature and unnecessary death. Those who still continue to enjoy and uphold "the American way of life," whose "best interests" first produced the war, "participate in the deeds of your fathers."

To make the preceding statement does not mean that yet another generation of young Americans is presently fighting and dying in southeast Asia. The point is rather that the American people as a whole continue to be guilty of the former conflict by virtue of their abiding commitment to the same domestic and foreign policies that originally caused it. And like the persons in 11:47–48 who build the tombs of the prophets, they are not released from such a legacy simply by erecting a monument.[61]

The last saying (2) requires no explanation. It does suggest, however, another aspect to the critique of tomb-building in 11:47–48, namely, that this kind of practice, especially when it becomes a form of piety, neglects the living. The Pharisees' (?) interest in honoring the prophets suggests a reciprocal disinterest on their part in attending to the needs and desires of existing persons. In this way, the same behavior that earlier killed the prophets is effectively repeated, insofar as disregarding present-day reality means minimally not heeding and thereby often opposing current efforts at reform and social change.

In summary: Criticized in 11:47–48 is tomb-building, perhaps by the Pharisees, specifically for the prophets, presumably to honor them. The basic problem with this kind of remembrance is what it forgets. In 11:47–48, the antecedent habits of opposition and murder that originally led to the prophets' demise are at stake. (In Diogenes' case, the contradiction occurs between his socially marginal existence while alive and the subsequent public exaltation of his corpse.) Those who build such tombs participate in the tradition of repression, insofar as they do not denounce but, rather, affirm and carry on the social order inherited from their killing ancestors. Another problem with this same concern for the dead is its concomitant neglect of the living.

11:52. Woe to you Pharisees, for you have lifted the key of knowledge; you did not enter, nor did you permit those who were entering to go in.

In this final woe, a point is scored similar to that of the fourth, namely, that while the Pharisees enjoy a certain position of social status, they do not use it in accordance with its function and possibilities, but simply hold on to the privilege of having it.[62] Of all the woes in Q, this one, if any, implies a certain self-consciousness to the Pharisees' imperfect righteousness. At the same time, the fundamental theme remains the same as in the preceding sayings, namely, the disjuncture between appearance (having a certain power) and reality (doing nothing constructive with it). It is a theme that admits of numerous variations:

1. Jesus said, "Woe to the Pharisees, for they are like a dog sleeping in the manger of some cows, for it neither eats nor let[s] the cows eat."[63]

2. The Athenians urged [Diogenes] to become initiated, and told him that in Hades those who have been initiated obtain first place. "Ludicrous," he said, "if Agesilaus and Epaminondas are to dwell in the mire, while certain folk of no account will live in the Isles of the Blest because they have been initiated."[64]

3. Jesus said, "The Pharisees and the Scribes have taken the keys of knowledge and hidden them. They have not entered nor let those who want to go in. You then be shrewd as snakes and innocent as doves."[65]

Comparison of Q 11:52 with *GThom* 102 (=1) leaves the Pharisees looking rather churlish. Nothing, however, more "serious" or significant than that is at stake. Like the dog in the manger, the Pharisees currently occupy a certain position of power, being able to control access to a specific experience of knowledge, seen as desirable by others. But neither the dog nor the Pharisees do anything with their power except maintain it and perhaps, it is implied, try to flaunt it. Both are accused, therefore, of basically silly behavior. Human folly is again in view.

The second saying listed above (2) discusses the particular question of privileged access to a culturally significant "religious" experience. Diogenes contends that this experience must be of dubious value, if persons otherwise of high repute and moral character are to be denied the opportunity to enjoy it merely because they failed to fulfill certain customary prerequisites. Better stated, these prerequisites make no sense, if only by virtue of their omission and for no other good reason the best of persons will not receive what "certain folk of no account" obtain merely for having carried out a few perfunctory acts. There is therefore neither virtue nor vice in having (or not having) availed oneself of such an "opportunity": in the case of Diogenes, being initiated; in 11:52, the special knowledge that the Pharisees "lock" up, thereby preventing access to it.[66]

Beyond being an immature thing to do, the very idea of locking people out is declared impossible if something truly important is thereby supposed to be denied. For to think that a given group could control the participation by others in the more significant experiences of life and death is simply ludicrous; thus, at any rate, Diogenes. If, nonetheless, the

Pharisees continue to conduct themselves on such a premise, then obviously they themselves "do not go in." The Pharisees will not experience what they are now attempting to prevent others from enjoying — who are said, in any case, to be "going in."

The woe in 11:52 concerns especially this pretense to lock up or out, just as the saying by Diogenes (2) centers on the practice of initiation. The problem with both activities is their evident uselessness, given the fact that, as Diogenes suggests, if what is guarded in this way were truly of value, no one could impede "those going in" from finally enjoying it.

Comparison of 11:52 and *GThom* 39 (=3) must highlight the difference between these two sayings. In *GThom* 39, the Pharisees (and scribes) are said to have hidden the keys to *gnōsis*. The problem is, therefore, where to find them. In 11:52, by contrast, there is no indication of any concern about location. The issue is rather the desired entrance into an experience of knowledge and the effort by the Pharisees to keep other people out.[67]

In summary: Human folly is again in view in the final woe of Q (11:52). Like the dog in the manger in *GThom* 102, the Pharisees enjoy a certain power or privilege without, however, doing anything constructive with it. The irony is like what Diogenes says about initiation, namely, that if what is "locked up" by the Pharisees truly mattered, they would finally not be able to deny anyone access to it. If, on the other hand, they succeed in keeping certain people out, then the experience is hardly worth the effort in the first place.

§

In different ways, all the woes in Q's formative stratum turn about the axis of appearance versus reality. Appearance is typically synonymous with the pretense of virtue, while reality is always less exalted. The constant tweaking of this contrast characterized the Cynics as well, who never ceased to bring their rhetorical inventiveness and sardonic sense of humor to bear upon the gap. Like other Cynic *bons mots*, the woes in Q play for the perceptual space in which current social norms could be relaxed and a type of moral relativity reign.

At least there is a sense in which the dominant social order was thereby rendered not inevitably supreme, though this is never expressed in any more positive or constructive terms. The social critique championed by the woes in Q was thus not tied to particular utopian desires for a specific cultural "restoration" or "renewal." It may be that the sheer press of established ways was such that, practically speaking, all the Q people could hope for was to unsettle things a bit.

Is the criticism "fair" that the woes in Q make of the Pharisees? Undoubtedly, the Pharisees would not have thought so. Unfortunately, we lack their reply to the charges. The matter is complicated even further by the fact that the woes in Q are possibly the earliest evidence that we have for the Pharisees as such. There is little else with which to compare this set of sayings in order to see if their critique of the Pharisees corresponds to the "facts" as we otherwise might know them. There is thus no way to be more "objective" in our assessment of the woes' veracity. Regarding their voracity, however, we can probably be less reserved.

CHAPTER FIVE

Memory: John and Jesus

Earliest Recollections
(7:24B–26, 28A, 33–34; 9:57–60; 14:26–27)

E VERY MOVEMENT has its antecedents: its designated precursors.
Subject to a variety of assessments, the memory of these persons
is always an integral part of any group's social identity. Thus we know
who "we" are, because "we" share the recollection of a common ances-
tor, idolize the same hero(s), venerate (or disparage) certain people as
having been particularly significant for our current self-understanding
and present way of life.

The Q people remembered John and Jesus as their "founder figures."
In this chapter, I review the earliest recollections of them in the document's formative stratum. The statements made here are marked by a
minimalist style. The dynamic duo have not yet become what they soon
will be in other early Christian literature. At the same time and perhaps
for this reason, it is more than likely that the Q people saw themselves
reflected in the image of these men whose distinctive social style they
recalled in a few peculiar sayings.[1]

7:33–34. **For John came neither eating nor drinking and they
say, "He has a demon." The son of man came eating and drinking and they say, "Look, a glutton and a drunkard, a friend of
tax-collectors and sinners."**[2]

Many things are remarkable about 7:33,[3] though the image of John
as an ascetic "neither eating nor drinking" is not one of them. This
depiction of the desert drifter essentially corresponds to what we otherwise know about John's personal habits.[4] Nowhere else, however, to my

87

knowledge is the same man ever said to have had a demon. Indeed, 7:33 is the only place in the synoptic tradition where the expression "have a demon" is used (except for the redactional formulation in Luke 8:27; cf. Mark 5:20).[5]

Both characterizations of John, namely, as demented and ascetic, are paralleled by similar well-known descriptions of the Cynics. The spare diet of many of these ersatz-mongrels, restricting themselves to water and a few mean vegetables, is common knowledge.[6] And Diogenes, the archetypal Cynic, at one point is supposed to have been called by Plato "Socrates gone mad."[7] At the level of Q's formative stratum, John appears as one more of these same "dog-gone" philosophers.

In 7:34, if we may assume that the expression "son of man" refers to Jesus,[8] the picture painted here of John's junior colleague portrays him in a rather different light, namely, as "a glutton and a drunkard, a friend of tax-collectors and sinners." In obvious opposition to the preceding description of John, Jesus is said in 7:34 to have eaten and drunk frequently enough and in sufficient quantity to become notorious for his generous consumption.[9]

The language itself of 7:34 is unusual. Both the word for "glutton" (*phagos*) and for "drunkard" (*oinopotēs*) are hapaxlegomena in the New Testament, found nowhere else in these writings.[10] The term for "friend" (*philos*), while common enough in itself, is never used by Mark nor otherwise in Matthew.[11] Both the word for "tax-collector" and for "sinner" appear only here indubitably in Q.[12]

What 7:34 says about Jesus matches the saying's peculiar diction. In modern slang, John's understudy appears here as a real "party animal." "Eating and drinking," he himself commits what elsewhere in Q (17:27) they are said to have done whom the deluge overwhelmed at the time of Noah.[13] Far from worrying about where his next meal would come from, as 12:22 admonishes not to, Jesus, according to 7:34, apparently ate and drank well and often enough to be suspected of overindulgence. Perhaps for this reason, he saw no cause for concern about these things. In any case, Jesus' behavior plainly did not conform to his contemporaries' image of a "serious" and "upright" man.[14]

As if such habits were not enough, Jesus is also characterized in 7:34 as having been "a friend of tax-collectors and sinners." The company he kept was obviously "not the best." It seems he chose to spend too much of his time with those whom local society did not approve or laud. This is what "sinners" were in general terms. The reference to tax-collectors specifies the impropriety.[15]

Here is a view of Jesus remarkably different from the usual scholarly perspective on him as either an apocalyptic prophet or a scribal teacher of wisdom. The picture that emerges from the "depths" of the synoptic tradition at the level of Q's formative stratum is one of a bit of a hellion and wanderer on the wild, even illicit, side of things — the original Galilean version of the 1950s rebel James Dean!

Lest we think, however, that such a view is only a polemical caricature, an isolated aberration, a false impression, the same distinctive memory tradition surfaces elsewhere in two other peculiar sayings from Q's formative stratum, namely, in the pair of sayings about "discipleship" or following the "son of man" in 9:57–58, 59–60. Presumably, what these texts have to say about "taking after" Jesus held true for him as well.

9:57–58. And someone said to him, "I will follow you wherever you go." And Jesus said to him, "Foxes have holes and birds of the air have nests; but the son of man has nowhere to lay his head."[16]

This well-known saying (9:57–58) identifies another aspect of the "life-style" of the "son of man," to whom reference was first made in 7:34. Again, the saying (9:57–58) is rife with linguistic oddities. Except for Luke 13:52, the Greek word for "fox" (*alōpex*) is found only here (Luke 9:58/Matt 8:19) in the New Testament. The term for "holes" (*phōleos*) is similarly a hapaxlegomenon in these writings, as is the word for "nests" (*kataskēnōsis*). The content of the saying is equally strange. As far as I know, this is the only place in early Christian literature (*pace* GThom 86) where the sleeping habits of the "son of man," i.e., Jesus, are discussed.[17]

The situation described in 9:58 is that of every tramp and street-person, though other persons in antiquity were also sometimes homeless.[18] Predictably, efforts have been made to give the saying (9:58) a more profound significance than this.[19] But the point of the dictum is essentially clear and hardly requires needlessly complex interpretation. In 9:58, the "son of man" is said to lead a less civilized existence than the animals seen regularly at the edge of ancient Galilean towns and villages.[20]

This characterization of Jesus, without a place to lay his head, may sound tamer than the statement in 7:34 referring to him as "a glutton and a drunkard, a friend of tax-collectors and sinners." But both descriptions amount to the same thing. In both sayings, Jesus is said to have habitually "transgressed" the normal bounds of conventional society. His behavior was consistently "abnormal," at variance with local cultural expectations.

In the present case (9:58), his sleeping habits, as previously in 7:34 how much Jesus ate and drank plus the kinds of friends he kept, all ignored (or defied) the usual ancient codes of proper comportment for upstanding community members. A person with no place to lay his head, precisely for this reason might end up sleeping anywhere. Not only prone to rowdiness, Jesus was also remembered in Q's formative stratum as someone decidedly shiftless.

> *9:59–60.* **And another said to him, "Lord, let me first go and bury my father." But he said to him, "Follow me, and leave the dead to bury their own dead."**[21]

The next saying (9:59–60) is even more subversive.[22] Implicitly, it challenges the entire family-based (patriarchal/kinship) construction of social relations in the ancient Mediterranean world by advocating complete disregard for the filial duty of burial. It is difficult to overemphasize the direct affront of such a pronouncement to the dominant created orders of classical antiquity.

It is important for interpretation of 9:59–60 to recall the well-known fact that the fundamental social institution of the ancient Mediterranean world was the household, at whose head stood the *paterfamilias*. Perhaps less well known but equally important to bear in mind is the great significance that members of the same society attached to being properly buried by their children. In 9:59–60, a direct swipe is taken at both convictions.[23]

Martin Hengel has described in considerable detail the "break with law and custom" that the saying in 9:59–60 represents. Unfortunately, Hengel's description is so skewed by erroneous assumptions about the "Jewishness" of Jesus and the charismatic quality of his speech and behavior that Hengel's basic insight threatens to fade from view. Hengel imparts a great deal of information about ancient (Jewish) laws and customs, but says strikingly little about the actual break with them by Jesus beyond the fact that it occurred. This is perhaps the inevitable consequence of Hengel's belief that we should view what is said in 9:59–60 "above all from an eschatological angle and — must we not say? — in the light of the messianic authority of Jesus."[24]

The saying itself in 9:59–60 does not require such an interpretation. What we have here is instead simply " 'anti-social' behavior," as Hengel himself characterizes the comparable comportment of Israel's classical prophets.[25] In this regard, Hengel betrays a curious habit, shared with others of his trade, of amassing impressive amounts of data, only to miss the point of it all. Consider the following example:

> The Book of Tobit...shows, as do the entire literature of the Testaments of the Patriarchs and Josephus, that the request for interment by one's own son was a generally widespread, conventional motif behind which there lay a firmly established freely accepted custom. Even Apollonius of Tyana, who is portrayed as being completely free of human prejudices and as condemn-

ing possessions and outward honors... "hurried, when he heard of his father's death, to Tyana, and interred him with his own hands beside his mother's grave" (Philostratus, *Vita Apoll.* 1.13). Conversely, refusal of burial had always been considered among the Greeks and Jews as an unheard of act of impiety and as the severest of punishments for criminals; behind this lies the old and widespread animistic idea that the unburied dead could find no rest. Basically there was on this point no difference between Jews and Gentiles: "Burial of the dead was for the ancients always both a human and a religious duty" (E. Stommel, RAC 2:200).[26]

Most telling is Hengel's quick conclusion that "behind this lies the old and widespread animistic idea that the unburied dead could find no rest." Are not social continuity and the proper succession or "passing on" of generations as much at issue? Is it really the animistic idea of the restless dead and not rather the particular values of honor-shame cultures like the ancient Mediterranean world that are here revealed?[27] Are we really to imagine that Jesus' retort finally represents religious enlightenment and the one true faith?[28] Is it not rather just another example of the specific social posture assumed by both Jesus and the people who recalled him in Q's formative stratum within and over against the "ethical" environment of first-century C.E. Galilee?

The references collected by Hengel in the footnote that supports his contention of an animistic background to 9:59–60 are extremely mixed in character.[29] Passages from the Babylonian epic of Gilgamesh (12.155ff) and Homer's *Odyssey* (11.51ff, 72ff) may indeed attest "the old and widespread animistic idea" of the restless unburied dead. But the prohibition of mourning for certain executed criminals described by Suetonius (*Tib.* 61.2) and the refusal to let them be buried (*Vesp.* 2.3) are more likely just further means of underscoring and accentuating the extreme act of expulsion that their capital punishment was meant to represent.

Not even in death were the condemned allowed to be remembered and thus readmitted as once again part of their former social group, whose requirements for continuing membership they were judged to have violated beyond forgiveness. Their identity as citizens has been thoroughly stripped away. This is dishonor, literally to lose face, to be deprived of all recognition of ever having belonged to one's own people.

Lack of burial as punishment for "the godless man" in the tradition of Israel likewise makes clear that this person, too, would not be recognized as ever having been a member of God's people. In this regard, Hengel refers to 1 En 98:13; 2 Macc 5:10; Josephus, *Ant.* 10.97; *War* 2.465; 3.377; 4.317, 385. Consider, however, to take but one example, the language of 2 Macc 5:10 in context. Jason, the person whose unburied corpse is here in view, is said "in the end [to have] got[ten] only disgrace" (v. 7) for his activities, was "hated" and "abhorred" (v. 8) by everyone, and as he was unmourned without a funeral, "had no place in the tombs of his fathers" (v. 10). Ultimate social ostracization is the fate depicted by these verses, not an agitated afterlife.

The fact that honor versus shame, not animism and the restless dead, is the basic issue at stake can be seen even more clearly when the "positive counterpart" or the act of burial itself is discussed. Hengel refers in this regard to Sir 44:4 [sic=44:14]; 46:12; 49:10. Note that in Sir 46:12 the reference to burial is followed in *parallelismus membrorum* by speech about "those who have been honored" in this way. Regarding Sir 44:14, the description of those whose "bodies were buried in peace" is preceded by an account of how "their glory will not be blotted out" (44:13). Hengel himself recalls "the related veneration of the graves of holy men in Jewish Palestine in the Hellenistic period." Of principal concern in these texts is thus the enduring value of social honor, not the possibility of wandering spirits.[30]

The "tale of the grateful dead man in Tobit" evokes from Hengel a round of references to secondary sources, only to conclude with the observation that in one instance of two versions of the tale, "in each case a living person who protects a corpse from desecration is rewarded by the resurrected dead person."[31] To protect a corpse from desecration means, however, continuing to guard the public respect due its erstwhile owner, whose physical self can now no longer be spared the malaise of biological decay.

Hengel's inference of an "old and widespread animistic idea" behind ancient interest in burial of the dead, especially filial burial of the parental dead, is simply not supported by the evidence that Hengel himself has adduced for this purpose. His own characterization of 9:59–60 is therefore unfounded.

It may be instructive to review at this point what Hengel otherwise writes about further possible parallels to the saying in 9:59–60. Regarding Ezek 24:15–24 and Jer 16:1–8, for example, Hengel states:

> Of course, these "parabolic actions" of the prophets do not constitute direct parallels, but they do show how Yahweh, to advertise his own future activities, could demand from individual prophets a rigorous break with the taboos and conventions of their environment, even specifically here, as regards customs relating to mourning.[32]

On the other hand:

> A real analogy which we shall have to investigate, does indeed exist in the fact that in this context [i.e., a speech] the accusation is

made against Socrates that he was educating his pupils to condemn their ancestors and relations . . . , *Memorabilia*, 1.2.51.[33]

Hengel refers again to this same passage (Xenophon, *Memorabilia* 1.2.51) — though he does not investigate it any further — when considering the call to follow Jesus and the accompanying need to break with one's parental family. Hengel cites as well certain other statements by Musonius Rufus and Epictetus of a similar sort:

> "Your father is a hindrance to you in philosophizing; but the common father of all men and gods, Zeus, admonishes and encourages you to do this. . . . Zeus' command enjoins man to be good which is identical with being a philosopher. . . . " Musonius continues to the effect that the use of violence on the part of the father must in the last resort remain without success, as he possesses no power over the capacity to think philosophically.[34]

> " 'And how is it possible that a man who possesses nothing and who is naked, without house and hearth, untidy, without slaves and without a home town can live a happy life?' 'Look at me. I am without house, without home, without property, without slaves! I sleep on the ground, I have no wife, no children, no palace from which to rule, but only the earth and sky and one rough coat. And what do I lack? Am I not without sorrow, am I not without fear, am I not free? . . . Who on seeing me will not consider that he is looking at his king and lord?' " H. Hommel draws attention to a related passage: " 'what is morally good (τὸ ἀγαθόν) therefore has priority over any relationships. My concern is not with my father but with the ἀγαθόν . . . .' "[35]

Hengel concludes:

> Here we certainly have the nearest philosophical analogy to the sayings about following in Q Mt 8.18–22 and Lk 9.57–62. Jesus too demands complete freedom of the person who follows him; though of course on the basis of an entirely different kind of reasoning and different objective.[36]

How much goes unsaid, assumed, and unexamined with the phrase, "of course"! It is clear, however, as the comparisons provided by Hengel himself suggest, that issues of considerable social weight were perceived to be involved in the matter of obedience to and respect for the memory of one's father. Burial was the moment par excellence to demonstrate expected and applauded filial loyalty. To ignore it, as Jesus proposed, could only reveal great indecency. Jesus was being simply shameless.

14:26. If anyone does not hate his own father and mother, he cannot be my disciple.[37]

The sayings in 14:26–27 again treat the topic of discipleship: what it meant for the persons whom Q represents to "take after" Jesus. The tone of these texts is consistent with the earlier statements made in 9:57–58, 59–60.[38] Like the saying in 9:59–60, 14:26 makes the first requirement for going with Jesus the breaking of familial bonds. Hating one's father and mother seems to be on a par with not burying them. The striking (i.e., revolting) character of such an attitude in the ancient world has already been discussed.[39]

14:27. He who does not take his cross and follow me cannot be my disciple.[40]

This saying (14:27) is most peculiar for Q, which otherwise shows neither interest in nor knowledge of "the cross," if by this expression we understand the death of Jesus to be invoked.[41] A close parallel to 14:27 exists in Mark 8:34, but the saying (14:27) is nonetheless attested for Q by the fact that both in Matthew (10:38; 16:24) and in Luke (9:23; 14:27) there are doublets of it. Such redundancy is typically understood to indicate that a given text was originally found in both Mark and Q and then rather mechanically repeated by the two later evangelists.

Except for Q 14:27 (and parallels), the Greek word for "cross" (*stauros*) is used only a handful of times in all four canonical gospels, and in each instance always to describe the execution of Jesus (a somewhat predictable occurrence, given that this act was remembered as a death by crucifixion). The same holds true for the related verb, *stauroō*.[42]

In Mark 8:34, the "parallel" saying to Q 14:27 is made to serve quite neatly the redactional agenda of this gospel. Indeed, if Burton Mack is correct, Mark 8:34 is now the opening statement of three sets of instruction that make of Mark, as the story of Jesus' death, a "model" for Christian existence. Mack writes:

> the sayings function as Mark's positive statement about the paradigmatic purpose of the gospel for his own time and community. They describe, in effect, Mark's own solution to the conundrum of Jesus' fate, the way in which he intended for his readers to make sense of the gospel and the crucifixion as irony. They are Mark's instructions as to what, then, one was to think and do in the meantime.[43]

The situation regarding Q is very different. It is hardly clear what relationship exists between 14:27 and the rest of the synoptic sayings source.[44] What precisely does it mean to say, "take his cross," in the midst of a series of sapiential maxims? Can language of this sort mean anything other than a reference to Jesus' crucifixion (which it most certainly does in Mark)? There is, however, nothing else in Q that would lead us irresistibly in this direction, were it not that we still tend to read the document, namely, Q with everything else in mind that we "already know" about early Christianity from other texts. What might an alternate reading be?

As one possibility, consider the following piece of advice from Epictetus:

> If you want to be crucified, just wait. The cross will come. If it seems reasonable to comply, and the circumstances are right, then it's to be done, and your integrity maintained.[45]

Epictetus here is not discussing anyone's death as a saving event. He is rather rehearsing one of a number of possible consequences of adopting and living in accordance with a certain philosophy. In 14:27, by analogy, the cost of assuming a similar way of life would likewise be graphically depicted. One doubts that in the cited instance Epictetus speaks from personal experience, although the example used may be based on known cases. The same would hold true for Jesus' first followers in Galilee. The fate imagined in 14:27 is certainly not inconceivable as a result of the social challenge and outrageous behavior otherwise recalled in Jesus' name by Q's formative stratum.

❧

The different sayings in Q 7:33–34; 9:57–58, 59–60; 14:26–27 are all peculiar in any number of ways. In the case of 7:33–34; 9:57–58; 14:27, linguistic oddities are evident. In every saying, the content is exceptional: what is described or enjoined in these utterances neither corresponds in general to widespread social conventions of the ancient Mediterranean world nor specifically to other later Christian images of Jesus.

The unusual memory of Jesus in Q 7:33–34; 9:57–60; 14:26–27 is nonetheless remarkably coherent. The distinctive character of each pronouncement is thoroughly compatible with that of the others. We are thus not dealing simply with isolated instances of strange phenomena. In view is rather a pattern of peculiarity. This makes the sayings even more . . . peculiar.

❧

As already seen in the discussion of 7:33–34, alongside Jesus in Q's formative stratum, there was also John. While the differences between the two men could hardly be overlooked, they were otherwise remembered as essentially of equal status, being "the same, but different": two sides, if you will, of the same coin; two burrs in the same mule's tail. Such con-joint status — both simultaneously "founding fathers," but each with his own distinctive style — is not unlike the similar dual memory of the twin "sires" of the Cynic tradition, whether the happy couple are said to have been Antisthenes and Diogenes or Diogenes and Crates.[46]

John is consistently portrayed in Q's formative stratum as someone of superior worth, at least regarding rigor. He is certainly never thought to have played second fiddle to anyone else. Indeed, he seems to exceed every possibility of adequate description through the usual categories of characterization.

7:24b–26. What did you go out into the desert to behold? A reed shaken by the wind? But what did you go out to see? A man dressed in soft clothing? Look, those who wear soft clothing are in the royal palace. But what did you go out to see? A prophet? Indeed, I tell you, even more than a prophet.[47]

The saying in 7:25, "But what did you go out to see? A man dressed in soft clothing?" is the medial term of a threefold characterization of John, beginning in 7:24b with the image of a shaken reed and ending in 7:26 with the reference to a prophet. Rhetorical "build-up" is apparent in the way the questions are ordered. The initial description of John is taken from the realm of "nature": an inert plant whose agitated movements are due to the tumult of the wind. The final portrait is "supernatural": John would be the latest manifestation of the spirit of prophecy, whose agitation reflects the tumult of God. The logical fulcrum of this progression is the saying in 7:25.

Despite the saying's obvious rhetorical importance, it is nonetheless virtually impossible to find a scholarly discussion of 7:25 beyond the requisite paraphrase of the verse by thorough commentaries.[48] Entire books devoted to John do not discuss the saying, except for a brief note. But, again, it is 7:25 that ultimately makes the argument of 7:24b–26 persuasive.[49] Why the "oversight"?

Some unstated presuppositions are plainly operative in 7:24b–26. One is why anyone would have ventured out into the ancient wilderness (*erēmos*) in the first place. Hence the opening question: "What did you go out into the desert [*erēmos*] to behold?" repeated then as: "But what did you go out to see?" Evidently, one could see "a reed shaken by the wind."[50] But the fact that no further comment is made before moving on to the next possibility implies that this was unlikely to have been the reason why anyone undertook such a foray. As Joseph Fitzmyer remarks, to see a reed shaken by the wind in the desert was "something quite ordinary, not really worth so long a trip."[51]

Sometimes, it is thought that the reference in 7:24b to a buffeted reed recalls John's personal drama.[52] The verse is thus subjected to a metaphorical or moral interpretation. Norman Krieger writes, for example, that the buffeted reed as an image of fragility represents the embassy of John, whose earlier certitude on the banks of the river Jordan at the baptism of Jesus subsequently wavered in prison.[53] Expanding the horizon of possibilities even further, C. Daniel thinks that 7:24b has the Zealots in mind.[54] But none of these interpretations is convincing.[55]

Returning to the question why anyone would have ventured out into the desert, a real possibility is that they hoped to find a prophet there. The appearance at this time of different dissentient persons and communities in the uninhabited regions of Judea and Galilee is well known. The final comment made in 7:26c suggests, moreover, that most would have agreed that such a prospect was sufficiently compelling to draw them out of their towns and villages into the surrounding wilderness. In fact, it is implied, this is precisely what many people expected John to be. Not a few persons went out to see him, thinking that he was a prophet. At the same time, 7:26 makes clear that such a belief was erroneous: "Indeed, I tell you [nai legō hymin], John is even [kai] more than a prophet."[56]

Both of these first and final reasons why one might have gone out into the desert receive in 7:24b and 7:26 a negative reply — the first (7:24b), though factually true, because of insufficient motivation; the final (7:26), though factually true and sufficiently compelling, because erroneous. John could have been a prophet, but he wasn't.

The suggestion in 7:25 that one might go out into the desert to see a man dressed in soft clothing is different from the other two sayings that surround it, insofar as 7:25 does not discuss a real expectation. Certainly, no one thought this way about John. The adversative imperative idou at the beginning of the verse, implying the self-evidence of commonsense, plus the reference to royal dwellings or palatial life later in the saying, make clear the proposition's essential irreality.[57] The usual interpretation is thus that, in 7:25, between the inadequate proposal of 7:24b and the improper one of 7:26, a certain fantastic, because absurd, possibility was imagined.[58] 7:25 would be a throwaway line.

Such an interpretation is improbable. The high degree of rhetorical craft apparent in the overall construction of 7:24b–26 makes it unlikely that a throwaway line would occur at its heart. The usual interpretation of 7:25 exists by default. Lacking any other idea what the verse might mean, perhaps because the ancient connotations of its discourse have been unknown, scholars simply impute whatever seems best to them. I wish to propose a new interpretation, one that finds the fact significant that John in 7:25 is opposed to the use of "soft clothing" and that such apparel is simultaneously and conversely said to be especially at home in "royal dwellings" and palatial life.

The diction of 7:25 is anomalous in the context of the synoptic tradition, the term *malakos* occurring only here. The implied subject matter is, moreover, not a typical topic of concern. Elsewhere in the New Testament, *malakos* occurs only in 1 Cor 6:9. The related term *malakia*, found only in Matthew in the synoptic tradition, there means "illness" and does not address the same issues as our text.

In Luke 7:25, the word *tryphē* is also employed. Like *malakos, tryphē* is found only here in the synoptic tradition.[59] In Luke 7:25, the initial reference to a man *en malakois himatiois* corresponds to the subsequent description of those *en himatismo endoxō kai tryphē*.[60] Use of the term *tryphē* in Luke 7:25 is likely due to the evangelist. It represents a redactional interpretation of Q. That Luke, however, understood the saying in this way is not insignificant for what follows. He too saw that a particular kind of characterization was being made here. Luke's association of "softness" with "luxury" (*malakos/malakia* with *trypheros/tryphē*) is, in fact, a commonplace of ancient moral philosophy.

The anomalous character of 7:25 vis-à-vis the synoptic tradition stands in marked contrast to the fact that the same terminology (*malakos, tryphē*) plus the more general theme of soft clothing and palatial life formed a standard part of the polemic waged by ancient Cynics against their own contemporary culture. Especially important in this regard are the so-called "Cynic epistles."[61] In ps-Diogenes, *ep.* 28, for example, at the beginning of a long harangue against almost everything about "the so-called Greeks," a telling weakness is taken to be the envy that they feel whenever they see someone who has "clothing that is a little softer."

In ps-Crates, *ep.* 19, an argument is mounted against calling Odysseus "the father of Cynicism," principally because he was the "softest" of all his companions. After equating in general terms this weakness of Odysseus with the enjoyment of pleasure, the discussion then settles on the question of his clothing. On one occasion, Odysseus is said to have put on Cynic garb, but otherwise his behavior exemplified a contrary desire for "the sweet life." At this point, it is extremely important to realize that the description of Odysseus in ps-Crates, *ep.* 19, effectively summarizes the Homeric epic, which records the trials of Odysseus returning to his royal palace on the island of Ithaca and Penelope, his wife. According to ps-Crates, *ep.* 19, Odysseus is wrongly called the father of Cynicism because his momentary adoption of rough apparel was only in the service of his larger effort to embrace once more the luxuries of his throne and queen.[62]

In ps-Crates, *ep.* 29, and ps-Diogenes, *ep.* 12, the Cynic way of life is said to be opposed to "softness." According to ps-Crates, *ep.* 29, not indifference but endurance distinguishes the philosophy of the Cynics, specifically, their ability to endure things others cannot handle "on account of softness." According to ps-Diogenes, *ep*. 12, the Cynic shortcut to happiness is soon forsaken by most of those who had at first so eagerly sought it out because of the shortcut's severity and the "softness" of these persons. In ps-Diogenes, *ep*. 29, the tyrant Dionysius is addressed. He is offered a pedagogue, clearly a Cynic, who "will turn you away from softness," that is, the life surrounding the tyrant in his palace.[63]

This polemic against soft clothing and the softness of character it revealed was extended to other things as well; for example, the use of soft couches and similar sleeping arrangements. Thus, Epictetus reports:

> "To be naked is better than any scarlet robe; and to sleep on the bare ground," [Diogenes] says, "is the softest couch."[64]

Likewise, Julian opines that the person "who is entering on the career of a Cynic ought first... [to] ask himself the following questions," among which is "whether he cannot do without a soft bed."[65]

The invective against "softness" formed part of the Cynics' wider campaign against the mores of the rich and lascivious. Ps-Lucian, for example, in "The Cynic" has his representative cur declaim:

> Therefore, my appearance is, as you see, to be dirty and unkempt with a worn cloak, long hair, and bare feet, but yours is just like that of the sodomites and no one could tell the difference either by the color of your cloaks, or by the softness and number of your tunics, or by your wraps, shoes, elaborate hairstyles, or your scent.[66]

In Lucian's "Dialogues of the Dead" (20.8), the last of the marks of the false philosopher, after he has been stripped by Hermes for Charon, is softness. At the other end of the spectrum, as Dio Chrysostom remarks, the ideal Cynic aggressively trains his body and does not permit it to suffer "baths and ointments and perfumes," lest thereby it become "too soft and unsound."[67]

A concrete example of what the Cynics may have had in mind as "softness" can be found in Philo (*de spec. leg.* 3.40–41). Persons who practice pederasty are under discussion. Philo thinks that in many nations, such people receive rewards for this "incontinence and softness." Among other things, Philo mentions that such "hermaphrodites" could be found in the crowded marketplace, leading the processions at the feasts, and performing various religious rites, most notably those of Demeter. At the same time, persons who emasculate themselves are "clad in purple like signal benefactors of their native lands" and walk around with bodyguards. Against the wishes of Philo, it would appear that the social status of many of these "softies" was quite high.

In ps-Diogenes, *ep.* 36 (really more a dialogue than a letter), part of the conversation revolves around whether or not poverty is something evil. The befuddled interlocutor stammers that it is because, among other things, poverty causes cold. The Cynic counters that most people think so only "on account of softness," going on to note that "even here there are allies: animal hides, woolly sheepskins, and the walls of caves and houses."[68]

It is only when placed in the context of such debate, one spearheaded in antiquity by the Cynics, that the "throwaway line" in 7:25 can be seen for the sharp statement that it is. The suggestion is made here that perhaps those who went out into the desert to John thought that they would see the sort of person otherwise excoriated by the popular philosophers for lurid living, the sort especially prone to gather in the royal court like flies at a banquet. Perhaps they thought for some strange reason that John too would be dressed like one of these sycophants, arrayed in cloth as purple as their prose, though John in the desert could hardly have been farther away from and more inimical to the official center of power and influence than he was.

*

It is sometimes suggested that 7:25 refers obliquely to Herod's court.[69] Such a perspective certainly coheres with the preceding interpretation of the saying's original rhetorical context, given that the Cynic polemic against softness found its most ready and telling target in the palace of contemporary tyrants and despots. In 7:25, John is characterized as one who, like the Cynics, was the very opposite of these persons.

The same interpretation of 7:25 may provide a clue as to why John and Herod were elsewhere recalled as having been such mortal enemies. Corroboration is given to what A. E. J. Rawlinson has termed the "bazaar rumor" about John's death in Mark 6:14–29.[70] As Ernst Lohmeyer recognized, this well-known tale of the Baptist's end is hardly clarified, if we think that John's censure of Herod's marriage to his sister-in-law, the pretext of John's imprisonment, "only renders concrete the general call to repentance."[71] As Rawlinson rightly notes, "Josephus assigns a political motive for the execution of the Baptist."[72] Like the Cynics, John appeared programmed for conflict with the highest civil authorities of the land, finding in them the most blatant instance of what was wrong with the surrounding culture.

The greatest resistance to this interpretation of 7:25 and its characterization of John as a social carper like the Cynics will come from those who still want to see John as a prophet. It is noteworthy, therefore, and not to be ignored that, as already discussed, immediately after 7:25 in the following verse (7:26) we read that John was "more than a prophet." This cannot mean that he was therefore somehow really quite a prophet or an exceptional one or a prophet as well as something else. Rather, it must mean what is flatly stated: that for the person(s) whose judgment is here recorded, John was "not a prophet, but more" than that. The term "prophet" as a generic category simply did not suffice to describe him.[73] An altogether different category of classification was required.[74]

Unlike the classical (canonical) prophets of Israel, whose identity resided especially in their opposition to the erosion and ignorance of traditional values by the developing and decadent monarchy,[75] John appears, at least in 7:25, to have defined himself as a Cynic through opposition to the reigning culture as such. The royal dwellings with their palatial life symbolized, both for John and for the Cynics, the dominant aspirations and pitfalls of advancing "civilization."

At the formative stage of Q, it was not the call to repentance or renewal of the religious patrimony of Abraham that especially distinguished John but, rather, his stance in the desert. Beyond the circuit of conventional society in an altogether different orbit from the one that united ancient kings and their customary critics, John stood apart, in fundamental disagreement with the current order of things — at whose margin, nonetheless, if barely, he could still be found.

The characterization of John in 7:24b–26 is best understood when we compare the saying as a whole, but especially v. 25, with the similar discourse of the Cynics. The rhetorically logical fulcrum of 7:25, linking the inadequate motivation of 7:24b with the negative conclusion of 7:26, rides on a certain sense of irony or humor.[76] Like the figure of Odysseus in ps-Crates, *ep.* 19, who only laughingly or scornfully could be called the father of Cynicism, so it is that only with an advanced sense of the ridiculous might one imagine John in the desert as "a man dressed in soft clothing." The sheerness of the contrast, whose impossibility borders on the inadequacy of the preceding suggestion, cultivates a climate of negative expectation for the subsequent and seemingly better proposal of John as a prophet.

At the level of expectation, the answer to the first question in 7:24b is strictly speaking yes, but actually no. The answer to the final question in 7:26 is strictly speaking no, even though most persons in antiquity would probably have answered yes. The intervening question in 7:25, whose answer is both strictly speaking and likely no, makes this inversion possible. At the same time, by virtue of its purely negative quality, a specific profile is implied for John in 7:25, not unlike the relation that exists between a shadow and its owner. The developed image would be precisely the opposite of what is stated. Cynic parallels to 7:25, as in the photographic process, help then to visualize concretely the sort of man we should imagine.

7:28a. I tell you, among those born of women there is no one greater than John.[77]

The "prehistory" of 7:28 remains uncertain.[78] If, as some think, 7:28a was once an "independent" saying, only subsequently conjoined to what both precedes and follows it, the view of John contained in this half-verse would belong to the same uncompromising memory tradition discussed above.[79] In John, the persons whom Q represents recalled "the greatest man ever born," much as Alexander the Great, the ancient world's supreme example of a kingly conquerer, is supposed to have said after meeting Diogenes: "Had I not been born Alexander first, I would have been Diogenes."[80] Diogenes himself was wont to say that there was likely no one more content than he.

❦

At the level of Q's formative stratum, John appears in 7:24b–26, 28a, 33 as a "serious" Cynic, critical of those around him and the cultural habits they pursued. For John's critics at this stage, the man's main mark of divinity was just the demon in him. His admirers, however, recalled John as "the greatest man ever born." He was certainly no "softie" like the sycophants at Herod's court, no toady of the local tyrant. Like the Q people, John was rather to be found in the desert, on the social margin, aggressively pursuing another "better" life.

Jesus emerges in the memory of Q's formative stratum as a more convivial, though no less demanding Cynic. He is plainly neither an apocalyptic seer nor a scribal sage. Instead, at this level of the document's composition history Jesus was recalled as rather a bit of an imp: in Socrates' terms, a social gadfly, an irritant on the skin of conventional mores and values, a marginal figure in the provincial context of first-century C.E. Galilee whose style of life and appeal to others was precisely to go a different way than the "normal" one.[81] For the persons whom Q represents, no one could have embodied better their own social practice.

CONCLUSION

Galilean Upstarts: A Cynic Q

W HAT IMAGE EMERGES when the preceding "takes" on the people whom Q's formative stratum represents are here combined within a single concluding frame? What larger picture develops, if we now endeavor to imagine in as full-bodied a form as possible the public profile of Jesus' first followers in Galilee according to the diverse testimony of Q's initial literary layer: those persons who otherwise would necessarily have remained unknown bit-players on the eastern stage of the ancient Roman empire?

In terms of ethos, the Q people looked very much like Cynics, moving about their regional haunts barefooted, penniless, sparsely robed, without staff or bag (10:4a), on certain occasions speaking to no one (10:4b), at other times quite pointedly direct and "witty" in their denunciation of what they perceived in the surrounding society to be so much "unnatural" nonsense (11:39–48, 52), embodying in this way a thoroughgoing "radical" critique of the local dominant culture.

Styling themselves "emissaries" or scouts of a more satisfying mode of existence (10:3), the Q people claimed to be acting as agents of "God's kingdom," whose power they felt would grant all those who took them up on their offer both the key to happiness in general (6:20b; 12:31) as well as on-the-spot effective treatment of "whatever ailed you" (10:9; 11:20) — much as the Cynics called their way of life a "short-cut" to contentment, believing that its different "ascetic" rigors, like other ancient forms of training and regimen, would cure the "disease" produced by the falsely touted "good" life.[1]

Wandering from town to town and house to house, the persons identified with Q's formative stratum looked to other men and women of good will or "sons of peace" for gestures of hospitality (10:5–6). In exchange for this uncertain benefaction, the Q people were prepared to trade the benefits of their own uncommon wisdom. Not an easy life, to be sure, it was made even harder by the additional restrictions that these beggars took upon themselves, abstaining from all intentional provision (10:4a; cf. 12:22ff).

Not surprisingly, the Q people soon learned to anticipate that a cool reception might be waiting for them at the hands of the persons whom they approached with no prior warning for a handout. Indeed, this experience of an unwelcoming response happened often enough and was sufficiently harsh to provoke the Q people's self-description as "sheep among wolves" (10:3) and to require their creation of a strategy for exiting hostile hamlets in disgrace (10:10–11). When taken in, however, a certain higher visitation was purported to transpire (10:16).

As part of Q's more extended ethical elaboration of this way of life, the exhortation to "love your enemies" in 6:27–35 seeks to "resolve" the crucial, because recurring, problem of inimical opposition: the diverse, if somewhat predictable, predicaments provoked and suffered by the Q people as a consequence of their decided social marginality.[2] The different strategies of resistance developed by these local *provocateurs* for dealing with such sporadic complications as the threat of personal insult (6:28), physical assault (6:29a), the loss of whatever goods they might have had (6:29b) and the desire of others for anything else they possessed (6:30) find expression in 6:28–30 in a series of proactive — though "ultimately unfulfilled" — acts of self-dispossession, eventually thematized in 6:27 as the oxymoron "love your enemies."

Hardly a lasting solution to the various problems looming any given day on the horizon, the goal of this "strange advice" developed by the Q people was not to enjoy as soon as possible our modern utopian ideal of the elimination of all such unwanted occurrences from the social scene. Rather, the suggestion to "love your enemies" in Q stemmed from a more concrete and immediate aspiration, uttered evidently from a position of relative "weakness," namely, just to keep going in the particular way that the persons whom the document represents had chosen for themselves despite adversity.

The "golden rule" slyly placed *in medias res* in 6:31, the blunt questions asked point-blank in 6:32–33, and finally the unsettling example of God in 6:35 bring the general exhortation to a close with a series of probing rationalizations, all of which sustain the earlier imperatives in 6:27–30 by further calling into question the standard behavior they so plainly oppose. Such wisdom was admittedly heterodox, but then so were the "wise guys" it was meant to sustain!

Repeated reference to the "kingdom of God" in Q's formative stratum belongs to this stage of the document's thoroughgoing transvaluation of local societal norms. A way of life that otherwise might have seemed poor and insignificant was hereby said to be instead quite simply satisfying, salutary (10:9), self-sufficient (6:20b), free of worry (12:31), full of possibility (13:18–21).

Plainly ascetic, in need of and enjoying only a few things, the promise of such an existence, identified as the "kingdom of God," included the knowledge it displayed of granting freedom from debilitating "ills" and "weakness" in the midst of otherwise unfavorable circumstances (10:9). Astute at defending itself under attack (11:15–20), the same approach to life taught the believing participant how to proceed one day at a time (11:2–3), like the ravens and the lilies, without property (12:22–31). A subversive view of things, insofar as the enterprise of human "civilization" was itself hereby put into question, like the mustard seed and the leaven, a form of political activity was simultaneously implied up to more than met the eye (13:18–21).

Like other Cynic "zingers," the woes in Q's formative stratum (11:39–48, 52) played, as social critique, for the perceptual space in which current social norms and ideal structures could be relaxed and a certain relativity reign. All of the woes in Q's formative stratum turn about the axis of appearance versus reality — appearance being synonymous with ostensive virtue, reality always rather less exalted. The Cynics, too, never ceased to underscore the same enduring contrast between pretense and performance, bringing their rhetorical inventiveness and sardonic sense of humor to bear in diverse ways upon this gap.

The Pharisees were chosen as the brunt of Q's occasionally more playful, sometimes harsher, "cultural criticism," mainly because the Pharisees, better or more zealously than anyone else in the context of first-century C.E. Galilee, promoted the Jewish people's officially sanctioned "covenanted" way of life.[3] And it was precisely this belief in the need for a normative ethos as the basis of a divinely "blessed" existence that the woes in Q's initial literary layer (11:39–48, 52) set out to scrutinize. Before their later escalation by Q's subsequent redactions into a rhetoric of condemnatory judgment, the sayings in 11:39–48, 52 were originally content merely to burst the bubble of all overweening claims to perfect righteousness.

The Q people looked back to John and Jesus as the precursors of their fledgling "movement." Jesus was remembered in Q's formative stratum essentially like Socrates as a social gadfly or imp, an irritant on the skin of local mores and values, a marginal figure in the provincial context of first-century C.E. Galilee whose style of life and appeal to others was principally to go a way different than the "normal" one. For the Q people, the tradition of his memory helped display and articulate further their own "dissident" social practice.

At the same level of Q, also recalled was Jesus' "alter-ego," John, a more "serious" Cynic, critical of those around him and the cultural habits they pursued. For John's critics at this stage, the man's main mark of divinity was just the demon in him. John's admirers, however, remembered the desert drifter as "the greatest man ever born."

Like the Cynics, the "Galilean upstarts" whom Q's formative stratum represents conducted in word and deed a form of "popular" resistance to the official truths and virtues of their day. Registered in their unorthodox ethos, ethics, ideology, and ad hoc social critique as well the sparse but vivid memory they maintained of certain "anti-heroes" of the recent past (John and Jesus) was both a decisive "no" to the typical habits and aspirations of their immediate cultural context, as well as a curious confidence in their own peculiar ability to achieve here and now, in the body and despite considerable adversity, a higher form of happiness. Such subversive wisdom, however fragile and quixotic its half-life and logic may have been, still gives rise, for some, to the uncommon pleasures of unsettling thought and action.[4]

The Formative Stratum of Q

Agreement and Disagreement with John S. Kloppenborg, *The Formation of Q*

A S STATED in the introduction, I take John S. Kloppenborg's basic thesis in *The Formation of Q* as a fundamental working hypothesis.[1] I agree with Kloppenborg that the theory of "Q" remains the best available solution to the so-called "synoptic problem"; that Q as used by Matthew and Luke was indeed a written document, originally produced and preserved in Greek; and that sufficient evidence exists to believe, as Kloppenborg has carefully shown, that the striking heterogeneity of materials in the synoptic sayings source is due, at least in part, to alterations made by two (or three) editions of the text.

To Q's formative stratum, Kloppenborg assigns the following "clusters" of sayings: (i) 6:20b–49;[2] (ii) 9:57–62;[3] 10:2–11, 16; (iii) 11:2–4, 9–13; (iv) 12:2–7, 11–12; (v) 12:22–31, 33–34; (vi) 13:24; 14:26–27, 34–35; 17:33.[4] To the secondary stratum, Kloppenborg ascribes: (i) 3:7–9, 16–17; (ii) 7:1–10, 18–35 (including 16:16); (iii) 10:12, 13–15, 21–24; (iv) 11:14–52; 13:34–35; (v) 12:39–59; (vi) 14:16–24; (vii) 17:23–30, 34–37; (viii) 19:12–27; 22:28–30. A tertiary redaction includes: 4:1–13; 11:42d; 16:17.[5] Unattributed in *The Formation of Q* are the sayings in 13:18–21; 15:4–7; 16:13, 18; 17:1–6.[6]

I agree with Kloppenborg in assigning to Q's formative stratum the "mission" instructions in 10:3–6, 9–11, 16 (chapter one); the discourse about "love your enemies" in 6:27–35 (chapter two); the different kingdom-of-God sayings in 6:20b–21; 10:9; 11:2–4; 12:22–31 (chapter three); and the "peculiar" memories of Jesus in 9:57–60, 14:26–27 (chapter five).

I disagree with Kloppenborg, however, regarding the status of 10:2,

7b (chapter one). Kloppenborg assigns these sayings to Q's formative stratum, but I believe that they belong, like 10:12, 13–15, to the document's secondary redaction. In addition, I disagree with Kloppenborg (or exceed the extent of his discussion) regarding the stratigraphical location of the Beelzebul debate in 11:14–20 (chapter three), the two parables in 13:18–21 (chapter three), the "woes" in 11:39–48, 52 (chapter four), and the recollections of John — and Jesus — in 7:24b–26, 28a, 33–34 (chapter five). Kloppenborg would assign all these sayings to Q's redaction, whereas I place them in the document's formative stratum.

In what follows, I explain why I disagree with Kloppenborg *on these points*. Let me repeat, however, that his general thesis in *The Formation of Q* remains a basic presupposition of my own work.

Q 7:24b–26, 28a, 33–34

Ascription of the sayings in 7:24b–26, 28a, 33–34 to Q's formative stratum rests essentially upon recognition of the basic discontinuity, indeed, incompatibility between what is said in these sayings and the image of John that the document's penultimate redaction has otherwise sought to create. It is finally impossible to imagine how the hand responsible for Q's secondary elaboration would ever have willingly included these sayings in its composition, were it not that they already had a place in Q's initial literary presentation.[7]

I do not dispute Kloppenborg's description of the way in which the two large blocks of material in 3:7b–9, 16–17, and 7:18–35 (including 16:16) generally display the work of Q's redaction. The final impression created of John in these texts is indeed that of "a prophet of the coming end," reflecting "the deuteronomistic pattern in which the prophets are interpreted as preachers of repentance and as heralds of judgment."[8] Both passages clearly intend, furthermore, to make John finally subordinate to Jesus.

In 7:18–35, the eventual portrait painted of John is roughly the following. In the first (7:18–23) of this section's three major divisions (7:18–23, 24–28, 31–35), in order to answer the question asked by John in 7:18–20 whether or not Jesus is indeed the coming one or should they look for another (=part two of the self-put-down begun by John in 3:16), the response given by Jesus in 7:22–23 clearly implies that Jesus is, in fact, the long-awaited figure, the designated successor to the final eschatological prophet. John thereby becomes Jesus' precursor, the anxious inquirer's self-knowledge being revealed that he was not the real thing.

John's sole purpose in this passage (7:18–23) is to provide a prominent point of departure for the further magnification of Jesus' person (at

John's expense). In 7:22–23, Jesus' plate is heaped with choice morsels of Isaianic prophecy, suggestive of their fulfillment by Jesus in some way, followed then with a concluding beatitude that vaguely threatens all who would be scandalized by such self-aggrandizement. John rapidly recedes into the background — so much so, in fact, that the abrupt transition in 7:24a to the suddenly exclusive characterization of John in 7:24b–26 seems forced and poorly motivated.[9]

In 7:27, John is significantly elevated to the rank of God's appointed endtime *aggelos*. Now essentially equivalent to Elijah, John is here characterized as the ultimate heavenly messenger due to appear just before the final day of the Lord. Such a promotion, however, only serves in the end to demote John once again below the rank of Jesus. That John was sent "before your face" means paradoxically for Q's redaction coming first but decidedly in second place: "to prepare your way before you."[10]

By the time of Q's redaction, it is made clear in 7:28b that the "least" person "in the kingdom of God" is henceforth to be considered "greater than [John]." Though once proclaimed the greatest of all mortals (7:28a), John is here put back in his place. Indisputably awesome and correct, he ceases to be the decisive player in the field. Indeed, he may no longer even be part of the game, given that Jesus and by extension all those identified with him "in the kingdom of God" are said to supersede the former "superman" — a destiny, as already noted, anticipated by John himself in 3:16.

In 16:16, John embodies the end of "the law and the prophets." They endured "until him." John is either the culmination of whatever they stand for or the premonition of something new. In either case, he becomes a transitional figure, pivotal and significant, but not "the thing itself."

In 7:35, it might seem that John is now suddenly seen as Jesus' equal. Both men are referred to in this saying as "children of wisdom" with no apparent distinction otherwise being made between them. Each participates — in the specific way that 7:33–34 has differently described — in the "deuteronomistic" scheme of divine envoys repeatedly sent to, but routinely rejected by, the "children of Abraham" (cf. 3:8; 7:32).

At this point, however, in the larger composition of 7:18–35, how best to characterize John and Jesus has ceased to be the main concern of Q's redaction. The focus of attention has shifted instead to another problem, namely, how adequately to describe "this generation" (cf. 3:7b; 7:31). Its equal disregard of both John and Jesus — who otherwise for Q's redaction, as seen above, have plainly distinct portfolios — is interpreted in 7:35 as patent evidence of this generation's clear culpability.

The example of John and Jesus' contrasting personal styles in 7:33–34 serves at the level of Q's redaction simply to sustain what John alone proclaims at the start of the secondary stratum, namely, the threat of "wrath to come" against this generation and its "brood" of unrepentant "vipers" (3:7b). John and Jesus are equally important in 7:35 merely to underscore the utterly feckless folly of this generation's irresolute regard. Otherwise, there is no suggestion of further parity between them.

This redactional view of John — and Jesus — apparent in the overall arrangement and general content of many of the sayings in Q 3:7b–9, 16–17; 7:18–35 contrasts sharply with the strikingly different character-izations made of the same men in the encompassed sayings in 7:24b–26, 28a, 33–34. In 7:33–34, for example, we are truly light years away from the portrait painted of the relationship between John and Jesus in 7:18–23. Instead of the messianic aura surrounding Jesus in 7:18–23, it is the fog of a hangover that envelopes the fearless feaster in 7:34. Any scandal provoked by Jesus from the perspective of this saying alone would not be the result of eschatological surprise and wonder, but the direct consequence of his low-life associations.[11]

In 7:33–34, John is fully Jesus' equal. At least, John stands on a par with the omnivorous sot, though at the opposite end of the behavioral spectrum. There is no hint of inferior ranking. Between the two men, a specific social style is defined that, whether eating and drinking or not, was consistently liable to denigration as perverse, in bad taste, out-to-lunch, politically incorrect.

The contrast between the sayings in 7:33–34 and 7:18–23 regarding John and Jesus is, again, simply too great for the initial inclusion of both sets of sayings in Q to be attributed to the same compositional stratum, as though the two discursive units were somehow merely variations on a theme. The rhetoric of each is much too strong, aggressive, and mutually inconsistent vis-à-vis the relative status of both John and Jesus for what is said in 7:33–34 to be taken simply as a different angle on a single per-spective, supporting as it were a la chiaroscuro the opening presentation of the two figures in 7:18–23.[12]

Regarding the second set of sayings in 7:24b–28, this ever more tightly wound jumble of alternating perspectives is roughly divisible into the following four discrete units: (i) 7:24b–26; (ii) 7:27; (iii) 7:28a; (iv) 7:28b. The image of John developed in the first of these segments (7:24b–26) through a series of leading questions is glossy indeed. The man emerges here as finally "even greater than a prophet" (7:26) — a statement on the face of it impossible to reconcile with John's subordi-nate inquiry of Jesus in 7:19 whether or not Jesus is "the coming one" predicted by prophetic literature.

Does someone "even greater than a prophet" look for another "stronger than he, who is coming" (cf. 3:16)? Or is this merely a coy ploy on Jesus' part (or Q's redaction) further to enhance the superior status of Jesus as already displayed in 7:18–23 by now elevating as much as possible the relative value of his supporting cast, namely, John? If so, it is a daring — and potentially fatal — move, for the kind of person evoked in 7:24b–26 could easily steal the show.

Nothing said in 7:24b–26 is guaranteed to keep John in his place. In fact, the *via negativa* whereby equivocal characterizations of the man are consistently surmounted encourages instead a growing sense of John's superlative character. Words can simply not be found with which adequately to describe this person (unlike Jesus, whose basic being has just been summarized with a few snippets of scripture in 7:22).

It is most unlikely that the editorial perspective responsible for the view of John in 3:16 as someone unable to untie the sandal-straps of his successor, would so quickly turn around in 7:24b–26 and praise the same man so unqualifiedly and with such exuberance. It is furthermore quite improbable that the two accounts of John's self-imposed self-diminution in 3:16 and 7:18–23 would compositionally have preceded those passages in the document where this person, namely, John, is exalted or seen as simply Jesus' counterpart. It is therefore most plausible to assume that at least the sayings in 7:24b–26 and 7:33–34 already belonged in some fashion to Q's formative stratum before 7:18–23, 27, 31–32, 35; 16:16 were subsequently incorporated into the document at the time of Q's redaction.[13] For similar reasons, it is also possible that 7:28a was similarly once a part of Q's initial literary layer.[14]

Q 10:2, 7b

In appendix two of *The Formation of Q:* "Formal Analysis of the Q 'Wisdom Instructions,'" Kloppenborg lists as part of the formative stratum of the document the various sayings in 10:2–11, 16; specifically, 10:2, 3, 4, 5–6, 7ab, 8–9, 10–11, 16. Kloppenborg's arguments, however, in the body of the book regarding the compositional status of 10:2, 7b make the assignment of these sayings to Q's earliest literary level anything but secure. Indeed, it seems to me that Kloppenborg himself provides many of the reasons for refuting his own unfounded conclusion.

I begin, therefore, by first citing a series of statements from Kloppenborg's own analysis of the composition-history of 10:2–16. Kloppenborg writes:

> Schulz views the commissioning speech [10:2ff] as a unitary composition from the beginning. This is unlikely. The harvest motif introduced in 10:2 does not reappear in the rest of the sermon [=10:3–16]; in 10:2 "the Lord of the harvest" is the immediate "sender" of the workers, while both 10:3, 16 imply a chain in

which Jesus is the proximate sender; 10:2 exists independently in *Gos. Thom.* 73; and as Zeller observes, the command to pray for more missionaries is not directed to those sent out in v. 3, "but to Christians who might be imagined to be gathered for prayer prior to the commissioning, as in Acts 13:1–3." This is, in short, a change of addressee between 10:3 [sic=10:2?] and the following equipment instruction.[15]

Q 10:3 has somewhat stronger connections with the rest of the speech.... 10:3 with its description of missionaries as "sheep" is particularly apt for 10:4–7, which enjoins them to travel without provisions or money (i.e., in an exposed and defenseless manner). ...although 10:3 may have been originally independent, it coheres well with the rest of the speech and may be, as Hahn claims, a relatively early accretion to the instructions.[16]

The Q version contains several elements not found in Mark.... While the proverb [in Q 10:7b], which also occurs in 1 Tim 5:18 and *Did* 13:1, may be a secondary accretion, it is usually agreed that the greeting of peace and the description of missionary activity are very ancient.[17]

[T]he connection of 10:16 with the mission charge was a natural one. It displays several similarities to 10:3: both anticipate the rejection of the preaching, and both represent the missionaries as the emissaries of Jesus.[18]

The status of 10:2 is more difficult to access. Jacobson argues that v. 2 as well as v. 7b belong to "late redaction," i.e., *subsequent* to the addition of 10:12, 13–15. He points out that both sayings enjoyed an independent circulation, both conceive of Christian missionaries as ἐργάται and both serve to "conform the mission instructions to early Christian mission praxis." But such reasons do not help us situate 10:3 [sic=10:2], 7b with regard to 10:13–15. Equally problematic is Lührmann's attempt to link 10:2 with 10:13–15 on the grounds that "harvest" implies consciousness of the Gentile mission and Gentile membership in the community. As seen above, "harvest" is not always invested with the significance of the judgment or gathering of the Gentiles. Even if 10:2 does point to engagement in a Gentile mission, this in itself does not provide a basis for distinguishing 10:2 from 10:3–11, 16. If 10:8b belonged to Q, there was already consciousness of the problems attending a mission to the Gentiles. A much more decisive observation is that 10:2 signals a shift in setting from missionary instructions as such to the broader setting of advice to a community involved in the preparation and commissioning (10:2) of preachers. The same shift is signaled by Q 10:7b, which is no longer directed at the itinerant preachers, but at those who are expected to *support* missionaries. Thus 10:2 and 10:7b appear to be later additions to 10:3–11, 16.[19]

Summary. Beginning as a cluster of instructions [10:4–11] specifically for missionaries, the composition was augmented by framing sayings (10:3, 16) and by the addition of 10:2 and 10:7b. Both of these sets of additions signal a shift in *Sitz im Leben* from missionary instruction to instruction for a church engaged in the sending and support of missionaries.[20]

Regarding the summary statement, Kloppenborg surprisingly fails accurately to recall his own previous observations when he says here that "both of these sets of additions," namely, 10:3, 16 and 10:2, 7b "signal a shift in *Sitz im Leben*." Only the sayings in 10:2, 7b as Kloppenborg has described them would correspond to "a church engaged in the sending and support of missionaries." The sayings in 10:3, 16 are rather directed at persons who already understand themselves to be instead "emissaries of Jesus." With its description of those sent out as "sheep," 10:3 is furthermore said by Kloppenborg to be "particularly apt for 10:4–7" and "coheres well with the rest of the speech," while the connection of 10:16 with the same materials is called "a natural one."

Indeed, it would appear to be only the lack of a parallel saying to 10:3 and to 10:16 in the Gospel of Mark, plus the fact that variant forms of 10:16 (and 10:3) may be found elsewhere in early Christian literature, that causes Kloppenborg to distinguish between the "core" of the "mission charge" in 10:4–11 and the otherwise thoroughly congruent "framing sayings" in 10:3, 16.[21] In fact, were it not for Kloppenborg's use of an "aggregation" model to account for the oral "growth" of the discursive "clusters" he describes as finally constituting Q's formative stratum, Kloppenborg's general description of 10:3–16 from every other point of view consistently remarks the basic internal coherency of this block of material.[22]

Kloppenborg's actual observations regarding the compositional character of 10:3, 16 stand in striking contrast to what he has to say about the sayings in 10:2, 7b. In essential agreement with Arland D. Jacobson, Kloppenborg recognizes that these utterances (10:2, 7b) do not cohere especially well in more than one way with the other statements in 10:3–11, 16.[23]

Kloppenborg disagrees with Jacobson and a number of other scholars only regarding the meaning of the harvest imagery in 10:2, specifically, whether or not some sort of relationship is implied thereby to a presumed "Gentile mission."[24] Beyond the limited scope of this deeply dubious discussion, Kloppenborg does not deny that Jacobson's more telling observations are essentially correct.[25]

In fact, the only reason why Kloppenborg does not finally ascribe 10:2, 7b to Q's redaction seems to be the lack or uncertainty or insufficient stridency in these sayings of the motif of the announcement of judgment and the polemic against this generation that Kloppenborg is otherwise at pains to isolate as a salient feature of the document's secondary elaboration.[26] Surely, however, the evident shift in *Sitz im Leben* that the same sayings (10:2, 7b) betray vis-à-vis the rest of 10:3–11, 16 is equally germane to the question, especially if Q's redactional polemic against "this generation" signals not only the announcement of judgment, but also and indeed precisely thereby the establishment of clearer social boundaries and the concomitant consolidation of a more distinctive group-identity by the later tradents of Q.[27] To this subsequent stage of development would belong most naturally the division of labor apparent in the designation of "workers" by 10:2, 7b versus those who send them forth (or take them in) as "hired hands" in the ripening fields of the Lord.[28]

Q 11:14–52

Kloppenborg assigns everything in 11:14–52 to the secondary redaction of Q. The compositional integration of all the materials making up this "lengthy block" of Q into the synoptic sayings source is said to be the work of its penultimate literary stratum. Everything is read under the aegis of "controversies," and controversy appears to be understood as essentially equivalent to "the theme of the opposition between Jesus and 'this generation,'" which is said to recur throughout the section (11:14–52). But while such an equation may be true for the two specific sets of sayings in 11:29–32 and 11:49–51, interpretation of the many other statements in this section as a whole (11:14–52) is seriously skewed by the same perspective.[29]

The "theological tendency of the Q composition" (11:14–52) is otherwise said by Kloppenborg to be discernible in "the principles of association" of its "many originally independent traditions." Comparison of the sayings in question with their parallels in Mark is also thought to be instructive. Again, however, these are at best debatable procedures.[30] Moreover, it seems to me that the most important, if least explicit, reason why Kloppenborg finally assigns everything in 11:14–52 to Q's secondary redaction is Kloppenborg's insufficiently critical acceptance of the prevailing form-critical characterization of many of these sayings as especially "polemical." For the theme itself of an overt opposition between Jesus and "this generation" actually occurs, as already noted, in only a couple of clearly circumscribed subsections of 11:14–52, namely, 11:29–32 and 11:49–51. In both these passages, furthermore, one finds many of the other features typical of Q's redaction.[31] But such is not the case for the rest of the sayings in 11:14–52.

In 11:39–48, 52, the six "woes" are specifically directed against the Pharisees. If my reading of these sayings' rhetorical "tenor" is correct, unlike the threat of judgment in 11:49–51, which charges "this genera-tion" with all the blood poured out from Abel to a certain Zaccharias and promises exacting punishment for these crimes in return, the "origi-nal set of woes" in 11:39–48, 52, as Kloppenborg himself describes them at one point, is content merely to tweak the nose of the Pharisees' too stiff approach to righteousness.[32]

Nothing in 11:24–26, 33, 34–36 polemicizes against "this genera-tion." Instead, these sayings essentially comment on different aspects of ancient medical "theory" and practice. The debate in 11:14–20 regard-ing exactly how it is that a certain mute was healed, acrimonious or acerbic as the exchange may be, did not become an argument about the destiny of separate social groupings until the "beatitude" in 11:23 was subsequently appended to it, changing the otherwise common scene of mistrust and assurance after the performance of any "magical" act into the polarized assessment: "whoever is not with me is against me."

Returning to 11:39–52, Kloppenborg himself records again most of the observations that account for why 11:49–51 "is almost unanimously regarded as a secondary insertion" in its present context:

> Despite the unitary appearance of 11:47–51, there is reason to believe that the woe-oracle form [of 11:47–51] is a secondary con-struction of Q redaction, and that 11:49–51 is an interpolation into a series of woes — an interpolation which separated 11:52 from the rest of the woes. Whereas 11:47–48 (like the rest of the woes) is directed against the Pharisees or scribes, 11:49–51 broadens this criticism to "this generation," i.e., to those who reject Wisdom's messengers (cf. 7:31–35; 11:29–32). Moreover, in the midst of woes attributed to Jesus it is unexpected to find a saying of Sophia speaking, apparently from her standpoint at the beginning of history (ἀποστελῶ). Finally, the character of the Sophia saying differs from that of the woes: whereas the woes of-fer reproaches, the Sophia oracle is a threat of retribution on this generation. Thus it appears that a saying of Sophia has been joined to a series of woes through catchwords and thematic associations to form a judgment oracle against "this generation."[33]

> The woes in Q 11:39–52 have a complex tradition-history. From a tradition-historical standpoint the oldest are 11:42, 39–41. Q 11:43, 46 are somewhat younger, while 11:44, 47–48 and 52 re-

flect increasingly acrimonious relations between the synagogue and the community. The latest insertion was 11:49–51, which broke up the original connection of 11:47–48 with 11:52, and which broadened the polemic from groups within Judaism to "this generation" itself. From the perspective of the latest editing of the Q woes, Israel is guilty of rejecting God's envoys, and her leaders actively attempt to thwart the unfolding of the kingdom. The editing of the Q woes has transformed them from intramural disputes into full-blown oracles and threats of judgment.[34]

What Kloppenborg fails to indicate in *The Formation of Q* is why he thinks that "the latest editing of the Q woes," i.e., the insertion of 11:49–51 into "the original set of woes" in 11:39–48, 52 must be imagined to have coincided with the introduction of this earlier composition (11:39–48, 52) into the document itself. Two reasons suggest themselves. The first is Kloppenborg's apparent assumption, already noted above, that every sign of social conflict and dispute in Q is somehow more likely to be part of the redactional stage's aggressive polemic against "this generation" than a further feature of the formative stratum's inversionary instruction. This is, however, hardly a self-evident conclusion, especially given the fact that the material content of Q's initial literary layer as Kloppenborg himself describes it differs in a number of significant ways from conventional ancient wisdom.[35]

The second reason stems again from Kloppenborg's assumption of an aggregation model for the oral "growth" of the discursive "clusters" making up Q's formative stratum, presupposed in phrases like the woes' "complex tradition-history." Granted that not every woe in 11:39–48, 52 says exactly the same thing in exactly the same way — why should they? must they? — and that some of these sayings, moreover, speak more strongly or directly than others, such variance in speech is in itself not bad rhetoric. The degree to which different attitudes towards the Pharisees might be discerned in the various pronouncements made in 11:39–48, 52 is insufficient, in my opinion, to warrant recourse to the kind of evolutionary myth of origins implicit in the aggregationist view of the development of early Christian tradition here maintained by Kloppenborg.[36]

According to the latter point of view, in the case of the "original set of woes" in Q (11:39–48, 52), there was first a "kernel" of sayings in 11:39–41, 42 that would correspond to "an early Jewish Christian and Torah-observing circle." An initial expansion (11:43, 46) was then made of this "core" group of materials, which supposedly disputed Pharisaic legal interpretation and leadership but otherwise provides no evidence of a fundamental break with early Judaism. Finally, a third stage of elaboration is thought to be attested by the woes in 11:44, 47–48, 52, which ostensibly stem "from an 'anti-synagogue "ecclesiastical" redaction' " in "bitter confrontation" with the Pharisees.[37]

Notice, however, how closely such a sketch of the antecedent "oral" development of the "original set of woes" in Q (11:39–48, 52) essentially follows the current order of their literary presentation in the document (except for 11:44, which is supposed to have originally followed 11:43, 46). Why not assume, however, that the rising rhetorical pitch of the successive woes in 11:39–48, 52, creating in this fashion a certain crescendo effect, results from the considered arrangement of these diverse materials by the "author" of Q's formative stratum? Here as elsewhere at this level of the document, a certain artfulness may be observed in the construction of a series of ever more penetrating and bolder critiques.[38]

Likewise, the sayings in 11:14–20, 24–26, 33, 34–36 constitute, at the level of Q's formative stratum, a similar catena of astute and witty criticism, centered on the theme of health and healing. With Q's redaction, the divisive proverb in 11:23 was later inserted between the two groups of sayings in 11:14–20 and 11:24–26, much as 11:49–51 was subsequently interjected between the sayings in 11:39–48 and 11:52, and 10:12, 13–15 was placed between 10:3–11 and 10:16. In every instance, an earlier line of sharp assessment and cultural distanciation has been converted into a program of blunt condemnation. Likewise, the sayings-complex in 11:29–32 takes the otherwise not uncommon desire for a "sign" not as the standard mark of a lamentable gullibility or weak reasoning, but as evidence of a perverse unwillingness to recognize what, in the mind of the composer, should have been as clear as day.

Regarding 11:23, Kloppenborg does not (cannot) indicate any integral relationship between this saying and the preceding Beelzebul controversy in 11:14–20, stating only that "Bultmann is undoubtedly correct in considering this [11:23] an originally independent saying."[39] Kloppenborg does suggest that 11:23 "continues the motif of the parable of the warring soldiers" in Luke 11:21–22 par.[40] For this suggestion to be relevant at all, however, one must first accept that Luke 11:21–22 par. was once in Q. Should one conclude that such is not the case, then 11:23 simply intervenes awkwardly between the sayings in 11:14–20 and 11:24–26, which otherwise are plainly and closely related to one another.[41]

Kloppenborg's argument for the redactional character of 11:14–20 and 11:24–26 depends wholly on his a priori view of them as polemical statements of judgment. Otherwise, the usual signs of "the theme of the opposition between Jesus and 'this generation' " do not appear in these passages. While comparison of 11:14–20 with the parallel text in Mark 3:22–26 may highlight what is peculiar here to Q, it hardly makes clear in and of itself the precise quality of the rhetoric of this text.

Kloppenborg's reading of 11:14–20 and 11:24–26 as somehow suffused with polarized social antagonism is neither self-evident nor inevitable. Regarding 11:14–20, my different appraisal of the meaning of this passage is presented in the body of the book.[42] Regarding 11:24–26, the precise significance of this unusual piece of "demonological" instruction remains fully to be determined.[43] Kloppenborg derives his understanding of the saying from its association with 11:23. Kloppenborg's explanation, however, of the import of this relation is difficult to follow and fails to convince.

The "parable," as Kloppenborg calls the saying, in 11:24–26 is said to "threat[en] those who, having been delivered of a demon, invite it back by failing to respond positively to divine power." The saying (11:24–26) is somehow supposed to "serv[e] as an illustration" of the principle that 11:23 has deduced from the Beelzebul controversy, namely, that "it is impossible to be free of demonic occupation if one has not positively responded to the kingdom. Neutrality is not an option in the face of a confrontation with divine power."[44] Such a reading, however, fails to take seriously the fact that in 11:24–26 the act itself of exorcism is finally put under scrutiny and comically burlesqued.

As Kloppenborg himself recognizes: "If taken as a teaching about the inevitable consequences of exorcism, the story [11:24–26] makes nonsense of the preceding materials [in 11:14–20] by implying that no exorcism can ultimately be effective."[45] Though Kloppenborg assumes that in the context of Q "this is not its function," in fact such lampooning fits quite well with both the preceding deconstruction or unraveling of the charge of practicing black magic in 11:14–20 and the subsequent depreciation of the pretenses of piety in the "woes" of Q's formative stratum (11:39–48, 52). Both 11:14–20 and 11:24–26 critique the "medical establishment" of their day by suggesting, first, that the skill and knowledge to "heal" was not a privilege reserved only for "your sons," and, second, that the "science" itself of exorcism could not finally deliver what it promised. A different kind of wisdom was required.

Kloppenborg's interpretation of 11:33, 34–36 too quickly moralizes the meaning of these otherwise straightforward pronouncements:

> The "sound eye" saying [in 11:34–36] which follows [11:33] functions as a commentary word, directing attention away from the objective fact of the "light" to the preconditions for subjective appropriation of that light, and to the fearful prospects that await those who do not respond adequately. When the moral disposition of the audience prevents it from apprehending divine activity when it is so openly manifest in Jesus' preaching, his exorcisms and his person, then that audience is benighted indeed![46]

The gnomic statement in 11:33 implies that this preaching/ sign [11:29–32] is plain for everyone to see. Then follows the metaphorical saying about the eye, which, like 11:24–26 [?], amounts to a threat pronounced upon all those who, because of their impaired moral vision, do not respond to the preaching of the kingdom.[47]

Such a reading of 11:33, 34–36 fails to appreciate the "realism" of ancient belief in the power of the eye, including and especially the evil eye.[48] Kloppenborg's effort to make the sayings in 11:33, 34–36 simply serve as moralizing extensions of what has already been said in 11:29–32, as though they merely underscored Jesus' preceding defense of his preaching as an adequate sign of his personal status, does not take seriously enough the degree to which the sayings in 11:33, 34–36 reflect both actual social practice (11:33) as well as widespread cultural assumptions about the nature of vision and the concomitant interplay of the "forces" of "light" and "darkness" in Mediterranean antiquity.[49] Whatever the final interpretation of 11:33, 34–36 may be, these sayings belong to the same world of social concern as those in 11:14–20 and 11:24–26, similarly mixing popular conviction and experience with astute observation and critical reflection. They can therefore also be seen without difficulty as having once been part of Q's formative literary stratum.[50]

Q 13:18–21

The two well-known parables about the kingdom of God being like a mustard seed and leaven in 13:18–19, 20–21 are scarcely discussed by Kloppenborg in *The Formation of Q*, due mainly to the lack of a secure literary context in which to place them. Kloppenborg refers to the sayings only three times in his book:

> Contrary to Schenk, 13:18–19 and 13:20–21 (two parables of growth) do not fit well with 12:39–59, but neither do they cohere with the following materials. They are best left on their own.[51]

It is for this reason that we do not treat the two growth parables (13:18–19, 20–21) in this context [namely, Q 13:24–30, 34–35; 14:16–24, 26–27; 17:33; 14:34–35] in spite of their proximity to 13:24–30. They concern the vigorous and ineluctable growth of the kingdom from something small and hidden to something of amazingly large proportions, rather than entry into the kingdom as such. Materially, they seem to relate to sayings such as 12:2, which likewise implies that the kingdom will be manifest by some hidden yet powerful internal dynamics.[52]

[F]or Q, the kingdom is currently in the process of self-manifestation (10:23–24; 11:20; 12:2; 13:18–21), and the mission of the Q preachers is part of the eschatological harvest (10:2).[53]

Because no larger literary context is apparent in which to place the sayings in 13:18–19, 20–21, Kloppenborg must exclude them from his argument in *The Formation of Q*. When, however, he says that "materially, they [13:18–19, 20–21] seem to relate to sayings such as 12:2," which Kloppenborg otherwise assigns to Q's formative stratum, we might therefore conclude on material grounds that the two parables are to be similarly located.[54]

On the basis of stratigraphical coherence, in terms of content the sayings in 13:18–19, 20–21 are more like the other kingdom-of-God sayings in Q's formative stratum (6:20b; 10:9; 11:2; 12:31) than they are like those of the redactional layer (7:28b; 13:29; 16:16). The latter group of utterances all speak of the kingdom of God as a locus of participation (or exclusion): at stake in these sayings is primarily the question of superior social status. Thus, for example, in 7:28b the least member of the group of persons identified with the kingdom of God is said to be greater than the previous greatest man that ever was, namely, John. In 16:16, the period following John is characterized as one marked by the struggle to enter into or seize possession of the new formation. In 13:29, the kingdom of God is pictured as a banquet, at which major figures from Israel's epic past (Abraham, Isaac, Jacob) and others from east and west will dine together, minus those against whom the saying (13:28–29) is directed. In all three instances, the kingdom of God, for Q's redaction, is the symbolic instrument of an us/them, in/out, now/then, better/worse polemical logic. None of this is evident in 13:18–19, 20–21.

The Text of Q:
Some Critical Problems

A s INDICATED in the introduction to this book, whenever possible I have used as the basis of my own translation into English the critical Greek text of Q now being established by the International Q Project (IQP). In what follows, I presuppose the data base, evaluation(s), and designated response(s) prepared by various members of the IQP for the sayings under discussion, limiting my remarks here to what might best be understood as an alternate or additional evaluation of this information. The arguments are meant to be intelligible on their own. Their relative strength, however, can obviously only finally be determined by comparison with the IQP data base.[1]

Q 6:27–35

Of primary importance for every reconstruction of Q 6:27–35 is deciding what the original order was of the different sayings in the passage as a whole. The English translation in chapter two has already revealed that I take the sequence of statements in Luke 6:27–35 to represent the original order of sayings in Q (6:27–35). Luke has amplified this text with certain additional materials of his own, especially in vv. 27–28 and vv. 34–35. But otherwise Luke maintains the basic structure of the original composition in Q. It is Matthew who has significantly dismantled the reasoning of the Q passage in accordance with the evangelist's own redactional interests: specifically, his construction of the series of antitheses in the Sermon on the Mount.

Not every scholar draws this conclusion. Despite widespread recognition that the presentation of materials in Matt 5:21–48 is otherwise unparalleled in the synoptic tradition and that, furthermore, the governing concerns of this series of texts and their style of argument coincide with characteristic features of the rest of Matthew's gospel, i.e., that Matthean redaction is likely responsible, at least to a significant degree, for the shape of the traditional material presented here, it has nonetheless been Matthew's rendition of Q 6:27–35=Matt 5:(38–) 39b–42, (43–) 44–48 that has seemed to not a few investigators to be most plausibly that of the synoptic sayings source as well.

The fact that many scholars still assume that Matthew preserves the earliest form of the sayings-complex on love of enemies ought at least to cause some pause for thought, given how utterly influential the Gospel of Matthew has been in otherwise determining the traditional scholarly imagination of Christian origins. To what extent, in other words, have New Testament scholars regarding the problem of the original order of Q 6:27–35 or the most "logical" form in which to reconstruct the primary sequence of these sayings not essentially continued to read the material in question from Matthew's point of view?

Perhaps the best advocate for Matthew=Q is Ronald A. Piper, who, however, wants to have his cake and eat it, too, in my opinion, when he states: "It is possible [likely]" that at an earlier stage of tradition these exhortations [(6:29–30) were separate from and possibly] preceded the love-of-enemies exhortations <as in Matthew> (although probably not in the antithetical form of Matthew)."[2] Thus, the presentation of Q materials in Matt 5:(38–) 39b–42, (43–) 44–48 is supposed to be both "probably not" that of Q and simultaneously "possibl<y> [likely]" the way it was originally in the same document.

R. Piper recognizes that: "It is of course possible to argue persuasively that Matthew is responsible for achieving the more 'logical' arrangement that his gospel reflects. Matthew's formulation of *antitheses,* however, need not suggest that he was also responsible for the division of the material."[3] Why else, however, apart from Matthew's antithetical interests in the first part of the Sermon on the Mount, would the sayings in Luke 6:29–30 ever have been separated from what is said both before and after them in Luke 6:27–28 and 6:31ff?

R. Piper's main reason for believing that the sayings in Luke 6:27–28, 29–30, 31ff did not always or originally appear together in Q is as follows:

There is a *striking [formal] discrepancy* in the Lukan formulation of these sayings, which provides a starting-point for any analysis. It consists of the switch from the second person plural (6:27–28) to the second person singular (6:29–30) and back to the plural again (6:31ff) in the opening series of exhortations. *Because* this apparent intrusion of the singular exhortations closely matches the material located in a separate block of teaching on non-retaliation by Matthew (Mt 5:39–42/Lk 6:29–30), it strongly suggests that the exhortations in Lk 6:29–30 have in fact been inserted into the series of exhortations about love of the enemies.[4]

Neither of these statements, however, is especially true — certainly not regarding the features that I am responsible for italicizing in the above citation. The shift, so often remarked and thought to be somehow significant, between use of the second-person plural in Luke 6:27–28, 31ff and use of the second-person singular in Luke 6:29–30 is, to put it bluntly, not really noteworthy at all. At least as Shawn Carruth has pointed out on the basis of Longinus, *On the Sublime* (26.3), such variation falls perfectly within the canons of ancient persuasive speech.[5] An explanatory mountain has thus been made out of a molehill of an observation.

R. Piper struggles to diminish the relevance of Carruth's apt reference to ancient rhetorical theory. But Piper's reasoning in this regard is even more problematical than his own original suggestion. Piper writes:

> S[hawn] C[arruth] offers another (purely stylistic) motive for the insertion of the singular sayings amidst the plural ones. As variant 6:29.1 [i.e., the original placement of 6:29–30], she suggests that it may be good rhetorical style (to catch the listener's attention). Assuming that this can be substantiated also in written works, it would provide as useful an explanation for *Luke's* procedure as for Q's. It would at least be arguable that Luke might be more familiar with and open to such rhetoric than Q. In view of the ambiguity which this stylistic argument still presents, the understanding of Luke's [imputed] motive in view of the content and motivation of the exhortations seems more compelling.[6]

Many questions are here begged. How, for example, is Carruth's so-called "purely stylistic" motive essentially different from R. Piper's "striking [formal] discrepancy"? Why would what Longinus *writes* not be applicable "also in written works," given that so much ancient writing otherwise betrays the influence of oral rhetoric? While Longinus's remark might theoretically "provide as useful an explanation for Luke's procedure as for Q," at issue is precisely whether or not the observation of a shift from plural to singular in Luke 6:27–28, 29–30, 31ff suggests the unlikelihood of a continuous composition here in Q. It is precisely this assumption, namely, that the difference in number must mean different compositional units, that Carruth's reference to Longinus has shown to be invalid. Why think that Q was somehow less "familiar with and open to such rhetoric" than Luke?

Returning to the previous citation, the fact that the sayings formulated in the second-person singular in Luke 6:29–30 essentially correspond to what appears as a separate block of teaching on non-retaliation in Matt 5:39b–42 hardly leads in the straightforward manner suggested by R. Piper's use of the conjunction "because" to the conclusion that, therefore, Luke has inserted this material into his larger series of exhortations about love of enemies. Logically, the same fact, i.e., difference in verbal number could explain equally well why Matthew has isolated and lifted out this particular set of sayings from the sequence in Luke 6:27–35 to form the antecedent and, as it were, anticipatory antithesis in Matt 5:38–42 to the concluding "contradiction" of the Sermon on the Mount (Matt 5:43–48), which emphasizes love of enemies as the more perfect imitation of God and constitutes the crowning example of the higher righteousness earlier enjoined to exceed that of the scribes and the Pharisees (Matt 5:20). Again, therefore, the significance of the shift between use of the second-person plural in Luke 6:27–28, 31ff and use of the second-person singular in Luke 6:29–30 is, minimally, inconclusive, if not, in fact, to be taken as further evidence of a certain rhetorical sophistication in Q.

According to R. Piper: "Once it is recognized that the exhortations on non-retaliation [6:29–30] have intruded into the teaching on love of enemies, it becomes clear why the love-of-enemies command had to be repeated later in the Lukan sequence [6:35a] in order to restore a connection with the motivation clauses found in Mt 5:45 (cf. Lk 6:35b)."[7] More precisely, the supposedly redactional insertion not only of Luke 6:29–30, but also of Luke 6:31–33 immediately after the initial commands to love and pray for your enemies (6:27–28) is said by Piper to have severed the original link between these opening imperatives and the *imitatio Dei* advocated in Matt 5:45/Luke 6:35c.

In Luke 6:35ab, however, not only the opening command to "love your enemies" (6:27) is recalled, but also a number of other redactional alterations and additions made by Luke in the immediately preceding verses (6:33–34). In view, therefore, in Luke 6:35ab is not so much a restatement of the original (Matthean) context of the final part of the saying (6:35c) but a recapitulation of the entire preceding discourse (6:27–34) — required, perhaps, because of Luke's unparalleled elaboration of it in 6:34. In any case, if the primary purpose of the additional material in Luke 6:35ab were to recall an original connection between Q 6:27–28 and 6:35c as attested by Matt 5:44–45, the ostensibly "restored" connection in 6:35aa was immediately interrupted by the same evangelist with a number of other sayings otherwise unparalleled in Matthew, thus vitiating the attributed rationale for the initial repetition.

According to R. Piper, on the assumption that Luke is responsible for inserting 6:29–30 after "the love command" in 6:27–28, in order to get back on track again: "this [was] achieved by resuming the 'love' theme of 6:27–28 in 6:32 and 35a after the diversion of teaching about not retaliating against violence in 6:29–30."[8] The reference to 6:32 is, however, wholly gratuitous, for it is actually — only — the "resumptive summary" in 6:35aa that is key to Piper's contention of an original link between Q 6:27–28 and 6:35c=Matt 5:44–45.

Did 6:32–33 precede (as in Luke) or follow (as in Matthew) the saying in 6:35c? An adequate answer to this question obviously depends to some degree on the decision made regarding the original position of 6:35c. Did 6:35c, therefore, originally appear at the end of the Q composition before 6:36; or did it follow 6:27–28 at the beginning of the sayings-complex as in Matt 5:44–45?

Versus an original location of 6:35c directly before 6:36, R. Piper discerns what he assumes to be an unacceptable tension between what is said of God in 6:35c and in 6:36. In both verses, God is similarly referred to as the model for the behavior that is advocated. In 6:35c, just as God does not distinguish between the good and the evil in bestowing the benefits of sun, so should the addressed "sons of God" likewise relate to others. In 6:36, just as God is merciful, so also should "you" be merciful.

R. Piper assumes that the contrast between God's "impartiality" or the readers' experience of the world in 6:35c and the emphasis in 6:36 on God's specific nature was highlighted by Luke's supposed displacement of 6:35c directly before 6:36, indeed, to such a degree that, according to Piper, "Luke finds it necessary to ease the transition between the two" by significantly altering the wording of 6:35: "This change in wording is necessitated by [Luke's] relocation of 6:35 next to 6:36."[9]

R. Piper, however, fails here to integrate a number of significant considerations into his explanatory scenario. First, Luke is not responsible for creating the contrasting views of God as a model for human behavior in Q 6:35c, 36. The same contrast exists in what is said of the supreme being in Matt 5:45 and 5:48, the only difference being that, in this case, two other verses (6:32–33=Matt 5:46–47) intervene between them. Are we therefore to assume that the "differences between the two sayings" (namely, Matt 5:45 and 48) were somehow only evident or troublesome when the two sayings were placed cheek to jowl in Luke 6:35c, 36?

If so, then Matthew can just as easily be imagined to have sought to separate the two theologically discordant utterances in Q (6:35c, 36) by creating between them a rhetorically "neutral space" — a type of "delay mechanism" or "pregnant pause" — through the insertion of the two divergent questions in Q 6:32–33, whence, then, Matthew could proceed to conclude in Matt 5:48 with the redactionally enhanced command to be "perfect as your father in heaven is perfect."

R. Piper, moreover, appears to assume — beguiled again, it seems, by

Matthew's text — that Q 6:36 is the original conclusion to the sayings-complex in Q 6:27–35. In fact, however, as is seen most clearly in Luke's version of Q's "inaugural" speech (6:20b–49), 6:36 is best understood as the introductory statement to the group of utterances concerning judgment in, at least, Q 6:36–38 and, more likely, 6:36–42.[10] It is Matthew — and only Matthew — who takes Q 6:36 not only as the final statement of Matt 5:44–48, but also as the concluding "punch-line" to the first section of his Sermon on the Mount.

If the sequence of sayings in Luke 6:(32–33) 35c, 36 represents the original order of Q, what, then, is the significance of the differing use of God in the final two sayings (6:35c, 36) as a model for human behavior, given that the contrast is not adequately explained — indeed, hardly at all — by R. Piper's interpretation of this difference as a sign of secondary redactional juxtaposition? Insofar as 6:36 was *not* in Q (nor in Luke, for that matter) the conclusion to 6:27–35, discussion of the meaning of this tension or "uneven" transition between 6:35c and 6:36 is relevant primarily regarding the *composition-history* of the opening "sermon" in Q. For the two sayings (6:35c, 36) together form — perhaps on the basis of a certain "catch-word" connection — the central turning-point in Q's inaugural discourse, seeing in the *imitatio Dei* the essential explanation of the way of life advocated in Q.

According to R. Piper, the status of those addressed in Q 6:27–35 as "sons of God" had to be established first before the rhetorical questions in 6:32–33 could meaningfully be asked, insofar as the logic of these latter sayings "requires them [the addressees] to go beyond what tax collectors and Gentiles/sinners do."[11] Is this, however, true? Only, perhaps, if we assume, as Piper does, that the rhetorical questions in 6:32–33 somehow resume the "love theme" of 6:27–28, elaborating this theme in some continuous fashion.

At issue, however, in 6:32–33 is not especially the question of love, certainly not love for one's enemies, nor how to respond to defamation, but, rather, the inadequacy of taking the general rules of reciprocity in the ancient Mediterranean world as a sufficient guide to one's own proper action. The sayings in 6:32–33 call into question the kind of social practice — "you scratch my back, I'll scratch yours"; "you hit me, I'll hit you" — encouraged in antiquity as the "normal" way that friends and strangers, kin and rivals should relate to one another, the type of "tit for tat" mentality — *do ut des* — implicitly challenged by the sayings in 6:27–28 and directly opposed in 6:29–30.

The sayings in 6:32–33 not only support what is said in 6:27–28 by contrast, but also through their rhetorical questions undergird the instructions given in 6:29–30. The typical "bottom-line" behavior shared in antiquity by even the socially disreputable tax-collectors and Gentiles could hardly be considered, therefore, a model of appropriate comportment. It is, then, on this basis, namely, the utter "baseness" of the conventional ethical view that in 6:35c the concluding rationalization/exhortation can be made to "be sons of God."

R. Piper is wholly at a loss what to do with the "golden rule" in 6:31. He agrees with most commentators in thinking that the saying's current location in Matthew (7:12) does not attest its original placement in Q, being due rather to the evangelist's redaction of the Sermon on the Mount. To refer, however, to 6:31 as finally "a floating unit of tradition" or as an "independent floating saying" simply confuses the categories of discussion, insofar as the question at hand is precisely (and only) whether Matthew or Luke or neither attests the original location of this saying in Q (6:31), which otherwise both evangelists agree was found in the document.

One might consider Luke's placement of the saying in 6:31 as equivalent to Q on the basis of *lectio difficilior,* insofar as the problems commentators have always had in understanding what the saying is doing here make it unlikely that Luke would have intentionally created such a problem. At the same time, as I have already tried to suggest, the same placement of Q 6:31 may originally have served to destabilize one step further the customary logic regarding how to manage social conflict in antiquity. It fits quite well, in other words, "as is" into the logic of the saying (6:27–35) as a whole.[12]

Q 6:35

Reconstruction of especially the first part of this saying depends heavily upon decisions made regarding the original order of Q 6:27–35. I assume, as just argued, that Luke=Q. Which conjunction, if any, stood at the start of 6:35 is still unclear. Most scholars nonetheless agree that the conjunction *hopōs* in Matthew (5:45) is redactional. Both Matthew (5:45) and Luke (6:35c) attest that, in the second position, one form or another of the verb "to be" then occurred (Matthew: *genēsthe;* Luke: *esesthe*). In either case, the verb was used imperatively (whether properly so, as in Matthew, or in the future indicative, as in Luke: i.e., "you shall be"). In Matthew's case, the evangelist obscured the subjunctive mood's original "jussive" quality by making it now part of the result clause dependent on *hopōs*.

Whose "son" you should be is basically clear, namely, "God's." The actual expressions, however, in Matthew ("your father in heaven") and in Luke ("the most high") are both plainly redactional. It is possible that just the phrase "of your father" (*tou patros hymōn*) occurred here in Q (see, further, Q 12:30). But it is difficult to be very confident about this decision.

I question whether the final phrase in Matt 5:45, *kai brechei epi dikaious kai adikous,* occurred in Q. Luke lacks any such second "parallel" statement, a fact that cannot simply be explained away as the inevitable consequence of Luke's redactional alterations in the first part of the clause (i.e., *autos chrēstos estin*). Luke is otherwise not adverse to the use of additional parallel statements, certainly not in the present context (see 6:27–28; also 6:34). Insofar as Matthew, on the other hand, is evidently eager, especially in the context of the Sermon on the Mount, to highlight the question of Christian "justice" (*dikaiosynē*), his addition of the final phrase in precisely these terms, complementing as it does the preceding image of the sun with reference to the "rain" and anticipating the call to perfection in Matt 5:48, is quite intelligible and thoroughly in keeping with Matthew's redactional agenda.

Q 10:7–8

Many scholars assume that, in addition to the proverb about the worker and his wage in 10:7b, some version of the other instructions in Luke 10:7–8, whether before and/or after this saying (10:7b), must also have occurred in Q. The main reasons for thinking so appear to be as follows:

(i) it is assumed that something else (besides the proverb in 10:7b) is finally needed here (10:7a) for the earlier composition in Q to be "intelligible";

(ii) the additional instructions in Luke 10:7(a)–8(b) correspond to the scholarly imagination of the likely concerns and challenges of Jesus' first followers in Galilee;[13]

(iii) the structural symmetry of the sayings in Luke 10:5–6, 8(a)–11 would be the mark of an original parallelism.[14]

Discussing these "reasons" in reverse order, beginning with the final one (iii) listed above, explicit structural symmetry is hardly the self-evident sign of an "original" formulation. Just as easily, it may reflect self-conscious enhancement by a later redactor. Like literary genre, the perception, elucidation, and even imposition of explicit structure in a given text is as much, if not more, a function of the reader (or editor) of a work (in this case, Luke) as it is a means of production (Q).

No doubt exists that the "mission" instructions in Q (10:2–16) discussed both the case of a "house" (10:5) and of a "city" (10:10). In the case of the "house," both Matthew (10:13) and Luke (10:6) agree in attesting for Q the explicit consideration of both a "positive" and a "negative" reception. Only, however, in Luke (10:8, 10) is the same sort of double possibility repeated at the level of a "city." In Matthew

(10:14) as in Mark (6:11), the discussion is limited in this regard to what to do whenever "someone" (or "any place") does not receive you. Thus, either Luke has elaborated the text of Q at this point beyond what either of his sources had to say about the city, or Matthew has followed Mark and ignored (i.e., eliminated) this feature once found in Q.

Hoffmann has tried to show that Luke has a decided interest in locating early Christian activity in the public context of the ancient city.[15] Certainly, one immediate effect of the reference to a hospitable *polis* in Luke 10:8 is to make what is said next in Luke/Q 10:9 about "treating the weak" and announcing that "the kingdom of God has arrived" a much less clandestine or conditional work than otherwise might be suggested by the direct association implied in Q between these particular activities and the domestic scene depicted in 10:5–6 of exchange with a "son of peace."

Regarding the second reason (ii) listed above, the assumption that Jesus' first "Jewish" followers in Galilee would naturally have been anxious about the "purity" of any food that they were offered is based upon at least two increasingly untenable stereotypes: first, a view of early Judaism in Palestine excessively influenced by the record of later rabbinic literature; and, second, a view of early Christianity in the same region as having been especially concerned about interpretation of the Jewish law — a view that Kloppenborg has shown to be quite erroneous for Q.[16]

Regarding the first reason (i) listed above, it may indeed be true that the proverb in Q 10:7b sits somewhat uneasily between the sayings in 10:5–6 and 10:9. It may do so, however, not because there was originally other material in addition to the proverb embedding it more firmly into the discursive flow of the "mission" instructions in Q's formative stratum, but, rather, because the proverb in 10:7b, like the sayings in 10:12, 13–15, was subsequently inserted into the formative stratum's earlier collection of utterances by Q's secondary redaction.[17]

Apart from the proverb in 10:7b, Luke 10:7–8 can be divided into the following six units:

(i) the imperative to stay in the house itself (10:7aa);

(ii) the imperative to eat and drink whatever there is (10:7ab);

   the proverb about the worker and his wage (10:7b);

(iii) the imperative not to change from house to house (10:7c);

(iv) the conditional clause about whichever city you enter (10:8aa);

(v) the possibility that they receive you (10:8ab);

(vi) the imperative to eat whatever they put before you (10:8b).

The first (i) and third (iii) of these units (10:7aa; 10:7c) essentially restate what is said in Mark 6:10 / Luke 9:4 / Matt 10:11: "Wherever you enter into a house, stay there until you leave from there." They do not constitute a "doublet" of any sort, insofar as there is otherwise absolutely no evidence — not even a "reminiscence" — in Matthew of any such instruction ever having been in Q, apart from the directive in Mark (6:10). Most likely, therefore, Luke has simply reiterated (twice) at this point in Q the same instruction which he otherwise found (once) in Mark (6:10).[18]

The conditional clause in Luke 10:8aa (iv) regarding whichever city you enter is a redactional creation by the evangelist. It anticipates the up-coming use of the same conditional construction in Q/Luke 10:10, whose precise phraseology in Greek, specifically, use of the particle *de* and the aorist tense of the verb *eiselthēte,* is the one properly paralleled in Matt 10:11.[19] The reference in Luke 10:8ab (v) to being received in a city likewise anticipates the subsequent instruction in Q/Luke 10:10 regarding what to do when "they do not receive you," paralleled in Matt 10:14. In both instances, Luke imitates the language of Q for the sake of elaboration.

Only in units·(ii) and (vi)=Luke 10:7ab; 10:8b is there any special material now associated with the "mission" instructions in Q (10:5–6, 7b, 9) that is otherwise unparalleled in either Matthew or Mark. Only here are the envoys of Jesus reminded to eat (and drink) everything put before them. Hardly an attack on Jewish ritual law, indicated hereby are rather general rules of proper "etiquette" to follow whenever someone actually provided the hoped-for hospitality.[20] As in units (i) and (iii)=Luke 10:7aa; 10:7c, the same statement is repeated twice.

Unlike Matthew, Luke is not generally supposed to have told his story of Jesus in order to provide a model for contemporary discipleship. Certainly regarding the specific content of the "mission" instructions, the evangelist in Luke 22:35–36 appears to leave no doubt that whatever might have been said by Jesus to the apostles at an earlier date in the Lord's "earthly" ministry, it no longer applied without further ado to the subsequent situation of later Christians. Does this truism hold true, however, with regard to eating and drinking?

In a word, no. In fact, what is said in Luke 10:7–8 regarding eating and drinking fits very well with everything that is said elsewhere by the author of Luke-Acts regarding Christian "deregulation" of the usual standards and social norms related to meals in the ancient Mediterranean world. Again, at issue is not the question of Jewish ritual law, but promotion of the alternate type of mealtime practice that Luke repeatedly depicts throughout his two-volume work as one of the tell-tale signs of the Christian way.[21]

There are thus numerous reasons to believe that Luke is responsible for everything (except the proverb about the worker being worthy of his wage) in Luke 10:7–8. If, nonetheless, despite the preceding considerations, one were to think that Luke has rather "preserved" here what Matthew eliminated; that Luke in 10:7–8 did not, in fact, "fill out" what he originally found at this point in the synoptic sayings source with what Luke already knew from Mark (6:10) and the other "mission" instructions in Q (10:10) to promote a recurring theme in his gospel and Acts; one would still need to explain why, then, Matthew has "left out" of his redactionally enhanced combination of Mark and Q every indication regarding how to behave properly in a household, if and when hospitality were shown. Specifically, one would need to explain why it is that here, unlike elsewhere in Matthew's gospel where the evangelist is clearly at pains to develop precisely the sort of regulations now found in Luke 10:7–8, Matthew would nonetheless have purposefully excluded from his version of the "mission" instructions these very verses. It is difficult to imagine a compelling answer to this question.[22]

Q 10:16

In my opinion, Matt 10:40 preserves the original wording of Q 10:16. The form of the parallel utterance in Luke 10:16 is therefore due to Lukan redaction.[23] Against this judgment, it is sometimes asserted that Matt 10:40 rather recalls Mark 9:37. But the first half of Mark 9:37 is instead recalled at its Markan location in Matt 18:5.

If the present wording of Matt 10:40 were indeed due to Mark 9:37, one would need to explain why the evangelist so wished to anticipate in Matt 10:40 what he subsequently states, following Mark (9:37), in Matt 18:5, that every evidence of the discursive variation found in Luke 10:16 — and ostensibly in Q — was therefore eliminated, thereby creating Matthew's strict — and ostensibly deliberate — uniformity of diction in this regard.

One would also need to explain how it is that this supposedly redactional standardization by Matthew (10:40; 18:5) of a saying otherwise known to him in two distinct forms, namely, Mark 9:37 and Q/Luke 10:16, furthermore happens to reflect so closely the remarkably similar pronouncement in John 13:20 — instead of assuming that the triangular agreement that otherwise exists between Mark 9:37, Matt 10:40=Q 10:16, and John 13:20 indicates the "traditional" wording of an "originally independent" saying, whose redundancy Matthew either did not notice or bother to change in the composition of his gospel.

Of course, a second possibility would be to conclude that Luke is responsible for the unique vocabulary of his version of Q 10:16 vis-à-vis Mark 9:37; John 13:20, perhaps to avoid the more obvious redundancy that would otherwise exist in Luke between Q 10:16=Matt 10:40 and Mark 9:37, the latter saying being recalled by Luke essentially verbatim shortly before in Luke 9:48. There are, however, additional stronger reasons for believing that Luke has changed the original wording of Q 10:16 into his current statement about "hearing" and "rejecting" in Luke 10:16.

The form of the saying in Luke 10:16 is uniquely tripartite. The first half describes two contrary scenarios: being "heard" and being "rejected." In both cases, whoever hears or rejects "you" is said to hear or reject "me." In the saying's second half, only the negative possibility of being "rejected" is discussed with reference to "the one who sent me."

Luke 10:16 is thus asymmetrical in its construction, unlike every other version of this not uncommon early Christian saying.[24] Furthermore, in equally unparalleled fashion, Luke 10:16 includes and indeed stresses the negative side of the representation in question. As such, what is said in Luke 10:16 functions essentially as a threat, whereas the other versions of the saying elsewhere serve primarily as a promise or an invitation.

On the basis of these descriptive observations, a satisfactory answer must now be given to two further questions in order for the redactional nature of Luke 10:16 to be established. First, why would Luke have cast Q 10:16 in terms of "hearing" (akouein) and "rejecting" (athetein) versus the language of "receiving" (dechesthai) as in Matt 10:40? And, second, why did Luke elaborate the first part of the saying (10:16a) in such a way as to create the present uneven parallelism between a "positive" and a "negative" experience?

A similar reference to "hearing" and "rejecting" occurs in Luke 7:29–30. Here, too, some (or all) the people "hear," while others, namely, the Pharisees and lawyers, "reject." Again, there is no obvious parallel to this saying (Luke 7:29–30) in either Matthew or Mark. The most probable conclusion would therefore seem to be that Luke is responsible for the formulation of both 7:29–30 and 10:16 in these terms.

According to Hoffmann, the contrast between "hearing" and "rejecting" discussed in Luke 10:16a recalls the similar set of alternate possibilities depicted in Luke 10:8, 10, namely, those of either acceptance or rebuff in a given city.[25] Everything described in Luke 10:8, 10f is the direct consequence of whether or not one is "received." (The same verb, dechesthai, is used in both instances.) In Luke 10:16, the same two possibilities continue to be imagined, only now specified, as in this case, positively (=10:8) a matter of being "heard" versus negatively (=10:10) a matter of "rejection."

Finally, understanding "acceptance" as primarily a matter of "hearing" reflects the instrumental role played by "hearing" elsewhere in Luke's drama of early Christian preaching, faith, and salvation.[26]

Q 11:39–41, 42

The IQP text places Q 11:42 before 11:39–41 as the original order of the woes in the synoptic sayings source, on the assumption that Luke found 11:39–41 a more fitting follow-up for his redactional introduction to these sayings: i.e., a stronger connection was hereby forged between the first woe in Q and the astonishment expressed in Luke 11:37–38 at Jesus' lack of hand-washing by the Pharisee who is his host. The issue of order is not especially important for my discussion of the woes in chapter five, insofar as I make no noteworthy claims based upon the sequence of their original presentation. Nonetheless, I agree with Bradley McLean that:

> while Luke's dining setting may very well be modeled on Mk. 7:1–2, it does not alter the fact that the setting was specified at the discretion of the redactor. Since there is no evidence that a narrative context accompanied Q 11:39b–44, Luke's hand was free to select or create any setting which, in his opinion, best suited the material. If the original order of the Q text was 11:42, 39b–41, 44, Luke could easily have created or selected a setting which better suited his material. In other words, if the Q woes began with the statement concerning tithing (v. 42), why would Luke not simply invent a setting in which a Pharisee came to Jesus with a question about tithing?[27]

On the other hand, there is no reason to assume that beginning in Matt 23:23, the evangelist (Matthew) has suddenly ceased actively to rearrange the order of his source materials. The whole final section of Matthew's enriched edition of the woes in Q (=Matt 23:27–39) is deliberately centered on the interrelated themes of tomb-building/being and the death of the prophets, redactionally purged of all "extraneous" material otherwise found at this point in Q/Luke 11:46, 52 and capped off with an additional lament taken from elsewhere in Q/Luke 13:34–35, to end Matthew's much more highly pitched harangue on a truly somber note. Precisely between this final section of the woes in Matthew (23:27–39) and the opening conglomerate of invective in Matt 23:2–22, generally acknowledged to be heavily redacted by the evangelist, the pair of sayings specifically under discussion here, namely, Matt 23:23–26=Luke 11:42, 39–41, occur in inverse order.

Can a motive be suggested why Matthew (and not Luke) would have rearranged the original sequence of the initial woes in Q (11:39–41, 42)? (It is generally agreed that Matthew is responsible for their mutual displacement from the head of the same sayings-complex to the middle of Matthew's composition.) A glance fore and aft at the sayings in Matt 23:16ff and 23:27ff suggests a couple of rather straightforward reasons why Matthew chose to switch the order of these utterances around. Of the two sayings, the one about tithing in Matt 23:23–24 continues much better the preceding discussion in Matt 23:16–22 about swearing in terms of the temple and the altar, insofar as tithing was precisely a temple-related enterprise.

Even more appropriately, however, the second saying in Matt 23:25–26 about cleaning the outside of the cup and the plate but not the inside, said to be full of extortion and rapacity, is a perfect introduction to the first of the series of concluding tomb-and-death sayings in Matt 23:27–28, which carries on in the same vein: "for you are like whitewashed tombs," outwardly beautiful, but full of all sorts of uncleanness within; "you also outwardly appear righteous, but within are full of hypocrisy and iniquity."

Unlike the unlikely process that must be imagined in order to explain why Luke would have altered the original sequence of the initial woes in Q (11:39–41, 42), whose general order Luke is otherwise supposed to have preserved intact, to assume that here as elsewhere in chapter 23 Matthew is again responsible for changing the presentation of his source materials not only does not require an elaborate explanation but accords perfectly with the evident structural design of the Matthean composition as a whole.

Q 11:40–41

Both Matthew (23:26 — "You blind Pharisee!") and Luke (11:40 — "You fools!") agree in introducing the first part of this saying with a denunciatory vocative. Beyond this, however, any agreement between them becomes intangible. Perhaps the translation into English should read: "You [expletive deleted]," as in the Watergate transcripts.

The subsequent statement in Luke 11:40, "Did not he who made the outside also make the inside?" has absolutely no correlate in Matthew. Unless a compelling reason can be given why Matthew would have excised this question, there is, then, no basis, in my opinion, on which to attribute such a saying (Luke 11:40) to Q.

The fact that a saying similar to Luke 11:40 occurs in the *Gospel of Thomas* (89) is essentially irrelevant, insofar as any posited (or demonstrable) relationship that might be held to exist between the *Gospel of Thomas* and Q — accepting that the *Gospel of Thomas* is not literarily dependent on the text of the canonical gospels — would exist only at the level of "tradition," a category otherwise broad enough to include "special material" found uniquely in Matthew and in Luke. As Robinson recognizes: "But when it is a question of whether a verse was in Q at all, *Gos. Thom.* really only supports the argument that it was in oral tradition."[28]

Robinson goes on to remark: "Of course this is not an isolated saying, but an appendix to another saying, and it is appended to the same saying in Luke and *Gos. Thom.*, which thus restores much of its force."[29] Except for the fact that one has still not explained why, then, Matthew would have excised this part of the saying. Furthermore, to accept the independence of the *Gospel of Thomas* vis-à-vis the text of the canonical gospels means presumably that, therefore, it can hardly serve in so direct and forceful a fashion to attest the text of one of the literary sources of Matthew and Luke, namely, Q.

Otherwise, the second half of the saying in Luke 11:41 and the rest of Matt 23:26(b) agree semantically in a number of significant respects: both (1) emphasize imperatively (Matthew: *katharison;* Luke: *dote*) the need (2) first (Matthew: *prōton;* Luke: *plēn*) to take care of (3) the inside (Matthew: *to entos;* Luke: *ta enonta*) in some fashion, (4) so that (Matthew: *hina;* Luke: *kai idou*) (5) also the outside or everything else (Matthew: *kai to ektos;* Luke: *panta*) will (6) be (Matthew: *genētai;* Luke: *estin*) (7) clean (Matthew: *katharon;* Luke: *kathara*).

Indeed, except for Luke's virtually unintelligible moralizing of the first part of this verse (11:41a), namely, "give the things inside as alms" or "give alms internally" (?), both Matthew (23:26b) and Luke essentially say the same thing, namely, "take care of what's inside, and everything else will be taken care of as a consequence." In the absence, however, of any clear criteria with which to choose the wording of one evangelist over the other, but recalling the imperatival mood shared by each, the priority given by both to "the inside" and the mutual reiteration of the goal as rendering "clean," I have simply translated Q 11:40–41 as: "Clean the inside . . . "

Q 11:43

I do not include Luke 11:43 par. among the woes in Q. The usual arguments for doing so are too abstract to be convincing and, even if granted, ultimately incapable of generating a reconstruction with any content.

The main arguments in favor of Luke 11:43 par. as once a saying in Q are as follows: (i) Luke 11:43 is a doublet, the similar saying in Mark 12:38=Matt 23:5b–7a being paralleled otherwise in Luke 20:46. (ii) Beyond the fact that both Matthew and Luke include a form of this saying in their respective versions of the woes in Q, there are two additional minor agreements between Luke 11:43 and Matt 23:5b–7a versus Mark 12:38, namely, (*a*) both in Luke 11:43 and Matt 23:6, the Pharisees are said to "love" whatever is mentioned next (though Luke 11:43 has the verb *agapate,* while Matt 23:6 uses *philousin;* only in Luke 20:46 does the same verb, *philountōn,* occur, unparalleled in Mark 12:38); and (*b*) both Luke 11:43 and Matt 23:6–7a agree in putting "first seat(s) in the synagogues" before "greetings in the marketplaces" versus the opposite order of the same phrases in Mark 12:38=Luke 20:46.

Even if one were to accept these observations, however, as evidence for the presence of a saying like Luke 11:43 par. in Q, there is not a single word beyond the term "love" to give the imputed utterance in Q any content not demonstrably dependent on (i.e., paralleled by) Mark 12:38. Thus, the final result would be: (i) the theoretical possibility that 11:43 was once in Q; (ii) the practical impossibility of establishing what was said in the original saying.

Notes

Introduction

1. For a general introduction to Q, see Jacobson, *First Gospel;* also Mack, *Lost Gospel;* Neirynck, "Recent Developments"; R. A. Edwards, *Theology.* For current stratigraphical description of the document, see below, p. 141, n. 31. For comprehensive bibliographies, see Neirynck and van Segbroeck, "Bibliography"; idem, "Additional List"; Kloppenborg, "Bibliography"; and the annual updates by Scholer in *SBLSP.* Scholars have generally assumed that Q was composed in or around Galilee. Cf. Lührmann, *Redaktion,* 88–89; Kloppenborg, "Social History," 85–86, 96–99. That Q was originally a "Christian" writing has sometimes been disputed. See, e.g., Mack, *Lost Gospel,* 4–5: "The people of Q were Jesus people, not Christians." Others would perhaps prefer to speak about the same persons as still part of "early Judaism." By referring to the Q people as "the earliest form of Christianity known to us," I merely wish to highlight the stark contrast between what eventually became "orthodox" Christianity and what is recalled in Q as part of this tradition's own official memory of its origins.

2. Regarding Q's "fragmentary state," cf. Polag, *Fragmenta.* Polag's reconstruction of the original text of Q is, however, often unreliable. See Neirynck, "L'édition." Other published reconstructions (or synoptic presentations) of the erstwhile document include: Harnack, *Sayings;* Schulz, *Synopse;* idem, *Spruchquelle;* Schenk, *Synopse;* D. Zeller, *Kommentar;* Havener, *Sayings* (an English translation of Polag); Kloppenborg, *Parallels.* See also below, p. 143, n. 36. For Q as "the first gospel," see above, n. 1 (Jacobson).

3. For the problems resulting from overstressing the significance of one or two texts of a particular type in Q without sufficient regard for how these texts represent (or do not represent) the document's overall generic patterns, see Kloppenborg, "Tradition and Redaction."

4. For a more "dissonant" but thoroughly compatible use of the same metaphor of montage to describe the practice of social description, see Taussig, *Nervous System,* 45.

5. See, e.g., Abrams and Hogg, *Social Identity Theory;* Camilleri, *Stratégies identitaires;* Mouzelis, *Back to Sociological Theory;* J. C. Turner et

al., *Rediscovering the Social Group; L'identité;* Davis, *Times and Identities;* Clifford, *Predicament of Culture.* Cf., further, Ricoeur, *Oneself as Another.*

6. See Rosaldo, *Culture and Truth,* 17. I have used Rosaldo's metaphor in a somewhat different manner.

7. For the category of "experience" in social/anthropological description, see Bruner and Turner, *Anthropology of Experience.* By using "experience" and "fictive" in the same sentence, I wish to make clear that by "experience" I do not imagine anything beyond the sphere of human artifice, and by "fictive" I do not mean something "unreal" or, at least, "purely" imaginary.

8. Perhaps the most fervent champion of the so-called "social-scientific" approach to the study of the New Testament is still Bruce J. Malina. See, e.g., his *New Testament World;* idem, *Gospel of John;* idem, *Christian Origins;* idem, *Calling Jesus Names* (with Jerome Neyrey). See, also, Neyrey, *Ideology of Revolt;* idem, *Paul, In Other Words;* idem, ed., *Social World of Luke-Acts.* See, further, the general bibliography by Duhaime, "Early Christianity and the Social Sciences"; specifically, Osiek, "New Handmaid"; Elliott, *Home for the Homeless,* esp. pp. 1–20; idem, ed., *Social Scientific Criticism;* J. Z. Smith, "Social Description." The "social-scientific" approach exemplifies what Ricoeur has characterized in the history of hermeneutics as the interpretative strategy of "explanation" versus "understanding." See, e.g., Ricoeur, "What Is a Text?"; idem, "Explanation and Understanding." The possibility of achieving "understanding" would now be identified by Ricoeur, as others, especially with the activity of narrative.

9. See Lévi-Strauss, *Savage Mind,* 16–22. Cf. Frye, *Great Code,* 37: "It apparently takes social scientists much longer than poets or critics to realize that every mind is a primitive mind, whatever the varieties of social conditioning."

10. See Auerbach, *Mimesis.*

11. See Vaage, "Archeological Approach."

12. See, e.g., Isenberg, "Millenarism"; Freyne, *Galilee;* idem, *Galilee, Jesus, and the Gospels;* Horsley and Hanson, *Bandits, Prophets, and Messiahs;* Horsley, "Popular Messianic Movements"; idem, "Like One of the Prophets of Old"; idem, "Popular Prophetic Movements"; idem, *Spiral of Violence;* idem, "Bandits, Messiahs, and Longshoremen"; idem, *Sociology.* Cf., further, Charlesworth, *Jesus within Judaism;* Dentzer and Orthmann, *Archéologie et Histoire;* Arav, *Hellenistic Palestine;* Kasher et al., *Greece and Rome;* R. H. Smith, "Southern Levant."

13. For more "conventional" descriptions of the tradents of Q, see, e.g., Hoffmann, *Studien,* 236–334; Theissen, *Sociology;* Schottroff and Stegemann, *Jesus,* 38–66; Horsley, *Sociology;* idem, "Renovation"; Kloppenborg, "Social History"; Kim, *Trägergruppe.* I critique these and other views of the original *Sitz im Leben* of Q in a forthcoming work.

14. Regarding the "reality" of the past, cf. Ricoeur, *Reality;* idem, *Time and Narrative,* 3:142–56.

15. When I say that the idea itself of history, as colloquially understood, has, as one of its by-products, the self-gratifying suggestion of our own moder-

nity (or postmodernity), I have in mind especially the yet influential cultural convictions of the previous century in Europe and North America as expressed, e.g., in the paradigmatic logic of Hegel's *Phenomenologie des Geistes,* the different "scientific" theories of human cultural evolution, the various "progressive" social programs of *fin-de-siècle* liberalism, and, most recently, the political-economic pretensions of late capitalist schemes of "development." Cf. White, *Metahistory;* Taussig, *Shamanism,* 366ff; idem, *Nervous System,* 44ff.

16. Cf. Frye, *Great Code,* 32–33. Said otherwise, myths would be "canonical" stories, limited regarding their narrative content and range, but read and rehearsed as though they were limitless with respect to their possible significance, whereas "literature," "folk-tales," and the like are simply but decidedly less so in both regards. For the term "canonical" as used here, see J. Z. Smith, "Sacred Persistence." For an intriguing (and ironic, because literary) representation of the social place and purpose of "myth" as precisely such a set of canonical stories among the Machiguenga people of the Peruvian Amazon, see Vargas Llosa, *El hablador.* I would not want to oppose "myth" to "literature" or "folk-tale" in any stronger ontological sense. The difference between these various forms of speech is, in my opinion, not inherent in the discourse itself, but stems rather from the specific social *use* to which a given story may be put at any given moment.

17. Any statement, however, that is not mere repetition — and even then, it can never be merely "mere" repetition, due to the fact of its selection and further recontextualization — is always "impure" invention. The use of documentation in writing history is thus rather like the artifice of form in poetry or ballast in a boat. Like documentary evidence in the hands of the historian, both are the constraints whose skillful management helps to create a tighter phantasy, a stabler floating on the surface of things. The texts assayed and weighed by the historian in the balance of informed judgment spread out before the reader as Homer's wine-colored sea: a formulaic expanse criss-crossed by the heroic warrior of the past fighting against oblivion, the wake of whose emergent book is formed by footnotes made of the same foam. Nothing is ever actually discovered, only recovered. Everything is thus made up, i.e., remade, redressed, and, in this sense, reconstructed as we go along. Cf. Crossan, *Historical Jesus,* 426: "Because there is *only* reconstruction.... If you cannot believe in something produced by reconstruction, you may have nothing left to believe in." To argue otherwise would demand the ability to demonstrate a sharp epistemological difference between what might be imagined, on the one hand, to be properly a "fiction" and, on the other hand, as written about "reality." Recall as well the notable shift that occurred only during the previous century in the classical historian's understanding of usually his proper task and manner of proceeding, namely, from the formerly favored "Thucydidean" canon of political "utility" to the previously disparaged "antiquarian" or "Herodotean" style of recollecting the past. See Momigliano, "Ancient History and the Antiquarian"; also idem, *Classical Foundations,* esp. pp. 54–79. For Ricoeur (see above, p. 138, n. 14) the importance accorded by historians to the "traces" of the past bespeaks a professional consciousness of the "debt" we owe to what has come before us, and thereby in some sense to the past's abiding presence. It remains

unclear to me, however, on what basis Ricoeur assumes that we are compelled or even eager to observe this debt.

18. Cf. Frye, *Great Code,* 46–47; Foner, "Restructuring," esp. p. 70. Regarding the notion of a "shared cultural memory," I recognize, of course, that the question of whether or not "we" might all yet be said still to share such a thing is increasingly a matter of often heated debate. See, e.g., the preface to Rosaldo, *Culture and Truth,* ix–xi; further, Bloom, *Closing.* At the same time, it would still appear to be true, if only at the level of sensationalism, that for many persons in both North America and Europe, a notable change in the way "we" now recall the life of Jesus and his first followers is perceived by friend and foe alike to imply something significant for the way in which "we" all understand ourselves today. This mutual sense of the "importance" of the issue is all that I presume to imply with the reference to "shared cultural memory." Of course, exactly how important (or unimportant) the topic "really" is, is part of the debate. The intensity of its felt significance (or lack thereof) will obviously vary from person to person, group to group, generation to generation. Many of the recent "new" visions of Jesus and his early disciples, both in film and in print, rather plainly belong to the development of a "post-Christian" culture, whose emergence nonetheless includes, perhaps because it yet requires, a continuing "review" of these central figures of the "classical" Western tradition.

19. The hidden "power" (or illusion) of narrative is not the only reason why certain historians have sought to elude this particular mode of rhetoric. See the analyses by Frei, *Eclipse;* Ricoeur, *Time and Narrative,* 1:95–120.

20. Cf. Cameron, " 'What Have You Come Out to See?' " 35: "One of the most pressing problems in the study of the New Testament is to clarify the various characterizations of its principal figures."

21. Cf. Aristotle, *de art. poet.* 1454a.15ff.

22. For the category of the "gaze," which I am correlating here with the discursive power of characterization, see Foucault, *Birth of the Clinic.*

23. See Bultmann, "New Testament and Mythology."

24. Cf. Ricoeur, "Preface to Bultmann"; idem, "Hermeneutical Function of Distanciation."

25. For the notion of "epistemic murk" and "implicit social knowledge," see Taussig, *Shamanism,* esp. pp. 127ff, 366–67, 393–95.

26. Cf. Taussig, *Mimesis and Alterity.*

27. See, e.g., Schürmann, *Untersuchungen;* idem, "Menschensohn-Titel"; idem, "Basileia-Verkündigung"; Wanke, "Kommentarworte"; idem, *"Bezugs- und Kommentarworte";* D. Zeller, "Redaktionsprozesse"; Kloppenborg, *Formation,* 98–100. The text of Q is itself, of course, the result of a certain reconstructive labor "beyond" or "behind" the "received" texts of Matthew and Luke. Note, however, that the so-called "critically established" texts of Matthew and Luke, used by most scholars as "closer to the original" than any currently extant manuscript, are equally "reconstructions" beyond or behind the texts "as we have them." Affirmation, moreover, of different stratigraphical layers in Q (whence reference to the "formative stratum" of the document) obviously belies any simple commitment on my part to "the text (of Q) as we have it." Thus, my refusal to pursue or to assume any knowledge about what-

ever it is that may have preceded the composition of Q's formative stratum is not another type of "canonical" criticism opposed to every investigation of the undersurface(s) of the biblical text. (Not every form of canonical criticism is opposed to this, either.) I merely wish to "draw the line," as it were, past which additional scholarly inquiry and debate have proven fruitless, in my opinion.

28. Cf. Güttgemanns, *Candid Questions;* Kelber, *Oral and Written Gospel,* esp. pp. 1–43.

29. I refer to source- and redaction-criticism to indicate those reading habits of traditional North American and European academic New Testament scholarship with which I am most in agreement. At the same time, I share the underdeveloped interest of early form-criticism in identifying the original (and subsequent) social setting(s) in which the discourse of the gospels was first produced, reproduced, and consumed over against a purely "literary" approach to these texts. See Theissen, "Einordnung."

30. For the question of Q's existence and related issues of a fundamental sort, see above, p. 137, n. 1; also Bellinzoni, *Two-Source Hypothesis;* Kloppenborg, *Formation,* 41–88. Cf., further, Longstaff and Thomas, *Synoptic Problem.* On the possibility and problems of reconstructing the "original" text of Q, see Vaage, "Ethos and Ethics," 531–51; also Robinson, "Critical Text." I abstain from all speculations about the likelihood of "special material" or *Sondergut* in either Matthew or Luke having also once been part of "Q" or indicative of later "editions" of the document used respectively by the two evangelists and known, especially to European scholars, as "QMatt" and "QLuke." By "Q" I mean only the "minimal" text of the synoptic sayings source mutually attested by both Matthew and Luke — beyond the level of "minor agreements" — recognizing the theoretical possibility, but finding it practically and methodologically impossible to implement, that either of the two evangelists could simply have left something out at any given point. Cf. Kloppenborg, *Parallels,* xxiii. What I call the "minimal text" of Q is divided by Kloppenborg into two distinct categories: "the minimal text of Q" and "the generally accepted extent of Q" versus a third order of reconstruction, "the probable and possible extent of Q," roughly equivalent to *Sondergut* and "triple tradition" material, which I reject.

31. See Kloppenborg, *Formation,* xv (reference is also made to an unpublished remark by Hans Dieter Betz); 1 n. 2. See, further, below, appendix one. Cf. Robinson, "LOGOI SOPHON"; Koester, "Apocryphal and Canonical Gospels"; also idem, "GNOMAI DIAPHOROI," 135ff; idem, "One Jesus and Four Primitive Gospels," 186–87. Kloppenborg identifies three distinct literary strata in Q on the basis of a number of related considerations. These latter may be summarized as essentially the twofold ability to discern: (1) the rhetorical disruption (or elaboration) of a given passage in Q through the insertion and/or addition of other material; and (2) the development of certain broad patterns of discourse throughout Q linking together the different individual sayings assigned to separate levels of the document's composition history. See Kloppenborg, "Literary and Stratigraphic Problems." In terms of literary genre, the formative stratum of Q, according to Kloppenborg (*Formation*), would correspond to that of similar ancient Near Eastern sapiential collections known as "instruction." The secondary redactional stratum, marked

especially by its polemical stance over against "this generation" and the correlative use of a "deuteronomistic" reading of Israel's history, was otherwise like a gnomologium. The third "light" revision of Q, essentially restricted to the addition of the temptation narrative (4:1–13) and a few other sayings (11:42c; 16:17), moved the document in the direction of ancient biography. Regarding this final "layer," see, further, Kloppenborg, *"Nomos* and *Ethos."* Perhaps it was for this reason that Q finally proved useful to the evangelists, Matthew and Luke, whose gospels represent more developed versions of the genre.

32. Q's initial literary layer is certainly older than the Gospel of Mark, including so-called *"Ur-"* and/or Secret Mark. The same stratum of Q is likewise less "developed" in its apparent "Christianity" than are the letters of Paul. It is, of course, always possible that certain "pre-Markan" or "pre-Pauline" traditions of comparable age to Q's formative stratum could be isolated. By calling the first "draft" of Q the earliest form of Christianity known to us, I am not arguing for this level of the document as the ultimate *Ursprung* of all other manifestations of the developing Christian movement. At the same time, however, no other "formative" level of tradition has been delineated to date of sufficient size and density like Q's initial literary layer to allow for a comparable social description of its tradents to be written.

At this point, someone is bound to ask: "Why the earliest and not the later, too?" In a climate of suspicion regarding every quest for the "original," my decision in this book to consider only that material belonging to Q's initial literary layer must appear problematical. And, indeed, it has recently been argued with some persuasiveness that the widespread tendency among biblical scholars to be especially interested in what might seem to us to be most "primitive" in the New Testament is actually part of a subliminal "Protestant" apologetic against "Catholic" accretions to (read: corruptions of) early Christianity's primordial "evangelical" substance. The farther back in time one goes or deeper down into the tradition, so the logic runs, the closer we would come to the pristine truth. See J. Z. Smith, *Drudgery Divine.* Given two or three literary layers in Q, each is presumably worthy of analysis and debate. As in any welldone archeological excavation, every level has a story to tell, and a responsible report will say something about them all.

In the case of Q, however, much more has been written about the document's final two stages, if only because the "expanded" version of Q is, in fact, Q itself: the recoverable state of the synoptic sayings source as used by Matthew and Luke in the composition of their gospels. On the other hand, very little has been written about Q's formative stratum, if only because until Kloppenborg's work, there was no consensus or even notion regarding what such an earlier text might entail.

33. See Kloppenborg, *Formation,* 51–64; further, Guenther, "Greek"; idem, "Quest for Aramaic Sources." Cf. Marshall, "Palestinian and Hellenistic Christianity"; Argyle, "Greek among the Jews of Palestine."

34. See esp. Taylor, "Order"; idem, "Original Order"; further, Vassiliadis, "Original Order"; Kloppenborg, *Formation,* 64–80.

35. Thus, e.g., Q 6:22–23 or simply 6:22–23 would indicate the beatitude from Q as found in Luke 6:22–23 and paralleled in Matt 5:11–12. This does

not necessarily imply, however, that Luke's wording or even always his order recalls that of Q. For the convention itself, see Robinson, "Critical Text," 19 n. 5; idem, "Sermon on the Mount/Plain," 451–52.

36. For a brief description and results to date of the work of the International Q Project, see Robinson, "Work Session 17 November 1989"; Asgeirsson and Robinson, "Work Session 16 November 1990"; Asgeirsson and Robinson, "Work Session 12–14 July, 22 November 1991"; Moreland and Robinson, "Work Sessions 31 July–2 August, 20 November 1992"; also Robinson, "Critical Text."

37. The most significant text-critical problems for the purposes of this book are discussed in appendix two.

38. Cf. Kloppenborg, *Parallels,* xxxi–xxxiii.

39. In general, I agree with Kloppenborg's conclusions in *Formation.* I explain my disagreements in appendix one. All other questions of interpretation beyond these technical considerations are discussed whenever pertinent in the body of the book.

40. Though I am not the only scholar to make this comparison. See, e.g., Downing, "Contemporary Analogies"; idem, "Cynics and Christians"; idem, "Ears to Hear"; idem, "Social Contexts"; idem, "Quite Like Q"; idem, *Christ and the Cynics;* idem, *Cynics and Christian Origins;* further, Wechssler, *Hellas im Evangelium,* 242–66; Schneider, *Geistesgeschichte,* 29–45; Hommel, "Herrenworte"; Mack, *Lost Gospel.* The debate regarding who exactly the intended subjects are of the enigmatic tirade in Aelius Aristides, *or.* 46 (ca. 180 C.E.), is instructive here as well. The fact that a case can be made for either Jews or Christians or the Cynics as the objectionable party in Aristides' view suggests that in antiquity distinguishing between certain representatives of these different groups may have been difficult for the uninitiated eye. See, further, de Labriolle, *La réaction païenne,* 79–87.

41. See Tuckett, "A Cynic Q?"; further, Horsley, *Sociology,* 116–19. For a fuller response to Tuckett's article, see Vaage, "Q and Cynicism."

42. See, further, above, p. 142, n. 32.

43. See J. Z. Smith, *Drudgery Divine,* 36–53.

44. For the phrase, "disciplined exaggeration," see J. Z. Smith, "Connections," 10: "Theory and its attendant operations (such as comparison) are disciplined exaggerations in the service of knowledge."

45. Droge and Tabor (*Noble Death,* 47 n. 28) may feel that "The literature on Cynicism is enormous," but it is also highly uneven both with regard to the different foci of investigation and the limits of each discussion. See, e.g., the representative bibliographies in Paquet, *Les cyniques grecs,* 303–28; Goulet-Cazé, *L'ascèse cynique,* 249–55; Billerbeck, *Kyniker,* 303–17. The standard introduction to ancient Cynicism, though increasingly dated, remains Dudley, *History.* See also E. Zeller, *Philosophie,* 2.1.280–336, 3.1.791–804; Ueberweg-Praechter, *Grundriß,* 173–85, 456–59, 526–36, 684–87.

46. For the relationship between "the Cynic" and "the Cyrenaic," see Steiner, "Diogenes' Mouse." For a comparison of the Cynics and the sophists, see Cappelletti, "Religiosidad e iconoclasía." For "la filosofia di Pirrone e le

sue relazioni con il cinismo," see Brancacci. For other schools of philosophy, see Goulet-Cazé, "Le cynisme à l'époque impériale," 2806–17.

47. See Tuckett, "A Cynic Q?" 352 n. 13: "One should therefore perhaps avoid terms like 'Cynic-Stoic' in the present discussion." For a succinct description of some of the differences between Stoic and Cynic "theology," see Malherbe, "Pseudo Heraclitus, Epistle 4," 45–51; idem, "In Season and Out of Season," 141; further, Ferrater Mora, "Cyniques et Stoïciens"; Rist, "Cynicism and Stoicism"; Harris, "Stoic and Cynic under Vespasian"; Goulet-Cazé, *L'ascèse cynique,* 141–91; idem, "Le cynisme à l'époque impériale," 2808–12.

48. See Seneca, *ep. mor.* 5.2, 4–5. Unless otherwise indicated, all references to and citations of ancient literature (except the Bible) are those of the Loeb Classical Library, whose translation, however, I have frequently modified.

49. At the opposite end of the spectrum stands the problem of "genuine" Cynic sources that contain "properly" Stoic material. See Goulet-Cazé, "Un syllogisme stoïcien"; idem, *L'ascèse cynique,* esp. pp. 210–18.

50. Cf. Goulet-Cazé, *L'ascèse cynique,* 12–13; Hoïstad, "Cynicism," 628: "The problem of Cynicism is essentially a problem concerning the sources." The difficulty of "no reliable sources" is not unlike the challenge faced by those who would write the history of "women in antiquity."

51. See Tuckett, "A Cynic Q?" 352.

52. See Tuckett, "A Cynic Q?" 353 n. 18.

53. See Vaage, "Ethos and Ethics," 362–72.

54. See Malherbe, "Self-Definition," 14. Reference is made especially to Gerhard (*Phoinix von Kolophon,* 64–72, 165–68; idem, "Legende") in support of the distinction made here by Malherbe between "two types of Cynicism: an austere, rigorous one, and a milder, so-called hedonistic strain." Elsewhere, however, Malherbe recognizes that this binary division — leaving aside for the moment the question of its validity per se — is insufficient to account for the full variety of flesh-and-blood Cynics in antiquity. Thus, for example, in discussing "the Cynic background to 1 Thessalonians 2," Malherbe (*Paul and the Popular Philosophers,* 38–47) speaks of *five* types of mainly "Cynic" philosophers, plus an ideal sixth type, mentioned in Dio Chrysostom, *or.* 32.

Regarding the distinction itself between two types of Cynics, it is not clear that Gerhard's characterization of Cynic divergence in these terms is, in fact, intended or able to constitute a proper typology of ancient Cynicism instead of being simply an ad hoc effort to articulate the fact of "difference" within the various traditions about Diogenes and his followers. Note, moreover, that the original debate concerning "hedonistic" versus "rigorous" or ascetic Cynicism had as its center of gravity a strangely familiar quest for the historical Diogenes. Beyond Gerhard, see, e.g., von Fritz, *Quellenuntersuchungen;* Hoïstad, *Cynic Hero,* 132–35; idem, "Cynicism," 631–32; Kindstrand, *Bion of Borysthenes,* 64–67. For both Gerhard and von Fritz, the terms "hedonistic" and "rigorous" finally function as the tradition-historical key to sorting out the seemingly confused and contradictory anecdotes associated with the premier dog-philosopher from Sinope. The significance of Cynic "diversity" is thus reduced to a question of confessional perspective: i.e., misanthropical versus philanthropical. Cf. Goulet-Cazé, *L'ascèse cynique,* 77–84.

55. Hoïstad's characterization of the Cynics (see above, n. 54) as followers of Socrates' "eudaemonistic asceticism" is more promising, insofar as it permits one to understand how it was that a given group of persons all shared a common goal — and thus with equal right were each called "Cynic" — at the same time that their behavior and individual pronouncements could vary to such a degree in accordance with particular circumstances. Hoïstad, however, does not extend this understanding of the Cynics beyond the time of Alexander the Great, given his belief that later Cynic "extremists" were influenced by contact with "oriental" asceticism and its practices of abnegation for abnegation's sake. Dramatic demonstration of self-control became in this fashion, according to Hoïstad, a virtue without concern for the attainment of contentment. These latter ideas are much less certain.

56. For a general overview, see the works cited above, p. 143, n. 45 (Dudley, E. Zeller, Ueberweg-Praechter); also Rankin, *Sophists, Socratics and Cynics,* 219–48; Döring, "Protestbewegung."

57. See Tuckett, "A Cynic Q?" 356.

58. For "Judaism" as a "buffer" concept in Western biblical scholarship and its generalized, if unacknowledged, effort to preserve a sense of early Christianity's historical "uniqueness," see J. Z. Smith, *Drudgery Divine,* 79–83, esp. p. 83. Regarding the question of "historical contact" between ancient "Judaism" and "Cynicism," see Fischel, "Studies in Cynicism"; further, Luz, "Salam, Meleager!"; idem, "Greek Cynic in the Jerusalem Talmud." Equally in error, however, would be the assumption that Cynicism was somehow restricted in its historical manifestations to only a few regions of the ancient Mediterranean world. Even a superficial review of Cynic geography quickly establishes the territory of these homeless hounds as roughly coterminous with the extent of Greco-Roman civilization in general, the exceptions being, perhaps, northern Africa (excluding Egypt) and the western provinces of Spain and Gaul. See Goulet-Cazé, "Le cynisme à l'époque impériale," 2731–34: "Les lieux de naissance et de résidence qui nous sont connus se situent, exception faite de Rome, en Grèce ou à l'est de la Grèce." According to Goulet-Cazé, the Cynics furthermore "étaient de grands voyageurs." It is important not to confuse our modern "disciplinary" maps of classical antiquity with its own rather more mingled cultural state.

59. For other summary descriptions of the Cynics, see Helm, "Kynismus"; MacCunn, "Cynics"; Sayre, "Greek Cynicism" (an idiosyncratic account); Hoïstad, "Cynicism"; Malherbe, "Cynics"; Caizzi, "Cinici"; also the review article by Goulet-Cazé, "Les cyniques grecs." Interesting as well are the efforts to express in a more contemporary vein the specific philosophical nature of ancient Cynicism. See, e.g., Sloterdijk, *Kritik der zynischen Vernunft;* Weber, *Diogenes;* Onfray, *Cynismes.*

60. Cf. Diogenes Laertius 6.64: Diogenes "was going into a theater, meeting face to face those who were coming out, and when asked why, he said: 'This is what I practice doing my whole life.'" See, further, Miralles, "Los cínicos, una contracultura"; Donzelli, "Un' ideologia 'contestataria'"; Shmueli, "Modern Hippies and Ancient Cynics"; Détienne, *Dionysos mis à mort,* 153–55; Hochkeppel, "Mit zynischem Lächeln"; Döring, "Protestbewegung." For

the category of "contracultural" versus "countercultural" and "subcultural," see Yinger, "Contraculture"; Roberts, "Generic Concept"; Robbins, "Rhetoric and Culture." Cf. Yinger, *Countercultures,* 3: contraculture=counterculture. Not everything said by these authors, however, about the specific sociological nature of a "contracultural" formation is accurate regarding the Cynics, specifically, the assumption that "contracultural" inevitably means short-lived, involving no more than one generation, incapable of sustaining an individual over an entire life span, with predictable behavior patterns. None of these traits seems to have been especially true for the Cynics.

61. See Diogenes Laertius 6.103–4; further, Rodier, "Morale d'Antisthène"; Henrichs, "Zwei Fragmente"; versus Niehues-Pröbsting (*Kynismus des Diogenes,* 22ff), who claims that "the first Cynics known to us historically were principally writers [*primär Literaten*]."

62. See Vaage, "Like Dogs Barking."

63. The juxtaposition in this sentence of "marginal" and "midst" is purposeful. To my knowledge, no Cynic ever sought the solitude of the desert, as did many Christian ascetics, or the forest, as in Indian asceticism. Instead, the Cynics appear to have deliberately practiced their form of cultural marginality within the usual settings of "normal" social life in antiquity. Thus, e.g., Diogenes, like many "street people" in our own day and age, set his tub up in the center of town near the Metroon.

64. For diverse perspectives on the idea and difficulties of (deliberate) social marginality, see, e.g., J. Z. Smith, *To Take Place,* 73, 154 n. 77; Rosaldo, *Culture and Truth,* 207–17; hooks, "Choosing the Margin"; Yinger, *Countercultures;* P. Brown, "Holy Man in Late Antiquity," 130–32. The Cynic "short-cut" was precisely both what assured contentment here and now, as well as the concrete expression of the Cynic's open opposition to the dominant culture. See, e.g., ps-Crates, *ep.* 6, 13, 16, 21; ps-Diogenes, *ep.* 12, 30, 44; Lucian, *vit. auc.* 11; Julian, *or.* 7.225c; Diogenes Laertius 6.38–39, 104; Emaljanow, "Note."

65. Thus I would account for both the concrete "diversity" of Cynics in antiquity, as well as the sometimes sharp discrepancies in the depiction of "Cynicism" by ancient authors. For Cynicism as a type of asceticism, see Diogenes Laertius 6.70–71; Capelle, "Altgriechische Askese," 679–99; Vaage, "Cynic Epistles"; idem, "Like Dogs Barking"; Goulet-Cazé, *L'ascèse cynique,* esp. pp. 53–71.

66. See Goulet-Cazé, "Le cynisme à l'époque impériale," 2734–36.

67. Derivation of the name "Cynic" from association with the gymnasium of Cynosarges in Athens has routinely failed to convince. See, e.g., Diogenes Laertius 6.13; further, Sayre, *Greek Cynics,* 93–94; Niehues-Pröbsting, *Kynismus des Diogenes,* 15–19.

68. For the Pythagoreans, see Burkert, "Craft versus Sect," 15–17. For the Epicureans, see Malherbe, "Self-Definition," 47–48.

Chapter One
Ethos: "Like Sheep among Wolves"

1. See Meeks, *First Urban Christians*.

2. The social description of Q is thus a first chapter in the longer history of Syrian Christianity. Such a perspective makes the present effort even more interesting, especially regarding the themes of both asceticism and Cynicism. Cf. Kretschmar, "Beitrag," esp. p. 65: "The actual historical origin of Christian asceticism in the region of Syria-Palestine lies, then, in the attempt to convert the call of Jesus to discipleship and his teaching of the disciples into a Christian way of life." Kretschmar has in mind especially the Gospel of Matthew with its ideal of perfection (*teleios*). Other texts of possible relevance are said to include Hebrews, certain of the apocryphal acts (e.g., *Acts of Thomas*), the book of Revelation, *Pseudo-Clementines* (esp. *ad virgines*), *Liber graduum*, *Didache* (1–6), James, *Didaskalia, Epistula Apostolorum, Epistle of Barnabas* (18–20). On the trajectory between Matthew and Q (Jesus and John), see Robinson, "Q Trajectory."

3. See Vaage, "Ethos and Ethics," 1–71; further, Hoffmann, *Studien,* 235–334; Theissen, "Wanderradikalismus," esp. p. 252 n. 20.

4. See Vaage, "Ethos and Ethics," 72–300.

5. For the text of Q 10:2–16, see Vaage, "Ethos and Ethics," 296. See also Asgeirsson and Robinson, "Work Session 16 November 1990," 496 (for Q 10:2–4); Moreland and Robinson, "Work Sessions 31 July–2 August, 20 November 1992" (for Q 10:5–6). The only noteworthy differences (thus far) between the IQP text and that of my dissertation are the tense of the opening verb in 10:2 (IQP: *eipen* vs. Vaage: *legei*); the spelling of the word for money in 10:4 (IQP: *argur..on* vs. Vaage: *argurion*); the reference "to this house" after the greeting, "peace," in 10:5 (IQP: omit vs. Vaage: *t...oik...*); and use of the locative adverb "there" in 10:6 (IQP: *ekei* vs. Vaage: omit). For 10:3–6, 9–11, 16 as part of Q's formative stratum, but 10:2, 7b, 12, 13–15 as due to the document's secondary redaction, see below, appendix one. For the text of 10:7–8 and 10:16, see below, appendix two.

6. Neither at Qumran nor among the Pharisees is there any evidence of these persons ever having undertaken a "mission" to Israel. See Schulz, *Spruchquelle,* 412. Cf. Townsend, "Missionary Journeys," who concludes that "the finding of a missionary-journey pattern in Acts corresponds quite well with the rise of modern missionary societies" in the seventeenth and eighteenth centuries C.E. One wonders to what extent the same holds true for the perception of an early Christian "mission" in the canonical gospel narratives of Jesus and his disciples.

7. See Epictetus, *diss.* 3.22.56; also 3.22.59. The Greek verb translated here as "sent" is *katapempein*.

8. See Epictetus, *diss.* 3.22.23–24: *aggelos apo tou Dios apestaltai;* further, ibid., 1.24.6; 3.22.38, 69, 97. See also Billerbeck, *Epiktet,* 78; who notes that the term *martys* is also relevant here. See, e.g., Epictetus, *diss.* 1.29.46f; 3.24.112f.

9. See Epictetus, *diss.* 4.8.30–31; also 2.16.47; 3.22.26, 23.34.

10. What the Cynics typically referred to as *eudaimonia,* the Q people called instead *makarios;* a word, however, hardly unique to Q. Among others, the Cynics, too, occasionally used it, as did the translators of the LXX for the Hebrew אַשְׁרֵי. See, further, Downing, *Christ and the Cynics,* 19. In the synoptic tradition, however, repeated use of the term *makarios* is a distinctive feature of Q. Neither *makarios* nor any word related to it occurs in Mark. In Matthew and Luke, virtually every instance of this word (*makarios*) is due either directly or indirectly to Q (e.g., the additional beatitudes in Matt 5:3–11). Only twice in the Gospel of John (13:17; 20:20) is anyone ever said to be "happy."

11. See *TDNT,* 1:399.

12. See *TDNT,* 1:410–11.

13. See *TDNT,* 1:411.

14. See *TDNT,* 1:412.

15. Ibid.

16. Ibid.

17. See Dio Chrysostom, *or.* 32.12; also 32.21.

18. See Dio Chrysostom, *or.* 34.4.

19. See ps-Diogenes, *ep.* 7. Unless otherwise indicated, all references to the Cynic epistles are to Malherbe, *Cynic Epistles.*

20. See ps-Socrates, *ep.* 1.

21. If the parallel text in Alciphron (*ep.* 2.38) is relevant, it was the writer's father who needed to be assuaged.

22. Cf. Hoffmann, *Studien,* 294; D. Zeller, *Mahnsprüche,* 52.

23. See below, p. 37f. Cf. Str.-B. 1:590.

24. See, e.g., Steck, *Israel;* ps-Diogenes, *ep.* 7: "I hear that you are grieved that the Athenian youths, drunk with wine, laid blows on me and that you suffer great distress that wisdom should be treated with drunken violence."

25. See Epictetus, *diss.* 1.23.7–8. Other interpretations of the contrast in 10:3 between sheep and wolves include those based on the single saying — and only parallel in Rabbinical literature! — of the Roman emperor Hadrian to R. Jehoshua, c. 90 C.E., cited in Str.-B. 1:574. See, e.g., Schlatter, *Matthäus,* 337; O'Hagan, "'Greet No One,'" 71; Grundmann, *Matthäus,* 291; Hoffmann, *Studien,* 295; Lignée, "Mission," 68. Equally unconvincing are the different interpretations by Bleek, *Erklärung,* 1:427; B. Weiss, *Matthäus und Lucas-Parallelen,* 268f; idem, *Markus und Lukas,* 442 (cf. Wellhausen, *Lucae,* 49); Loisy, *Les évangiles synoptiques,* 868, 875 n. 7; Zahn, *Lucas,* 411; idem, *Matthäus,* 401; Easton, *Luke,* 157; Lagrange, *Luc,* 294; Manson, *Sayings,* 75; Schlatter, *Lukas,* 277; Grundmann, *Lukas,* 209; Schürmann, "Mt 10, 5b–6," 143 n. 28; Haenchen, *Weg,* 224; Wiater, *Komposition,* 126; Schulz, *Spruch-quelle,* 413; Minear, *Heal and Reveal,* 10; Riesner, *Jesus,* 464; Jacobson, "Lc 10, 2–16," 422; Kloppenborg, *Formation,* 194. Beyond Isa 11:6; 65:25, other "biblical" texts occasionally referred to include: Jer 50:8; Ezek 22:27; Zeph 3:3; Prov 28:15 (LXX); PssSol 8:23; 2 Esd 5:18; 1 En 89:13–14.

26. See Diogenes Laertius 6.92. Cf. Paquet, *Les cyniques grecs,* 119.

27. On the meaning of "temptation," see Harpham, *Ascetic Imperative,* 45–66.

28. See, e.g., 2 *Clem.* 5.2–4 (citing, perhaps, the *Gospel of the Egyptians*, according to Hennecke-Schneemelcher, *New Testament Apocrypha*, 1:172; also 1:175–76).

29. See Lucian, *fug.* 14; further, Diogenes Laertius 6.47.

30. See Epictetus, *diss.* 2.9.4; further, 2.10.3.

31. See Epictetus, *encheir.* 46.

32. See Epictetus, *diss.* 3.3.7; further, 1.23.7–8; 2.4.11.

33. See Dio Chrysostom, *or.* 8.25 (a pig or a wolf); ps-Diogenes, *ep.* 40. In the latter case (ps-Diogenes, *ep.* 40) interestingly, one reads that "not even wolves do, and no animal is more wicked and harmful than they," what the worst of human beings regularly do, namely, "always waylaying those who happen by." The wolf here symbolizes not apocalyptic persecution, but merely moral baseness.

34. Cf. Plummer, *Luke,* 273 n. 1.

35. Cf. Zahn, *Matthäus,* 401; Lagrange, *Luc,* 294.

36. Scholarly explanations of the "real" meaning of 10:4 tend to make it regularly say something other (less severe) than what it literally says. See, e.g., Krauss, "Instruktion," 96; Schniewind, *Matthäus,* 128. Some scholars refer to *Ber.* 9.5, which discusses how properly to enter the temple area. See, e.g., Schniewind, *Matthäus,* 129; Plummer, *Luke,* 273; Manson, *Sayings,* 181f; Grundmann, *Matthäus,* 290; Hengel, *Nachfolge,* 84 n. 146; Schweizer, *Matthäus,* 154. Cf. Hoffmann, *Studien,* 321–24; Legrand, "Bare Foot Apostles?" 209–10. Josephus's description of the Essenes (*J.W.* 2.124–27) is occasionally invoked. See, e.g., Lang, "Grussverbot oder Besuchsverbot?" 76. Cf. Spitta, "Verbot," 45; Dalman, *Orte und Wege,* 215; Krauss, "Instruktion," 97; Hoffmann, *Studien,* 313, 317. Additional (unpersuasive) biblical references include: Gen 32:10; Deut 29:5–6; Josh 9:3–6; 2 Kings 4:29; Isa 20:1–4; Tob 5:17–18.

37. See Theissen, "Wanderradikalismus," 248–49; also Hoffmann, *Studien,* 312, 315; Schulz, *Spruchquelle,* 415.

38. See, e.g., Schlatter, *Matthäus,* 331; Hoffmann, *Studien,* 328–29; Schulz, *Spruchquelle,* 414–15; Wiater, *Komposition,* 126; Lignée, "Mission," 68; Polag, *Christologie,* 67; Schenk, *Synopse,* 52; further, Hirsch, *Frühgeschichte,* 209; Liechtenhan, *Mission,* 22; Michaelis, *Matthäus,* 2:83; Georgi, *Gegner,* 208; Kraft, *Entstehung,* 149.

39. Cf. above, p. 147, n. 2; Diogenes Laertius 6.103–5. Regarding the *enstasis biou* of the Cynics, in the midst of his concluding summary of their common "doctrines," Diogenes Laertius (6.104) simply says: "They also hold that we should live frugally, eating food for nourishment only and wearing a single garment. Wealth and fame and high birth they despise. Some at all events are vegetarians and drink cold water only and are content with any kind of shelter or tubs."

40. See Hoffmann, *Studien,* 313–14; further, Spitta, "Verbot," 44; Zahn, *Lucas,* 411; Lagrange, *Marc,* 151 (quoting Maldonat); Manson, *Sayings,* 181; Schlatter, *Matthäus,* 332. Schenk (*Synopse,* 52) thinks that two garments on a journey were "a mark of contemporary Hellenistic luxury travel." But

Hoffmann (*Studien,* 241) indicates otherwise. See, also, Str.-B. 1:566; Bleek, *Erklärung,* 1:422.

41. In any case, traveling light formed part of Antisthenes' general recommendations. See Diogenes Laertius 6.6: "The right outfit for a voyage . . . is such as, even if you are shipwrecked, will go through the water with you."

42. Diogenes was infamous in antiquity for having "defaced the currency" of Sinope. See Diogenes Laertius 6.20–21, 56, 71; further, Dudley, *History,* 20–22, 54–55. Cf. Diogenes Laertius 6.50; also 1 Tim 6:10.

43. See Diogenes Laertius 6.87. Cf. ps-Diogenes, *ep.* 9; Lucian, *Tim.* 56; *vit. auc.* 9.

44. See Diogenes Laertius 6.82.

45. See Julian, *or.* 6.195b. The reference to having "not even a household slave" likely tells us more about Julian than it does about Diogenes. Cf. the parallel saying in Diogenes Laertius (6.38) where no slave is mentioned.

46. See Lucian, *cat.* 19.

47. See Dio Chrysostom, *or.* 6.60.

48. See Dio Chrysostom, *or.* 10.14.

49. See, e.g., ps-Crates, *ep.* 16, 23; ps-Diogenes, *ep.* 7, 15, 19, 22, 26, 30, 34, 38, 46; Epictetus, *diss.* 3.22.10; Lucian, *vit. auc.* 7, 9; *bis acc.* 6; *dial. mort.* 20.2; *Peregr.* 15; *fug.* 14; Diogenes Laertius 6.13, 22, 23, 83. Julian (*or.* 6.200d) lists the *pēra* among the Cynic *gnōrismata.*

50. See, e.g., Hengel, *Nachfolge,* 31–37, esp. p. 36; Schürmann, *Lukasevangelium,* 502; Hoffmann, *Studien,* 240–42; Bosold, *Pazifismus,* 71; Schenk, *Synopse,* 52; Horsley, *Spiral of Violence,* 230f; idem, *Sociology,* 47, 117.

51. See Teles IVA.182–85 (O'Neil, 46f).

52. See ps-Crates, *ep.* 11 (my translation; Wimbush, 110).

53. See Diogenes Laertius 6.37; further, ps-Diogenes, *ep.* 6, 13. Although the wallet is not here explicitly eliminated from the Cynic "outfit," the possibility is plainly established that it, too, could be discarded with equal consistency.

54. See ps-Diogenes, *ep.* 22. Cf. P. Brown, *Body and Society,* 6: "Our book is set in a society that was more helplessly exposed to death than is even the most afflicted underdeveloped country in the modern world. Citizens of the Roman Empire at its height, in the second century A.D., were born into the world with an average life expectancy of less than twenty-five years. Death fell savagely on the young. Those who survived childhood remained at risk. Only four out of every hundred men, and fewer women, lived beyond the age of fifty. It was a population 'grazed thin by death.' "

55. See ps-Diogenes, *ep.* 26.

56. See Diogenes Laertius 6.85; further, Apuleius, *apol.* 22.1; Clement of Alexandria, *paed.* 2.93.4. In the first two lines of the poem, Crates parodies Homer's *Odyssey* (19.172). See Paquet, *Les cyniques grecs,* 110 n. 3.

57. See Deissmann, *Light,* 109; further, Lucian, *Luc.* 35. Cf. Krauss, "Instruktion," 100.

58. See *Const. Apost.* 3.6 (M. Metzger 2:134); Deissmann, *Light,* 109 n. 1.

59. Though part of Lucian's critique of the Cynics is precisely that some of them had made the beggar's bag into a pouch of greed. See, e.g., Lucian, *Tim.*

57; *pic*. 45; *Peregr*. 30; *fug*. 31; further, Diogenes Laertius 6.99; Epictetus, *diss*. 3.22.50.

60. See, e.g., Str.-B. 1:566; B. Weiss, *Markus und Lukas*, 443; Loisy, *Les évangiles synoptiques*, 87; Plummer, *Luke*, 273; Zahn, *Matthäus*, 339; Krauss, "Instruktion," 101; Lagrange, *Marc*, 153; idem, *Luc*, 295; Michaelis, *Matthäus*, 2:83; Schlatter, *Matthäus*, 332; Gächter, *Matthäus*, 325; Degenhardt, *Lukas*, 61 n. 7; Lohmeyer, *Markus*, 114 n. 2; Schürmann, *Lukasevangelium*, 501; Beare, "Mission," 4; Schweizer, *Matthäus*, 154; Legrand, "Bare Foot Apostles?" 209, 212–14; Kraft, *Entstehung*, 149. Cf. Schniewind, *Matthäus*, 128. In comparison with his interpretation of the staff, Hoffmann (*Studien*, 325) essentially ignores the prohibition of sandals.

61. Beyond the following examples, see also Teles IVA.109ff (O'Neil, 40ff); Dio Chrysostom, *ep*. 66.25; Dio Cassius, *hist. rom*. 65.13. Cf. Diogenes Laertius 2.28; 6.44.

62. See ps-Anacharsis, *ep*. 5.

63. See ps-Socrates, *ep*. 6.

64. See ps-Aristippus, *ep*. 13.

65. See Dio Chrysostom, *or*. 6.15.

66. See Dio Chrysostom, *or*. 10.7–8.

67. See Lucian, *cat*. 15; also 20.

68. See Lucian, *Icar*. 31.

69. See ps-Lucian, *cyn*. 1; also 13–14.

70. See ps-Lucian, *cyn*. 17.

71. See Alciphron, *ep*. 2.38.2.

72. See Diogenes Laertius 6.31.

73. For some scholars, the prohibition of the staff is one of the most important features of Q 10:4. See, e.g., Zahn, *Lukas*, 411; Lohmeyer, *Markus*, 114 n. 1; Hoffmann, *Studien*, 324–26; Schweizer, *Matthäus*, 154; Bosold, *Pazifismus*, 87f; Schenk, *Synopse*, 52.

74. See, e.g., ps-Crates, *ep*. 23, 33; ps-Diogenes, *ep*. 7, 19, 26, 30; Epictetus, *diss*. 3.22.10, 50; Alciphron, *ep*. 3.19.5; Lucian, *cat*. 13; *vit. auc*. 7; *dial. mort*. 20.2; *bis acc*. 6; *Peregr*. 15, 37; *fug*. 14; Diogenes Laertius 6.13. Julian (*or*. 6.200d) lists the staff among the Cynic *gnōrismata*.

75. Cf. Diogenes Laertius 6.23: Diogenes "did not lean upon a staff until he grew infirm; but afterwards he would carry it everywhere, not indeed in the city, but when walking along the road with it and with his wallet."

76. For the staff as a defensive weapon, see Schweizer, *Matthäus*, 154 (versus snakes). For its prohibition as a sign of defenselessness, see Hoffmann, *Studien*, 324–26 (signifying *Friedfertigkeit* and *Friedensbereitschaft*); Krauss, "Instruktion," 96; Lagrange, *Marc*, 152. For the staff as sometimes an offensive weapon, see ps-Diogenes, *ep*. 26; Lucian, *conv*. 19; *fug*. 14.

77. See, e.g., ps-Diogenes, *ep*. 20; ps-Socrates, *ep*. 1; Dio Chrysostom, *or*. 34.2; 72.2; Diogenes Laertius 6.90–91. Cf. Diogenes Laertius 6.33.

78. See Dio Chrysostom, *or*. 6.60. Cf. ibid., 7.8–9.

79. The book is Bosold, *Pazifismus*. For a critical overview of "modern" interpretations of 10:4b, see Vaage, "Ethos and Ethics," 140–48.

80. On the Cynic virtue of *parrēsia,* see, e.g., Julian, *or.* 6.201a; Lucian, *Dem.* 3; *pic.* 29–37; *fug.* 14; Epictetus, *diss.* 3.22.19, 50, 93; Dio Chrysostom, *or.* 77/78.37, 45; ps-Diogenes, *ep.* 50; ps-Socrates, *ep.* 1; further, Vaage, "Like Dogs Barking." Cf. Philo, *rer. div.* 14; *de spec. leg.* 1.321.

81. See Lucian, *vit. auc.* 10. The last phrase is: *katalysis gar ta toianta tēs archēs.*

82. See Diogenes Laertius 6.31.

83. See *Gnom. Vat.* 12 (Sternbach, 9).

84. See, e.g., B. Weiss, *Matthäus,* 199; Grundmann, *Lukas,* 209; Haenchen, *Weg,* 225; Hoffmann, "Lk 10, 5–11," 48.

85. With a predictable inflation of meaning, see, e.g., B. Weiss, *Matthäus und Lucas-Parallelen,* 265; idem, *Markus und Lukas,* 443; J. Weiss, *Schriften,* 1:309; Loisy, *Les évangiles synoptiques,* 872; M'Neile, *Matthew,* 137; Zahn, *Lucas,* 412; Lagrange, *Luc,* 295; Manson, *Sayings,* 181, 257; Grundmann, *Lukas,* 209; idem, *Matthäus,* 291; Schürmann, "Mt 10, 5b–6," 147; idem, *Lukasevangelium,* 503; Haenchen, *Weg,* 225; Hoffmann, *Studien,* 296–97; Schulz, *Spruchquelle,* 416; Schweizer, *Matthäus,* 154; Lignée, "Mission," 69; Bosold, *Pazifismus,* 77, 89–91. Use of the term "peace" in the New Testament is nonetheless not without its peculiarities. In Matthew (10:13, 34), for example, the word *eirēnē* occurs only twice (actually, four times: twice in each instance). In both cases, a text from Q is involved. In Luke (24:36) and John (20:19, 21, 26) the actual greeting, *eirēnē hymin,* is employed only by Jesus and only after the resurrection. Virtually the same construction, most often in the form of *charis hymin kai eirēnē* and typically elaborated by a prepositional phrase and/or participle, constitutes the core of the standard epistolary greeting in Rom 1:7; 1 Cor 1:3; 2 Cor 1:2; Gal 1:3; Eph 1:2; Phil 1:2; Col 1:2; 1 Thess 1:1; 2 Thess 1:2; Phm 3; 1 Pet 1:2; 2 Pet 1:2; Jude 2; Rev 1:4. In 3 John 15, *eirēnē soi* means simply "goodbye." The conventional benediction, "Go in peace," in Jas 2:16 and Mark 5:34 (the only occurrence of *eirēnē* in this gospel) amounts to the same cliché.

86. See, e.g., B. Weiss, *Matthäus,* 199; Loisy, *Les évangiles synoptiques,* 872; Zahn, *Lucas,* 412–13; Schenk, *Synopse,* 53; Lang, "Grussverbot oder Besuchsverbot?" 77.

87. See, e.g., B. Weiss, *Matthäus und Lucas-Parallelen,* 266; idem, *Markus und Lukas,* 443; J. Weiss, *Schriften,* 308; Plummer, *Luke,* 273; Zahn, *Lucas,* 412; Schulthess, "Sprache," 247; Loisy, *Luc,* 294; Easton, *Luke,* 157; Lagrange, *Luc,* 295; Manson, *Sayings,* 257; Grundmann, *Lukas,* 209; Haenchen, *Weg,* 225; Hoffmann, *Studien,* 74–78, 310–11; Schulz, *Spruchquelle,* 416. Cf. the description by Josephus (*J.W.* 2.135) of the Essenes as *eirēnēs hypourgoi.* Polag (*Christologie,* 68) says simply that the expression, "son of peace," is "indeed dark."

88. Is there any other reason but the hope thereby of establishing an amicable relationship with the dwelling's unknown occupants? There is no indication in 10:5–6 that the Q people already have a relationship with the residents of the house at whose entrance they eventually come to stand. The conditional phraseology employed in the saying: "whichever house...if a son of peace is there...if not...," makes it clear that no nascent network exists on which

the Q people could depend (versus, e.g., Horsley, *Sociology,* 117; Kloppen-borg, "Social History," 86). Nor is there any reason to imagine that there were "sympathizers" awaiting the arrival of these persons in the different towns and villages of Galilee (versus, e.g., Theissen, "Wanderradikalismus," 262; idem, *Soziologie,* 21–26). The kind of set-up enjoyed by the Essenes (Josephus, *J.W.* 2.124–27), and even the loose arrangement presupposed by the *Didache* (11–13), are not apparent in Q (10:5–6). For a critical assessment of Josephus's representation of the Essenes in this regard, see Bauer, "Essener," 24.

89. Both Theissen and Stegemann are plainly uncomfortable with the idea of Q and beggars, but do not (because they cannot [?]) discard the possibility. See Theissen, "Wanderradikalismus," 260; idem, "Legitimation und Lebensun-terhalt," 202, 205, 208; Stegemann, "Wanderradikalismus?" 113. Cf. Pliny the Elder (*nat. hist.* 5.17.4) for an imputed relationship between the Essenes and "worldweary 'refugees' "; further, Bauer, "Essener," 6; Theissen, "Legitimation und Lebensunterhalt," 204. The word itself, "beg," is admittedly not used in 10:5–6. Every interpretation that suggests a meaning not explicitly stated in the text runs the risk of speculation. (For a particularly spectacular example of this in the history of religion, see J. Z. Smith, "When the Bough Breaks," esp. pp. 213–14, 217–19). On the other hand, every interpretation that fails to con-sider the concrete social situation implied by a text like 10:5–6 often gives way all too easily to the worst sort of romantic phantasizing. Ordinary terms like "house" and "peace" become nostalgic ciphers for arcane powers and habits.

90. Beyond the following examples, see also ps-Diogenes, *ep.* 36; Dio Chry-sostom, *or.* 32.9; Epictetus, *diss.* 3.22.10, 50; Lucian, *pic.* 35; Diogenes Laertius 6.99; 7.17. Cf. ps-Anacharsis, *ep.* 3; Dio Chrysostom, *or.* 8.5.

91. See Lucian, *fug.* 14 (*epiphoitōntes*).

92. See Lucian, *Dem.* 63.

93. See Diogenes Laertius 6.86.

94. Predictably, Lucian does not depict the Cynics as reacting in this way. See, e.g., Lucian, *fug.* 17; *conv.* 12; *pic.* 35.

95. See Diogenes Laertius 6.49.

96. See ps-Diogenes, *ep.* 11.

97. See Dio Chrysostom, *or.* 7.82.

98. Cf. above, p. 152, n. 88. The issue of hospitality is not discussed much, at least not explicitly, in the New Testament. Only twice, in Rom 12:13 and Heb 13:2, is the word itself (*philoxenia*) actually used. As a rule, the pro-jected recipients appear to be limited to other Christians. See, e.g., Rom 12:13; 1 Tim 3:2; Tit 1:8; 1 Pet 4:9; 3 John 5–8. The word for "stranger" (*xenos*) does not appear in any of the canonical gospels, except for two *Sondergut* pas-sages in Matthew (25:35, 38, 43, 44; 27:7). Notably, in the first of these (Matt 25:31–46) describing the "great judgment," among the criteria for salvation or damnation is the fact that "I was hungry and you gave me (no) food, I was thirsty and you gave me (no) drink, I was a stranger and you (did not) wel-come me." Are "the least of these/my brethren" (Matt 25:40, 45), to whom the imposing "I" who judges refers, here as elsewhere only other Christians? Or should we see in Matt 25:40, 45, recalling the instructions in Q 10:5–6, a further instance of concern for the "entertainment of strangers"? In Heb 13:12,

the reader is told not to "neglect to show hospitality to strangers, for some thereby have entertained angels unawares" (cf. Gen 18:1–8; 19:1–3). To what extent does Q 10:5–6 look for the same sort of openness? Cf. Fox, *Pagans and Christians,* 107; Homer, *Od.* 17.485: "All sorts of gods in the likeness of foreign strangers range in their prime through men's cities, watching over their insolence and orderly behavior."

99. See, e.g., ps-Crates, *ep.* 19.

100. See ps-Crates, *ep.* 2; further, Diogenes Laertius 6.67. For the idea of "demanding back what belongs to you," see ps-Diogenes, *ep.* 10, 34; ps-Crates, *ep.* 26, 27; Diogenes Laertius 6.37, 72.

101. Cf. ps-Crates, *ep.* 22, 36; Josephus, *J.W.* 2.134, 138. Cultic purity is not the issue here. Cf. Hoffmann, *Studien,* 316–17. Most scholars assume that Matthew is responsible for the references to worthiness in Matt 10:11–13. See, e.g., Wernle, *Frage,* 66, 184, 189; M'Neile, *Matthew,* 136; Easton, *Luke,* 160; Klostermann, *Matthäus,* 87; Schmid, "Matthäus und Lukas," 263; idem, *Matthäus,* 178; Schlatter, *Matthäus,* 333; Grundmann, *Matthäus,* 291; Beare, "Mission," 5; Hoffmann, "Lk 10, 5–11," 38; idem, *Studien,* 272; Schulz, *Spruchquelle,* 405–6; Schweizer, *Matthäus,* 155; Laufen, *Doppelüberlieferung,* 215; Vaage, "Ethos and Ethics," 199, 202. Cf. B. Weiss, *Matthäus und Lucas-Parallelen,* 267; Harnack, *Sayings,* 80; Loisy, *Les évangiles synoptiques,* 871–72; Wiater, *Komposition,* 315 n. 13. This consensus, however, ignores certain peculiarities about "worthiness" in the New Testament. At least in the canonical gospels, it is striking how the word *axios* seems to be used almost exclusively in contexts associated with Q. The term (*axios*) never occurs in Mark. It is found only once in John (1:27) and, notably, in a parallel saying to Q 3:16. Every instance of *axios* in Matthew either cites or concerns a passage from Q. See Matt 3:8/Luke 3:8; Matt 10:10/Luke 10:7; Matt 10:11, 13/Luke 10:5–6; Matt 10:37, 38/Luke 14:26–27; Matt 22:8/Luke 14:21. The situation is somewhat more complicated for Luke. Beyond Q/Luke 3:8 and 10:7, there is the recollection in Acts 26:20 of Luke 3:8=Q, and the "Johannine" reference in Acts 13:25 to Luke 3:16=Q. (Both John 1:27 and Acts 13:25 use *axios* instead of *hikanos,* which is the reading in Luke 3:16/Matt 3:11/Mark 1:7.) The term *axios* also occurs in Luke 7:4 — a Q passage. Every other instance of *axios* in Luke (12:48; 15:19, 21; 23:15, 41) is then either *Sondergut* or a text in Acts (23:29; 25:11, 25; 26:31) that recalls *Sondergut* in Luke (23:15; except for Acts 13:46, but cf. Matt 22:8).

102. Cf. ps-Crates, *ep.* 17; Diogenes Laertius 6.62. See also above, n. 100.

103. See ps-Diogenes, *ep.* 38. Cf. Lucian, *Dem.* 63.

104. In Q 10:9, the persons addressed by this saying are then told to "treat the weak," just as in ps-Diogenes, *ep.* 38 we next read that "I did not dine with everyone, but only with those in need of therapy" (cf. Mark 2:17). Both in Q (10:5–9) and ps-Diogenes, *ep.* 38, the concluding reference is finally to a king (or kingdom): the "ones who imitate the kings of the Persians" are "those in need of therapy," just as in Q 10:9 the "weak" who have been treated are told that the "kingdom of God has arrived." For some of the theoretical problems raised by this kind of comparison in the history of religion, see J. Z. Smith, "In Comparison a Magic Dwells"; idem, *Drudgery Divine,* 51–53.

105. In the social context of first-century C.E. Galilee, marked as it was by Roman military rule, rising brigandage, and increased economic difficulty, the Q people made sure that their unexpected arrival at the door of strangers would not be mistaken for one more unknown threat by using the standard greeting formula, "Peace to this house." For "peace" as a conventional greeting, see Str.-B. 1:380–85; Zahn, *Matthäus*, 400 n. 26; Schlatter, *Matthäus*, 333; Polag, *Christologie*, 68; further, above, p. 152, n. 85.

106. See Schürmann, *Lukasevangelium*, 501.

107. See Hoffmann, *Studien*, 299. The "other statements of Q" are 7:22; 10:23–24; 11:20, 23, 24–26; cf. 7:1–10; 17:6.

108. See Schulz, *Spruchquelle*, 417.

109. The phrase in Greek that I translate "treat the weak" is *therapeuete tous astheneis*, often rendered as "heal the sick." The latter is not incorrect, as far as it goes, but obscures the multiple possible connotations of both the verb and the adjective in antiquity. For *asthenēs*, see below, p. 156, n. 120.

110. See below, pp. 56–57.

111. Cf., e.g., ps-Heraclitus, *ep*. 5, 6; Foucault, *Birth of the Clinic*; J. Z. Smith, "Devil in Mr. Jones"; Taussig, *Shamanism*; Sullivan, *Icanchu's Drum*, 449–60; Pilch, "Sickness and Healing," esp. p. 182.

112. See, e.g., M. Smith, *Jesus the Magician*. Cf. Fox, *Pagans and Christians*, 117.

113. All three of these passages, namely, 7:1–10, 7:18–23, and 11:14–20, are assigned by Kloppenborg (*Formation*) to Q's redaction. In my opinion, however, 11:14–20 belongs instead to the document's formative stratum (see below, appendix one). Cf. Kloppenborg, *Formation*, 168: "Q is well aware of the miracle tradition (see 7:22; 10:20; 11:14–15; 17:5–6)," but is not especially interested "in the miraculous as such." This is even less the case if the lack of a parallel saying to Luke 10:20 in Matthew means that 10:20 did not in fact appear in Q. Cf. Kloppenborg, *Parallels*, 76. 17:5–6 is not about healing. Thus, the only other texts related to health and healing in Q would be 11:24–26 and 11:34–36.

114. The verb in 11:20 is *ephthasen*; in 10:9, *ēggiken*. The difference in vocabulary, however, means little. See Polag, *Christologie*, 69: *ēggiken* can "hardly be meaningfully distinguished in terms of content" from *ephthasen*. The variation in terminology has nonetheless been thought to be significant in the history of historical Jesus research. See, e.g., Zahn, *Lucas*, 416; Hoffmann, *Studien*, 300.

115. Even though nothing in 10:9 has struck most scholars as being especially noteworthy, no one, as far as I know, has ever produced a parallel to the combination of concerns found here. It may be that what in 10:9 is so tersely fused, linking bodily health with heavenly rule, was simply not part of a common parlance. If so, then the significance of the following comparisons is only further enhanced.

116. See Diogenes Laertius 6.102.

117. See Lucian, *Peregr*. 28, 41; further, Bernays, *Lucian und die Kyniker*, 10.

118. Cf. *Ap. Jas*. 3.25–27.

119. Cf. Schulz, *Spruchquelle,* 417.

120. There is no reason to assume that the weak referred to in 10:9a were not really ill, i.e., suffering disease in some fashion, although the term itself, *asthenēs,* also belongs to the diagnostic vocabulary of ancient moral philosophy. See Malherbe, " 'Pastoral Care,' " esp. pp. 377–81.

121. Cf. Be Duhn, "Regimen for Salvation."

122. See Acts 13:51. The numerous parallels listed by Str.-B. (1:571) for this saying (10:10–11) deal only with the ritual removal of unclean (Gentile) dirt in general. The persons who enacted what is said here supposedly "compared the [unreceptive] place to the region of the Gentiles, and had no association with its residents." For interpretation of 10:10–11 along these lines, see, e.g., Loisy, *Les évangiles synoptiques,* 873; M'Neile, *Matthew,* 137; Manson, *Sayings,* 76; Degenhardt, *Lukas,* 63; Grundmann, *Markus,* 124–25. But neither the specific gesture of removing the dust from one's feet nor the particular situation in which such a deed was to be done, namely, when "they do not receive you," are evident in the parallels adduced by Str.-B.

123. Some interpreters simply imagine an altogether different meaning for 10:10–11 from what is said. See, e.g., Schlatter, *Matthäus,* 334: "Shaken, however, is not the foot, but the clothing"; further, Gächter, *Matthäus,* 328; Grundmann, *Markus,* 124. Other scholars make the saying mean too much. It must be a "prophetic sign." See, e.g., Grundmann, *Lukas,* 210; Lignée, "Mission," 70; Schürmann, *Lukasevangelium,* 505: "a prophetic sign, and more."

124. See Knox, *Sources,* 49.

125. See Gächter, *Matthäus,* 328: "The gesture does not consist in taking off one's sandals and slapping them together.... In such a case, one would have to walk with bare feet in the dust, making oneself laughable [*lächerlich*]."

126. See B. Weiss, *Matthäus,* 199. Cf. Hoffmann, "Lk 10, 5–11," 48.

127. See Diogenes Laertius 6.33.

128. See Diogenes Laertius 6.35.

129. See Diogenes Laertius 6.41. The term translated here as "man" is *anthrōpos.*

130. See Diogenes Laertius 6.89. Cf. Gregory Nazianzus on Antisthenes (below, p. 48).

131. There is some evidence of Cynic conflict with an entire "city." See, e.g., ps-Diogenes, *ep.* 28; ps-Heraclitus, *ep.* 7, 9.

132. Of course, many scholars do think that eschatological judgment is precisely what the gesture in 10:10–11 portends. See, e.g., Loisy, *Les évangiles synoptiques,* 873; Haenchen, *Weg,* 222, 226; Lohmeyer, *Markus,* 114; Schille, *Kollegialmission,* 82; Wiater, *Komposition,* 126. A sense of urgency is supposedly revealed here on the eve of the imminent end that did not permit any dallying about with prolonged attempts at conversion. See, e.g., J. Weiss, *Schriften,* 309; Loisy, *Les évangiles synoptiques,* 873; Manson, *Sayings,* 75; Schille, *Kollegialmission,* 82 (the Lord was due to arrive before nightfall), though the ultimate responsibility for all and any ill effects suf-

fered later as a result would squarely rest on the shoulders of the dawdling damned. See, e.g., J. Weiss, *Schriften,* 126; Manson, *Sayings,* 76; Gächter, *Matthäus,* 328.

133. Many scholars interpret the gesture as a dramatic suspension of all future relations. See, e.g., B. Weiss, *Matthäus,* 200; J. Weiss, *Schriften,* 126; Loisy, *Les évangiles synoptiques,* 872; idem, *Luc,* 296; Zahn, *Matthäus,* 401; M'Neile, *Matthew,* 137; Haenchen, *Weg,* 222; Grundmann, *Matthäus,* 291; Polag, *Christologie,* 69; Schenk, *Synopse,* 55. O'Hagan (" 'Greet No One,' " 71) says that the saying (10:10–11) demonstrates "positive hostility."

134. The key word in 10:16 is the verb *dechesthai,* used four times, not the penultimate participle *aposteilanta.* Cf. Klostermann, *Matthäus,* 93; Georgi, *Gegner,* 209 n. 1. For *dechesthai*=Matthew (10:40) as the original reading in Q (10:16) and not "hearing" and "rejecting" as in Luke (10:16), see below, appendix two. Variants of 10:16 occur in Mark 9:37/Matt 18:5/Luke 9:48; John 5:23; 12:44–45; 13:20; 1 Thess 4:8; *Did* 11:4; Ign., *Eph.* 6.1. Cf. Kloppenborg, *Formation,* 196.

135. Most scholars nonetheless assume that 10:16, like 10:3, is principally about authority or authorization. See, e.g., Loisy, *Les évangiles synoptiques,* 897; Lagrange, *Luc,* 300; Schmid, *Matthäus,* 187; Gächter, *Matthäus,* 351; Beare, "Mission," 6; Hoffmann, *Studien,* 304; Schulz, *Spruchquelle,* 458; Polag, *Christologie,* 70; Kloppenborg, *Formation,* 197. See, also, above, p. 22. Other (unconvincing) explanations are given by Loisy, *Les évangiles synoptiques,* 897; Zahn, *Matthäus,* 415; Schlatter, *Matthäus,* 351; F. C. Grant, "Mission," 309.

136. For 10:16 as forming an *inclusio* with 10:3/10:2, see Hoffmann, *Studien,* 304; Schenk, *Synopse,* 57. Cf. Gächter, *Matthäus,* 351.

137. Wisdom and her envoys are sometimes seen hovering in the background here. See, e.g., Hoffmann, *Studien,* 304; Schulz, *Spruchquelle,* 458; Schenk, *Synopse,* 57. Cf. Steck, *Israel,* 286 n. 9; Kloppenborg, *Formation,* 197 n. 113: "The closest Jewish parallel is the principle of agency found throughout rabbinic literature: שלוחו של אדם כמותו 'The agent of a man is like him.' "

138. For the Cynic way of life as both a form of asceticism and a shortcut to happiness, see above, p. 146, nn. 64, 65.

139. See, e.g., ps-Diogenes, *ep.* 6, 16, 36, 42; Diogenes Laertius 6.22, 23, 38; ps-Lucian, *cyn.* 15; Julian, *or.* 6.187d, 191, 193d. Cf. Dio Chrysostom, *or.* 6.26; 10.30; Plutarch, *aq. ig. ut.* A glance at the Stoic concept of nature as Diogenes Laertius (7.148–49) describes it makes clear how differently the Cynics deployed the same terminology.

140. Cf. Lovejoy and Boas, *Primitivism.* Cynicism is discussed in chapter four, although I do not find the category of "primitive" especially helpful for understanding the social posture of the Cynics in antiquity.

141. Cf. Sedley, "Philosophical Allegiance."

Chapter Two
Ethics: "Love Your Enemies"

1. I derive this understanding of ethics as a "second-order" reflection from Paul Ricoeur's hermeneutical philosophy of the will.

2. To discuss Q's ethics as a whole will require another book. In this work, I comment on only one text of the formative stratum as exemplary, namely, Q 6:27–35, initially selected because it appeared the most likely to resist accommodation to the characterization of the Q people advanced in the preceding chapter and thus a good test case, insofar as the usual interpretations of "love your enemies" did not seem to be especially compatible with my description of these persons. A second reason for maintaining the selection is recognition of the importance of "conflict management" and the definition of one's relationship to hostile "outsiders" and "others" in the formation of social identity. For 6:27–35 as part of Q's formative stratum, see below, appendix one.

3. See below, p. 44. The history of interpretation makes clear that the question raised explicitly by Theissen has always been implicit in the various efforts to "understand" the "true" meaning of this saying.

4. For the text of Q 6:27–35, see below, appendix two. Other (different) reconstructions of 6:27–35 include Hoffmann, "Tradition und Situation," 51–72; Sauer, "Erwägungen," 5–14; R. Piper, *Wisdom,* 78–82. That the unit ends at 6:35 and not 6:36, see Kloppenborg, *Formation,* 180.

5. See Kloppenborg, "Social History," 81–82. Cf. R. Piper, *Wisdom,* 83–86; Douglas, "Once Again"; Mullins, "Topos," esp. p. 544.

6. For the different redactional interpretations of "love your enemies" by Matthew and Luke, see, e.g., Theissen, "Gewaltverzicht und Feindesliebe," 176–83; Hoffmann, "Tradition und Situation," 82–103; Vaage, "Ethos and Ethics," 572–81; Horsley, *Spiral of Violence,* 262–70; also Bartsch, "Feldrede und Bergpredigt," esp. pp. 11–14; Furnish, *Love Command,* 45–59. For Luke's understanding, see, further, van Unnik, "Motivierung," 284–300. For Matthew, see Strecker, "Antithesen," esp. pp. 63–69; Rausch, "Principle of Nonresistance." For Matt 5:38–39a, see Bryant, "Matthew v. 38, 39"; Daube, "Matthew v. 38f.," 178–81; Sutcliffe, " 'Not to Resist Evil' "; Currie, "Matthew 5:39a," esp. pp. 143–45; Rathey, "Talion im NT?" For Matt 5:43 ("hate your enemy"), see I. Heinemann, "Nochmals."

7. See Vaage, "Composite Texts."

8. See Kloppenborg, *Formation,* 176.

9. Cf. Theissen, "Gewaltverzicht und Feindesliebe," 161–64.

10. Cf. Theissen, "Gewaltverzicht und Feindesliebe," 164–66. My translation of the apodosis of both 6:32 and 6:33 as "So what?" in order to highlight the rhetorical function of these questions in the argument of the sayings-complex obscures the fact that the term *misthos* is used in Q 6:32/Matt 5:46.

11. See Haas, *Idee und Ideal.* Cf. Waldmann, *Feindesliebe.*

12. See Klassen, "Love Your Enemy," 156. Cf. Neugebauer, "Wange," 868–69; Horsley, *Spiral of Violence,* 262–63, 266–67.

13. Cf. Horsley, *Spiral of Violence,* esp. pp. 259–73. Horsley is anxious that the reference to "enemies" in 6:27 not be understood as referring (exclusively? especially?) to foreign political foes. See also idem, "Ethics and Exegesis," 7–11, 17–18. Cf. Moulder, "Who Are My Enemies?"; further, Seitz, "Love Your Enemies," 49–51. I use the word "liberation" as a synonym for what in Greco-Roman antiquity was variously called *eleutheria.* See, e.g., Epictetus, *diss.* 4.1; *TDNT,* 2:487–96; Vollenweider, *Freiheit,* esp. pp. 23–169.

14. By characterizing as I have the socio-cultural "climate" of first-century C.E. "prerevolutionary" Galilee under Roman "colonial" rule since the middle of the preceding century (63 B.C.E.), I recognize that it is still debatable exactly how fraught the region actually was at any given moment with these particular kinds of tension. At the same time, I want to insist on the pervasive and seriously destabilizing nature of all colonial rule as such, so that even if "organized" political projects of resistance and revolt—for example, the "Zealots"—did not become fully articulated in Galilee and Judea until much closer to the outbreak of the first Jewish war than used to be assumed, it could hardly have been "business as usual" after the Romans arrived on the scene (even though commercial and other businesses were compelled to function more productively than before).

15. See J. Piper, *"Love Your Enemies,"* 27.

16. See Tannehill, *Sword of His Mouth,* 68–72; also Horsley, *Spiral of Violence,* 265–66. As will soon become apparent, I do not agree with Tannehill's description of the sayings in 6:29–30 as "focal instances" of the introductory command to "love your enemies" in 6:27, except as an observation on rhetorical construction. Tannehill is quite correct when he notes that "these commands [in 6:29–30] do not generalize concerning love or non-resistance," though Tannehill himself then generalizes when he asserts that "although these commands deal with specific situations, we unconsciously assume that they have implications for many other situations as well." Tannehill assumes that the different sayings in 6:29–30 are held together by "the simple device of reversing man's natural tendency." I would rather argue that what holds them together is instead the leading statement, "love your enemies," created by the editor of Q 6:27–35 in order to extend the significance of a number of peculiar acts to other situations as well. By placing these various behaviors all under the aegis of "love," the different sayings in 6:29–30 are each made to say more than they otherwise would on their own.

17. See Ricoeur, "Nabert on Act and Sign."

18. See, e.g., Douglas, "Once Again."

19. Cf. Horsley, *Spiral of Violence,* 263–64. Rhetorically, one might begin with the general concept. But ethically, at the level of concrete action, assuming that human behavior is not absolutely governed or determined by social convention, i.e., the rules of conduct codified as law and custom, variable options for personal comportment are first discerned and developed on the basis of specific "trial" acts. At some point, a set of these reactions and proposals could be grouped and classified together under a given "name," thereby suggesting through association with one another some deeper internal coherence among them, akin to that between the member "species" of a given "genus," as well

as providing a certain orientation for their subsequent review and rehearsal. Such is the phrase "love your enemies": a reflective effort by Q's formative stratum to combine in a "meaningful" series, as though variations on a single theme, the scattered "trials and errors" of prayer for pain-producers, sporadic gifts of further cheek, occasional collaborative robbery, the periodic granting of all requests, and when funds were available, loans without a due date.

20. See Theissen, "Gewaltverzicht und Feindesliebe," 191.

21. For the "golden rule" in antiquity, see Dihle, *Goldene Regel;* also Bartsch, "Traditionsgeschichtliches," 128–32.

22. This perplexity is lessened somewhat if the original link between the promulgation of the golden rule and the problem of the never-ending cycle of vengeance remained in force when Q was written. See Dihle, *Goldene Regel.*

23. See Matt 7:12.

24. Cf. Ricoeur, "Golden Rule." I would not share, however, Ricoeur's assumption that the "ethically wise," i.e., "secular" golden rule has here been placed in a "religious" context. This supposition by Ricoeur is due in part to his philosophical interest in the way in which "autonomous" moral "reason" is affected when deployed within the framework of a religiously constructed symbolic universe. More helpful, I think, is Ricoeur's discussion of competing "logics": in Ricoeur's words, the logic of reciprocity versus that of gift and superabundance, though, again, the logic of gift-giving is anthropologically difficult to distinguish from that of reciprocity. And the religious ideal of superabundance, promised theologically by the Protestant tradition and pursued by its capitalist children, is less securely superior in its social wisdom to that of reciprocity than Ricoeur seems to imagine.

25. A certain tension exists between the preceding "philosophical" analysis of 6:27–30 as a piece of moral instruction, according to which the saying in 6:28 is more like the subsequent commands in 6:29–30 than the antecedent imperative in 6:27, and the traditional exegetical observation by New Testament scholars of a certain *parallelismus membrorum* conjoining 6:27 and 6:28 into a single two-part utterance. This latter reading, however, has certainly been aided by the "gap" in Matthew's version of the Q passage between the phrases "love your enemies; pray for those who persecute you," placed at the beginning of the sixth antithesis in Matt 5:44, and the subsequent commands in Q 6:29–30, displaced by Matthew to become the body of the fifth antithesis of the Sermon on the Mount in Matt 5:39–42. The shift from second-person plural in 6:27–28 to second-person singular in 6:29–30 has also been a factor. The evangelist Luke is responsible for the four-part parallelism of Luke 6:27–28. In Luke 6:27, "love" is restated as "do good" and "enemies" as "those hating you," while in the second saying (6:28) "bless" anticipates "pray" and "those cursing you" sets up "those reviling you."

26. Beyond the sayings discussed in the text, see, further, Kloppenborg, *Parallels,* 29, esp. *Did* 1:3ff. For *Did* 1:3b–2:1 as a later second-century C.E. interpolation, see Layton, "Sources, Date and Transmission"; also, Kloppenborg, "Sayings of Jesus," esp. pp. 186–206. Cf. Jefford, *Sayings of Jesus,* 38–53.

27. Is it significant that the word "love" appears to be routinely avoided? See Bauer, "Gebot der Feindesliebe," who makes plain how thoroughly un-

welcome the teaching was to "love your enemies" in both early and later Christian antiquity. Cf. Klassen, *Love of Enemies,* 84; who claims (on the basis of Koester, *Synoptische Überlieferungen,* 44, 76) that "love your enemies" was "the most quoted saying of Jesus" in the second century C.E.

28. See Kloppenborg, *Parallels,* 29.

29. The middle statement in *P.Oxy.* 1224 fr. 2 that "he who is not [against you] is for you" specifically recalls Luke 9:50 (cf. Mark 9:40). Unlike Q 11:23, where everyone not "with me" is "against me," *P.Oxy.* 1224 fr. 2, as Luke 9:50 (and Mark 9:40), maintains a more open posture, willing to imagine and acknowledge forms of possible collaboration not based exclusively on strict identity. Otherwise, the logic linking the three parts of this papyrus fragment (*P.Oxy.* 1224 fr. 2) is not especially tight, at least regarding the placement of the middle statement. For "your enemies" are, presumably, precisely those who are "against you." Note, however, that both phrases are editorial reconstructions. The conjunction "for" after the opening imperative may have introduced a new perspective on the usual understanding of this language.

30. Beyond the examples cited in the text, see, further, Downing, *Christ and the Cynics,* 23–25; Kindstrand, *Bion of Borysthenes,* 205; versus, e.g., Waldmann, *Feindesliebe,* 57–58. I am *not* suggesting that notable parallels to 6:27–28 occur *only* in Cynic literature. See above, p. 158, n. 11; also Klassen, *Love of Enemies,* esp. pp. 12–42; Kloppenborg, *Formation,* 179 n. 37. Cf. Neugebauer, "Wange," 868–69. Reference is often made to Lev 19:18. See, e.g., Schulz, *Spruchquelle,* 134; Lührmann, "Liebet eure Feinde," 426; Horsley, *Spiral of Violence,* 271. This correlation, however, was first made explicitly by Matthew and should not be read back into Q. See, further, Kloppenborg, *Formation,* 178–79.

31. See *Gnom. Vat.* 187 (Sternbach, 76); further, Plutarch, *mor.* 21F; 88B.

32. The tendency of New Testament scholars to confuse discussion of "love your enemies" in Q 6:27–35 with the other "love commandments" of early Christianity, including the injunction to "love your neighbor as yourself" (Matt 22:39/Mark 12:31/Luke 10:27) and the parable of the good Samaritan (Luke 10:29–37), has had the not inconsequential effect of "washing out" of the critical appraisal of "love your enemies" the social fact of abiding enmity as the concrete problem under discussion in 6:27–35. See, further, Schottroff, "Gewaltverzicht und Feindesliebe," 197ff. The resulting interpretation of "love your enemies" becomes, then, roughly equivalent to the counsel of Pythagoras "so to behave to one another as not to make friends into enemies, but to turn enemies into friends." See Diogenes Laertius 8.23.

33. See Epictetus, *diss.* 3.22.54. This saying is frequently cited in the commentary literature on Luke 6:27/Matt 5:44, only to be immediately disregarded or blithely underestimated. See, e.g., Furnish, *Love Command,* 49.

34. See Stobaeus 3.20.61.

35. See Plutarch, *de prof.* 82E; Kindstrand, *Bion of Borysthenes,* 116 (for further discussion, ibid., 204–5). What those making progress are supposed to hear is a combination of Homer, *Od.* 6.187 and 24.402.

36. For a postmodern exploration of such an altruistic ethic, see Wyschogrod, *Saints and Postmodernism.*

37. See, e.g., Moffatt, "Matthew v. 39," 189: "Origen's argument [in the *Philocalia* (i.19)] seems to imply that he regarded the blow as an attempt to hurt or injure. But it also proves that for him [namely, Origen] the impossibility of interpreting the command literally rested upon this physical incongruity [as a description of direct frontal assault]"; Borges, *Literaturas germánicas medievales,* 76–77, on the later poetic work, *Der Heiland:* "El poeta se exalta cuando Simón Pedro saca la espada y le corta la oreja derecha al siervo del pontífice.... Omite la advertencia: Al que te golpeare en una mejilla, dale también la otra." For the *Didache* (1:4) the injunctions in 6:29 appear to be counsels of perfection (cf. Matt 5:48). Horsley ("Ethics and Exegesis," 18; idem, *Spiral of Violence,* 267–68) describes what is said in 6:29a as a "mere" insult. In an honor-shame culture, however, like the ancient Mediterranean world, there could be no such thing as a "mere" insult. Horsley wishes to emphasize the purely local "personal" character of what is said in 6:29a. Cf. Daube, "Matthew v. 38f.," 181–85, esp. pp. 182–83: "the case of smiting a man's cheek appears in Rabbinic argument as a typical case of insult, of insult unqualified, without actual damage to the person. The same is true of Roman law, where the praetor's edict gave as example of actionable insult the case that *Aulo Agerio pugno mala percussa est.* In fact already the first Roman codification, the XII Tables, in VIII 4, laid down a penalty of 25 asses for *iniuria,* understanding by this such modes of insult as a box on the ears.... Why was the word *iniuria,* the native meaning of which is 'an unlawful act' or 'illegality,' used to denote a slap in the face? ... it was only in cases like a slap in the face that unlawfulness alone, so to speak, [versus bodily damage] constituted the offense, that the rather abstract notion of 'violation of another person's rights' was in the foreground, not concealed behind any more concrete facts like a broken limb or a torn out eye, that the plaintiff could show the judge no glaring damage but appealed for redress on the sole ground that 'a wrong,' *iniuria,* has been done to him." For other interpretations of 6:29a, focused especially on the meaning of the "right" cheek in Matt 5:39, see Moffatt, "Matthew v. 39," 89; Davison, "Note."

38. See Gregory Nazianzus, *or.* 4.596B. If Horsley's suggestion (*Spiral of Violence,* 265, 268) is correct that the successive disrobing referred to in 6:29b would soon result in "nudism," the social effect would be the same as in the case of Antisthenes and his response to his abuser.

39. See Epictetus, *diss.* 4.5.8–9.

40. See Epictetus, *diss.* 3.12.10. Note the similar progression of topics here to the sequence in 6:28–29, namely, first "you are reviled/insulted," then "if someone strikes you." Cf. above, p. 31.

41. See Epictetus, *diss.* 3.22.100.

42. See Epictetus, *diss.* 2.16.28. Regarding certain gnomic sayings in the proverbs of Ahikar from among the Elephantine papyri, Montgomery ("Some Correspondences," 428) writes: "By [reading papyrus 57, col. 1, l. 13f. a certain way] I obtain the following sense: 'If a bad man take hold of the skirts of thy clothing, leave it in his hand. After he has bethought himself of Shamash (the god of justice), he will take of his own and give it to thee.' "

43. See Powell, *Collectanea Alexandrina,* 218. Cf. Teles II.82f (O'Neil, 11); Stobaeus 4.44.76 (quoting Favorinus).

44. See Tannehill, *Sword of His Mouth,* 70–71; further, above, p. 159, n. 16.

45. See Stobaeus 4.33.31. The passage continues: "When you choose to make a profit, you will do so easily; and when you have nothing, you will not want. But you will live content with what there is and not desire what is not there nor be distressed by whatever happens."

46. For further discussion of this point, see Vaage, "Q, Diogenes, and Jesus."

47. See Diogenes Laertius 6.29.

48. See Diogenes Laertius 6.62.

49. See Diogenes Laertius 6.46.

50. See *GThom* 95; Layton, *Gnostic Scriptures,* 396.

51. See, e.g., *GThom* 64.

52. See, e.g., Kloppenborg, *Formation,* 176 n. 26. Cf. Horsley, *Spiral of Violence,* 268. In a more recent article, Kloppenborg ("Social History," 88) contends that "Q 6:30 is obviously formulated from the point of view of persons [scribes] that were in a position to make loans. This extraordinary counsel to make loans without expectation of return should be viewed as a response to predatory lending practices and the chronic problem of indebtedness that ensued." But this is hardly so obvious or self-evident a conclusion. There is nothing in the language itself of 6:30b that requires one to assume the formalized institutional setting that Kloppenborg presupposes in his interpretation of the saying. There is no reason to believe that to "lend" was in this case any more specialized a form of social activity than to "give" is in the preceding statement (6:30a).

53. The Cynic term for this was *autarkeia.* See Rich, "Cynic Conception of αὐτάρκεια."

54. The "golden rule" (6:31) has already been discussed; see above, p. 45. The same saying (6:31) occurs elsewhere in both a "positive" form, as here, and a "negative" version, as, e.g., Tobit 4:15: "And that which you hate, do to no one" (LXX). The "negative" version, "Do not lie, and do not do what you hate," occurs in the *Gospel of Thomas:* both in Coptic (*GThom* 6b) and in Greek (*P.Oxy.* 654.36–37). Again, Thomas specifies what he especially opposes — in this case, lying — and then agrees with Q.

55. For discussion of the reference to "reward" in Matt 5:46 (*tina misthon echete*) and the parallel phrase in Matt 5:47 (*ti perisson poieite*), see, further, Sidebottom, "'Reward.'" According to Schottroff, "Gewaltverzicht und Feindesliebe," 218: "The main idea in Matt 5:46–47/Luke 6:32–35 is as follows: the Christian identity created by the obligation to love your enemies is opposed to the social identity of all other groups. Christians should transgress the bounds of group-solidarity and precisely thereby establish their own identity as a group" (my translation; cf. idem, "Non-Violence and the Love of One's Enemies," 25). Schottroff's language is somewhat overdrawn, in my opinion. Commendable, nonetheless, is her attention to the question of alternate social identity. The social values at work in 6:27–35 are not those of tradi-

tional "group-solidarity." They do not belong to the customary manners of most human societies. They may even be impossible to sustain in a "normal" community context, where some sort of "give and take" must seemingly be the order of the day.

56. See Seneca, *de ben.* 4.26.1. Kloppenborg (*Formation,* 177) refers to Sir 4:10 as well, but for different reasons.

57. See Epictetus, *diss.* 3.22.81–82.

58. See J. Piper, *"Love Your Enemies,"* 26.

59. See Tuckett, "A Cynic Q?" 366. Tuckett's rejection of the "genuine parallel" in Epictetus to "love your enemies" on the basis of Cynic "inconsistency" could also be applied to the memory tradition of Jesus in the synoptic gospels. Like the Cynics, Jesus is depicted in these writings as alternately advocating forbearance and acquiescence under siege with outbursts on other occasions of polemical rage and promises of divine retribution.

Chapter Three
Ideology: "The Kingdom of God Has Arrived"

1. For a similar, though not identical, understanding of ideology (versus the "social sciences"), see Geertz, "Ideology as a Cultural System." Cf. Ricoeur, "Science and Ideology"; idem, "Hermeneutics and the Critique of Ideology"; idem, "Ideology and Utopia."

2. For 6:20b; 10:9; 11:2, 20; 12:31; 13:18–21 as all part of Q's formative stratum, see below, appendix one. For the remaining kingdom (-of-God) sayings in Q (4:5; 7:28b; 13:29) as part of the document's secondary redaction, see Vaage, "Monarchy, Community, Anarchy," 60–61.

3. See, e.g., Schweitzer, *Kingdom of God;* Bright, *Kingdom of God;* Schnackenburg, *Gottes Herrschaft;* Camponovo, *Königtum;* Chilton, *Kingdom of God;* Willis, *Kingdom of God.* Especially suspect is the practice, often apparent in scholarly writings on the theme, of interpreting the kingdom-of-God sayings in Q and other early Christian texts on the basis of what we "otherwise know" about the meaning of the phrase on the lips of the historical Jesus, given that Q is one of our principal sources for this knowledge in the first place.

4. For Paul, see Vaage, "Monarchy, Community, Anarchy," 53–60.

5. See esp. Perrin, *Language of the Kingdom;* Wheelwright, *Metaphor and Reality;* also Scott, *Hear Then the Parable,* 61.

6. For the text of Q 6:20, see Asgeirsson and Robinson, "Work Sessions 12–14 July, 22 November 1991," 501. Cf. Schwarz, " 'Ihnen gehört das Himmelreich?' " who proposes that 6:20b originally read: "Happy are the poor, for they shall become rich," in accordance with the same inversionary logic as the subsequent sayings in Q 6:21. McEleney ("Beatitudes," 6) remains rightfully unconvinced, although his reasons for doing so are equally problematical.

7. The Greek term *ptōchos* in 6:20b refers to the poorest of the poor: the destitute, the beggar, the utterly disenfranchised, versus the lowly but still socially inscribed *penēs.* New Testament scholars have generally been loath to leave the significance of the saying (6:20b) at this level of reality. See, e.g.,

the ambiguous statements by Strecker, "Makarismen der Bergpredigt," 261: "Originally the promise applied to the materially poor, whereby in accordance with Jewish tradition 'poor' was understood as a religious concept"; Schweizer, "Seligpreisungen Jesu," 126 n. 1: "This is the danger of the Lukan formulation, especially since 'poor' in Greek can be understood in purely social terms, while the corresponding Aramaic formulation also but not exclusively indicates one's social status." The Old Testament, specifically Isa 61:1ff, is frequently invoked as part of the "background" or scriptural meaning of the utterance. But see the critical remarks by Frankenmölle, "Makarismen," 60: "…to dare the thesis that…there was no prior relation to the messianic prophecy in Isa 61:1f. Who would want to see this proven solely and simply through the word, οἱ πτωχοί? The frequency with which this term is found in the Old Testament as well as rabbinic and Greek literature points to a different frame of reference for understanding and a different literary genre." For Frankenmölle, unfortunately, these are the wisdom psalms and the eschatological proclamation of the historical Jesus.

8. Beyond the following sayings, see, further, Downing, *Christ and the Cynics,* 19–20. Cf. Schumacher, *Small Is Beautiful.*

9. See ps-Crates, *ep.* 11 (my translation; Wimbush, 119). Cf. Diogenes Laertius 2.27: "Socrates used to say that the fewer his needs, the nearer he was to the gods" (Downing, *Christ and the Cynics,* 69).

10. See ps-Crates, *ep.* 18 (my translation; Wimbush, 119).

11. Cf. McEleney, "Beatitudes," 8.

12. See Teles II.34–36 (O'Neil, 8). Cf. Xenophon, *mem.* 1.6.5.

13. Cf. the discussion of the "macarism of the wise man" (in fact, "anti-macarism") by Betz, *Essays,* 30–33 (with reference *inter alios* to the Cynics): "it is consciously formulated in opposition to the conventional macarism and stands its values on its head." For Diogenes "defacing the currency," see above, p. 150, n. 42. New Testament scholars have more frequently claimed that promised in 6:20b is an eschatological "reversal" of earthly fortune. See, e.g., Braun, *Qumran,* 13: "According to the Lukan version [6:20] Jesus shares with Qumran the endtime ideal of poverty"; Dodd, "Beatitudes," 4–6 (regarding the combination of "makarisms" and woes in Luke 6:20b–26). Dodd ("Beatitudes," 5) suggests that "All this has its setting in the secular thought of the time," citing Toynbee's discussion (*Study of History,* 4:245–61) of "the conception of περιπέτεια in the changing Hellenistic society."

14. See above, pp. 33–36.

15. For Cynic belief in the conquest of *eudaimonia* through living *kata physin,* see Hoïstad, *Cynic Hero,* 132–35. Cf. Plutarch, *de esu carnium,* 995 C–D: *ton bion apothēriōsai;* Détienne, *Dionysos mis à mort,* 159 n. 42 ("ensauvager la vie"); Baltzer, *Pythagoras,* 118: "um das menschliche Leben zur thierischen Wildheit zurückzuführen."

16. For the text of Q 11:2(–4), see Robinson, "Work Session 17 November 1989," 500; also idem, "Critical Text," 21–22.

17. See, e.g., Str.-B. 1:408–10; R. E. Brown, "Pater Noster," 229, 232 (though comparison with the Kaddish is not crucial to Brown's interpretation); Perrin, *Language of the Kingdom,* 28–29, 43, 47; Schürmann, "Zeugnis," 151:

"The peculiar nearness to the Kaddish could lead to the thought that Luke 11:2 par. Matt 6:9–10a was already a prayer of Jesus in Nazareth, which depended on a form of synagogue prayer and anticipated the Abba-address characteristic of Jesus"; Fitzmyer, *Luke,* 2:900; Manns, *La prière d'Israël,* 165. In his massive book on the Lord's prayer, Carmignac (*Recherches,* 32, 379) appears not to find this parallel worth much consideration. Another reason why the initial petitions in 11:2 are often read with one another over against the subsequent demands in 11:3–4 is the shift from use of the singular possessive pronoun "your" in 11:2 to the use of "us" and "our" in 11:3–4. This ignores, however, the close and complementary relationship that must exist between the opening vocative address of "Father" and the subsequent statement that "your name be honored."

18. See Jeremias, *Prayers of Jesus,* 98; further, idem, "Lord's Prayer," 144; idem, "Vaterunser," 1236; idem, *New Testament Theology,* 198. Cf. Petuchowski, *Lexicon,* 315–16: "It is more likely that both the Lord's Prayer as well as the Kaddish prayer created the combination of God's kingdom coming and the hallowing of the divine name from a common source, namely, Palestinian Jewish piety. This combination of ideas is finally also already contained in Ezek 38:23, whence the two first statements of the Kaddish prayer are otherwise borrowed."

19. See *Encyclopedia Judaica,* 10:661; further, Elbogen, *Gottesdienst,* 92 n. 527; J. Heinemann, "Prayers," 269: "already in regular use by the beginning of the fourth century as the prayer concluding the Haggadic sermon...its nucleus...and almost certainly also its beginning...are of Tannaitic origin." The effort by Fitzmyer (*Luke,* 2:901) to rescue the traditional comparison falls lame: "Even though many of the Jewish prayers that are often used for such comparisons...date from centuries well after the NT...and may have been themselves influenced by the NT forms, the parallels reveal the basically Jewish form and content of the prayer."

20. See Jeremias, *New Testament Theology,* 198. Cf. Elbogen, *Gottesdienst,* 94. The Aramaic of the Kaddish was not a colloquial dialect, but a cultured idiom spoken in the schools. The section of the Kaddish cited by Jeremias is not historically the first beginning of the prayer. The earliest attestation of the prayer is ca. 150 C.E. See Elbogen, *Gottesdienst,* 93; *Encyclopedia Judaica,* 10:661.

21. For Aramaic and Q, see above, p. 8, esp. n. 33.

22. See Jeremias, *New Testament Theology,* 198.

23. In fact, as already noted, the Kaddish "was not originally part of the synagogue service," but developed in the "academic setting" of rabbinic study, whence it "passed...to the synagogue." See, also, DiSante, *Jewish Prayer,* 172; Posner et al., *Jewish Liturgy,* 115; J. Heinemann, "Prayers."

24. See Jeremias, *New Testament Theology,* 198 n. 1; also idem, *Prayers of Jesus,* 98; idem, "Vaterunser," 1236.

25. See Elbogen, *Gottesdienst,* 93; also ibid., 96–97; further, De Sola Pool, *Kaddish,* XII.

26. See Jeremias, *New Testament Theology,* 198. According to Str.-B. (1:418) one never says in rabbinical literature, "May God's kingly reign come,"

but rather, "May it be revealed" or "reveal itself" or "appear." The single exception is apparently *Targ. Micah,* 4:8.

27. Cf. above, p. 165, n. 17.

28. Cf. the "eucharistic" interpretation of 11:3 by R. E. Brown, "Pater Noster," 241–43.

29. For other references to God as "father," see Downing, *Christ and the Cynics,* 51–52, esp. Dio Chrysostom, *or.* 36.36. Cf. the "much ado about nothing" in Jeremias, *Prayers of Jesus,* 11–65; also R. E. Brown, "Pater Noster," 225–28.

30. For a summary of the different interpretations of *epiousios,* see Fitzmyer, *Luke,* 2:904–6 (bibliography on pp. 908–9); Carmignac, *Recherches,* 121–43 (an extensive catalogue of opinions); R. E. Brown, "Pater Noster," 239–40; further, B. Metzger, "How Many Times?" 64–66; Jeremias, *New Testament Theology,* 199–201; Deissmann, "Ἐπιούσιος," in *Studien,* 115–19; also Boff, *Lord's Prayer,* 78–83, 103 n. 87. Metzger concludes that "the cautious lexicographer must perforce rely only on the context of the Lord's Prayer, on etymological considerations, and on patristic and versional evidence in seeking to ascertain the precise meaning of ἐπιούσιος." Cf. *Did* 11:4–6; Preisigke, *Sammelbuch,* 1:5224.

31. Cf. Epictetus, *diss.* 3.12.13; Heinen, "Göttliche Sitometrie," 72–79.

32. For the text of Q 11:(15–)20, see Moreland and Robinson, "Work Sessions 31 July–2 August, 20 November 1992," 503–4. (For 11:14, see Asgeirsson and Robinson, "Work Sessions 12–14 July, 22 November 1991," 503.)

33. See, e.g., Kloppenborg, *Formation,* 122.

34. The form-critical question as to which parts of 11:15–20 were and/or could (or could not) have once been independently transmitted as separate units should not obscure recognition of the unified argument that the text now constitutes as a whole (11:15–20). Indeed, insofar as the line of reasoning evident in the present arrangement of the sayings in 11:15–20 is as tightly coherent as I suggest, it is questionable how plausible it even is to posit a prior "circulation" of the different disarticulated member parts. Kloppenborg (*Formation,* 122–24) summarizes well the history of this discussion, but does not question its underlying assumptions about the "growth" of early Christian tradition. Cf. Robbins, "Rhetorical Composition." The different versions of the Beelzebul controversy in Matt 9:32–34; 12:22–37; Mark 3:19a–30; Luke 11:18–28 are all read by Robbins as variable instances of epideictic rhetoric.

35. The charge of practicing "black" magic is not uncommonly hurled at one another by competing "traditional" healers. See, e.g., Malina and Neyrey, *Calling Jesus Names,* 3–32; Taussig, *Shamanism,* passim (remarking the relationship between envy and the suspicion of sorcery).

36. Kloppenborg (*Formation,* 124–25) interprets the "assertion" in 11:19b that "therefore they will be your judges" as a direct threat to those who have accused Jesus and his followers of practicing black magic, on the assumption that the Q composition here (11:19b) "changes its rhetorical posture" from an initial exposure of the absurdity of the Beelzebul accusation "and shifts to the offensive, declaring that Israel's heedlessness of divine activity will lead to her

eschatological condemnation." This interpretation, however, does not cohere especially well with Kloppenborg's own tradition-historical assessment of an original break between 11:19 and 11:20, as "successive additions to the core" (11:[14], 15, 17–18a). It also fails to observe how the expression, *dia touto,* in 11:19b suggests, in fact, not a "shift" but continuity: the next (and final) step in a process of deductive reasoning, which is the preceding *reductio ad absurdum.* Are we furthermore really to imagine that the Q people presumed that the "sons" of their accusers would actually judge the "fathers," rather than understanding this "logical conclusion" to be instead a highly effective way of underscoring the deep impossibility of the accusation in the first place? In Q 11:31–32, to which Kloppenborg appeals for parallel support, the Queen of the South and the Ninevites are hardly in the same relationship to the members of "this generation" as are "your sons" to the accusers in the Beelzebul controversy. For "your sons" as meaning simply "your people" and referring to the "forgotten" fact of other Jewish exorcists, see Fitzmyer, *Luke,* 2:921. For the expression, "finger of God," in 11:20a, see ibid., 2:922; further, Deissmann, *Light,* 306; George, "Note"; Couroyer, "Le 'doigt de Dieu.'" Cf. Q 11:46, where the Pharisees are charged with loading burdens hard to bear on people, "and you yourselves do not move your finger."

37. It is sometimes thought that the verb *ephthasen,* translated here as "appeared," differs significantly in meaning from the similar verb, *ēggiken,* used in parallel statements (Q 10:9; Mark 1:15). But see above, p. 155, n. 114. Cf. Fitzmyer, *Luke,* 2:922. For the same reason, 11:20 has often been seen as important for the (various) quest(s) of the historical Jesus, though typically the preceding account of healing and polemical exchange in 11:14–19, at least in its present form, is not accorded equal "authenticity." Nonetheless, it is this literary context that has plainly influenced interpretation of 11:20 as somehow an "apocalyptic/eschatological" utterance.

38. For the "kingdom of Satan," see Kruse, "Reich Satans."

39. Cf. Otto, "Kingdom of God Expels Kingdom of Satan." Note, however, that it is especially the "parable" about the kingdom divided against itself in Luke 11:21–22 par. that Otto's interpretation primarily rides on — a text, in my opinion, not originally in Q. Cf. Kloppenborg, *Parallels,* 92; Moreland and Robinson, "Work Sessions 31 July–2 August, 20 November 1992," 504.

40. The interpretation of *ara* by Otto ("Kingdom of God Expels Kingdom of Satan," 30–31) begins similarly, but then quickly gets lost in groundless speculation. See, further, Vaage, "Ethos and Ethics," 486 n. 39.

41. For the text of Q 12:(22–)31, see Moreland and Robinson, "Work Sessions 31 July–2 August, 20 November 1992," 504–5.

42. 12:31 is never referred to, for example, in any of the essays in Chilton, *Kingdom of God,* except for the introduction by Chilton himself, who describes the saying (12:31) as one of the texts in which "Nothing is said about the kingdom" (p. 3). Dillon ("Ravens, Lilies, and the Kingdom of God") simply assumes the traditional scholarly apocalyptic/eschatological interpretation of the kingdom of God in the preaching of Jesus, in order to explore in the present instance its relation to Jesus' ethical instruction.

43. A certain tension exists in the saying as a whole between the earlier

examples of the ravens and the lilies, which presumably do no work in order
to be fed and clothed, and the final injunction to "seek," which presumably
requires some effort.

44. 12:22–31 neither advocates subsistence as a way of life nor program-
matically denounces such a condition as obviously "inhuman," insisting on its
immediate amelioration as a substandard living situation. Rather, the saying
simply takes for granted as "just the way things are" the ancient social reality
of precarious supply with its attendant anxieties and preoccupations and, in the
midst of this obviously difficult set of circumstances, proposes how to achieve
a fuller form of contentment. Cf. Schottroff, *Hope of the Poor,* 38–66.

45. Solomon is the only Old Testament "personality" to be mentioned in
Q's formative stratum. All others (few in number though they be) belong to the
document's redactional layer. See Vaage, "Son of Man Sayings," 121–22.

46. For the disreputable character of ravens in antiquity, see Fitzmyer,
Luke, 2:978. The bird (*korax*) is mentioned only here (Luke 12:24) in the
New Testament. Cf. Ps 147:9; Job 38:41; Lev 11:15; Deut 14:14. See, further,
Servius on Virgil, *Georg.* 1.414 (Thilo, 3.209); Fuchs, "Verkündigung Jesus,"
385–88; Schulz, *Spruchquelle,* 150: "unreines Tier." Cf. Pliny the Elder, *nat.
hist.* 35.7.23.

47. For the Cynic way of life as being "in accordance with nature," see
above, p. 165, n. 15. For characterization of this way of life as a "short-cut"
to virtue and felicity, see above, p. 146, n. 64.

48. See Dio Chrysostom, *or.* 10.15–16; further, ibid., 6.31–34. For other
parallels, see Downing, *Christ and the Cynics,* 68–71: "Apart from references
to the short life of grass — Isa. 40.7–8, etc. — there seem to be no close Jewish
parallels" (p. 68).

49. See Seneca, *de ben.* 7.10.6.

50. For the text of Q 13:18–19, see Robinson, "Work Session 16 November 1990," 497. Cf. McArthur, "Mustard Seed," 200; Laufen, *Doppelüberlieferung,* 176; Fleddermann, "Mustard Seed and Leaven," 224.

51. Cf. Kloppenborg's *vorgeschichtliche Vermutungen* in "Parables of
Jesus." Of course, discussion also continues about the "original" meaning of
these sayings *im Munde Jesu.* See, e.g., Scott, *Hear Then the Parable,* 373–87;
Crossan, *Historical Jesus,* 276–79.

52. I obviously disagree with the tradition of New Testament scholarship for which the parables of Jesus as a form of speech and the kingdom
of God as a "world-shattering" experience are *mutatis mutandis* two sides
of the same coin. See, e.g., Dodd, *Parables;* Jüngel, *Paulus und Jesus,* 87–
174, esp. pp. 135ff; Crossan, *In Parables,* 23–36, esp. pp. 27 and 35; Scott,
Jesus, Symbol-Maker; idem, *Hear Then the Parable,* 56–62, esp. pp. 61–62.
Cf. Perrin, *Rediscovering,* 83: "It is a remarkable and little noted fact that,
pace Jüngel, there is only a very limited number of parables which are concerned to proclaim the Kingdom of God *per se*"; further, Breech, *Silence,* 71:
"Luke's versions of these two parables [13:18–19, 20–21] show that the Q
community understood both the mustard seed and the leaven as illustrations
of the way the community grew and spread in the ancient world. The Q versions of these parables, then, together with their introductions, give evidence

of early Christian thinking, but do not provide evidence of how Jesus might have connected the kingdom and his parables." In fact, Breech (*Silence,* 76–78) argues that the "original" version of Q 13:18–19, 20–21 on the lips of Jesus had nothing whatsoever to do with the kingdom of God at all. Bultmann (*History,* 174–75) questions whether the sayings in 13:18–19, 20–21 are even "parables": "All the same [despite a certain narrative aspect] these similitudes describe typical events, so that they do not amount to parables." A parable, according to Bultmann's rephrasing of Jülicher's definition, "gives as its picture not a typical condition or a typical, recurrent event, but some interesting particular situation." The suggestion by Kloppenborg ("Parables of Jesus") that "the two parables [13:18–19, 20–21] served as a conclusion for Q 12:2–12, 13–14, 16–21, 22–31, 33–34, *visualizing* the process of the disclosure of the kingdom,... [and] would, then, function in much the same way as 6:47–49 to provide a concluding visualization and 'witness' for the preceding argument," is thoroughly compatible with my perspective, only narrower in scope regarding the discourse in Q that it clarifies. Note that as Kloppenborg describes the place of 13:18–19, 20–21 in Q's formative stratum, the two parables would have been almost directly appended to the preceding kingdom-of-God saying in 12:22–31. Only 12:33–34 intervenes between the longer exhortation not to worry about food and clothing and the two short examples in 13:18–19, 20–21 illustrating or explaining more precisely the sense of the final rationale in 12:31, namely, "seek his kingdom and everything else will be yours as well."

53. Cf. Kuss, "Sinngehalt," esp. p. 651. For the category of "growth parable," see Dodd, *Parables,* 131ff; also Dahl, "Parables of Growth." The appropriateness of this category, "growth parable," to 13:18–19, 20–21 has been questioned by Crossan, *In Parables,* 50–51, who proposes instead "parable of advent." See idem, *Historical Jesus,* 278: "The point is not just that it starts small and ends big but that its bigness is not exactly a horticultural or agricultural desideratum." See also Scott, *Hear Then the Parable,* 383. According to Kloppenborg ("Parables of Jesus") following Laufen (*Doppelüberlieferung,* 178), the reference to the person (*anthrōpos*) who sows the mustard seed in the Q version of the parable (versus Mark 4:31; *GThom* 20) is a significant innovation, assimilating the structure of 13:19–20 to the parable of the leaven in 13:20–21. But beyond underscoring the fact of human agency in the process described, the basic point remains one of "results out of proportion to the initial state."

54. Much ink has been spilled on the question of exactly what kind of mustard seed is referred to in 13:18–19, as well as how such a seed was perceived in antiquity. On the "mustard" seed's precise botanical identity, see, e.g., Jülicher, *Gleichnisreden,* 575–76; Sproule, "Mustard Seed"; Pace, "La senapa del vangelo"; Granata, "La sinapis del vangelo"; idem, "Some More Information"; Oakman, *Economic Questions,* 124; Crossan, *Historical Jesus,* 278. For perceptions of the mustard plant in antiquity, see Scott, *Hear Then the Parable,* 380–81. Reference is otherwise commonly made to Pliny the Elder, *nat. hist.* 19.170f; 20.236ff; Theophrastus, *Enquiry into Plants,* 7.1.3. Jülicher (*Gleichnisreden,* 575) also refers to Dioscorides, *de mat. med.* 1.47; 2.183.

55. For the question whether or not anyone and, if so, who in ancient Palestine would have actually *sown* mustard seed, see Cotter, "Mustard Seed and Leaven," 50 n. 18: "Mustard was indeed cultivated in Palestine, as proved by the decision to introduce Egyptian mustard (a much better quality) into Palestine's agriculture" (vs. Oakman, *Economic Questions,* 125). In support of her position, Cotter refers to Heichelheim, "Roman Syria," 4:132, whose evidence, however, is limited to a single passage from the Mishnah (*m. Kilaim,* 1.2). Cf. Scott, *Hear Then the Parable,* 376: the action of the man in 13:18–19 is "at odds with the requirements of Palestinian custom as represented in the *Kalayim* . . . a metaphor of impurity: the planting of mustard seed in a garden." See, further, ibid., 381–83. For such sowing as a furtive act, like the "hiding" of the leaven in 13:21, see below, pp. 64–65. Cf. Kloppenborg, "Parables of Jesus" n. 99.

56. For the tenaciousness of mustard, see Pliny the Elder, *nat. hist.* 19.170: "when it has once been sown it is scarcely possible to get the place free of it, as the seed when it falls germinates at once." Cf. Theophrastus, *Enquiry into Plants,* 7.1.3: cress (*kardamon*) and mustard (*napy*) are said to take five days to germinate. For the "sowing" of seed as a stock metaphor in Greco-Roman antiquity for teaching, see Mack, *Myth of Innocence,* 159–60. Cf. Crossan, *Historical Jesus,* 278: "The point, in other words, is not just that the mustard plant starts as a proverbially small seed and grows into a shrub of three or four feet, or even higher, it is that it tends to take over where it is not wanted, that it tends to get out of control, and that it tends to attract birds within cultivated areas where they are not particularly desired."

57. For the phrase "birds of the air nested in its branches," see Ezek 17:22–24; 31:3, 6; Dan 4:10–12; Ps 104:12ff. Cf., further, Scott, *Hear Then the Parable,* 386: the contrast between the parable of the mustard seed and the actual content of the biblical passages alluded to with the reference to the birds nesting in its branches "burlesques the expectation of the kingdom under the symbol of the cedar or apocalyptic tree"; Crossan, *In Parables,* 48 (regarding Mark 4:31): "When one starts a parable with a mustard seed one cannot end it with a tree, much less the great apocalyptic tree, unless, of course, one plans to lampoon rather rudely the whole apocalyptic tradition." For Cynic criticism of Homeric epic, see *Pap. Genev.* 271; Kakridis, "Cynic Homeromastix."

58. For the text of Q 13:20–21, see Robinson, "Work Session 16 November 1990," 497.

59. Cf. Bultmann, *History,* 194–95; Jeremias, *Parables,* 90ff.

60. Significance is often attributed to the fact that in 13:20–21 the "actress" is a woman, whereas in 13:18–19 the actor is a man, with the corresponding gender-specific roles of domestic life in 13:20–21 versus agriculture in 13:18–19. See, e.g., Waller, "Leaven"; Schottroff, "Wanderprophetinnen," 335–38. Cf. the dissenting appraisal by Levine, "Feminist Food for Thought"; also idem, "Who's Catering the Q Affair?" It is striking how the same pattern of man/woman (male/female) repeats itself elsewhere in Q. See, e.g., 11:31, where a woman, the "queen of the south," comes to hear the wisdom of Solomon, while in 11:32 it is "the men of Nineveh" who repent at the preaching of Jonah. In 17:34, the "two men on a couch," one of whom will be taken, one

left, are followed by "two women grinding/in a field," one of whom will be taken, one left. Both of the latter groups of sayings belong to Q's redaction (see below, appendix one). Cf., further, 15:4–7 [8–10]; 17:26–27 [28–29] (the sayings in square brackets are found only in Luke).

61. Growth occurs in both 13:18–19 and 13:20–21. But growth is not the main point, not the focus of attention, not the governing interest. Of primary importance is, rather, the stark contrast between the way some things first appear and what they finally prove to be.

62. Cf. Kloppenborg, "Parables of Jesus": "there is an ineluctable process at work that will bring to fruition what was initially small and hidden."

63. See, e.g., Scott, Hear Then the Parable, 61, 324–29; Levine, "Feminist Food for Thought," 13.

64. Cf. Cotter, "Mustard Seed and Leaven," 43; Oakman, Economic Questions, 128.

Chapter Four
Critique: "Woe to You ... "

1. For a brief review of form criticism of the "woe," see Schulz, Spruchquelle, 62. According to this research, the "woe" was either part of the teaching of wisdom regarding who was "blessed" (or unblessed), or a way of cursing, rendering prophetic judgment, or giving apocalyptic warning. For the "woe" as part of "wisdom," according to Schulz, see, e.g., Amos 5:18; 6:1; Isa 5; 28–33; Hab 2. As part of apocalyptic "curse" and "judgment," see, e.g., 1 En. 92ff; 94.6, 7, 8; 95.5ff; 96.4–8. For the "woes" in Q, see, further, Bultmann, History, 113–14; Berger, Formgeschichte, 202–7. Curiously, the term ouai is not discussed in TDNT, neither in the English translation nor in the German original.

2. See, e.g., Matt 23:1–39; further, below, p. 173, n. 12; also Haenchen, "Matthäus 23"; Kümmel, "Weherufe"; Freudenberg, "Weherufe"; Pesch, "Redaktion von Matthäus 23"; Garland, Intention; Vaage, "Woes in Q," 602–4.

3. By "social debate and interactive conflict," I mean the "steady" state of ongoing social "tensions," constant bickering, interested squabbling, sometimes heated exchange, and the perennial mix-up of envy and desire forming part of every human group. For conflict of this sort as typical of most societies, see, e.g., Taussig, Shamanism, chap. 25: "Envy and Implicit Social Knowledge," 393–412; Bolton and Bolton, Conflictos. Cf. Horsley, Sociology, versus the calming effects of Theissen's "functionalist" approach to the study of early Palestinian Christianity with its heavy investment in social integration and control. See, also, Malina, New Testament World, 20: "Wherever there is social life, there is conflict."

4. For the woes in 11:39–48, 52 as part of Q's formative stratum, see below, appendix one. For a recent "tradition-historical" interpretation of the growth of these sayings, see Jolliffe, "Woes on the Pharisees." Cf. Mark 12:38–40.

5. For the text of Q 11:39–48, 52, unless otherwise indicated, see Asgeirsson and Robinson, "Work Sessions 12–14 July, 22 November 1991," 504–5.

6. For the order of Q 11:39–41, 42 and the wording of 11:40–41: "Clean the inside...," see below, appendix two.

7. For 11:42d as due to Q's tertiary redaction, see below, appendix one. Against the inclusion of 11:43 in Q, see below, appendix two.

8. By "critical literature," I mean every sort of writing that comments critically or passes judgment on something else. Criticism is nonetheless not inevitably an alien or alienating activity, though obviously it may be. Criticism is also an integral part of the process whereby a given group or set of persons define for themselves a social identity. It is the means whereby different members of a particular human network determine how they will relate to one another. For the woes in Q 11:39–41, 42, see Kloppenborg, *Formation,* 140: "The dispute with the Pharisees is still *intra muros.*" See also Schulz, *Spruchquelle,* 113: "because even their sharpest critique of Pharisaism proves 'finally to be an inner-Jewish critique.'"

9. The two styles of interpretation could be characterized as follows. On the one hand, there is the effort to determine exactly what a given saying is driving at. The other kind of interpretation asks: And what does the fact that the saying is driving at such and such in these terms tell us about the author(s), those opposed to and/or by it, the cultural situation in which both speaker and audience were originally found? Cf. Bultmann, "Problem of Hermeneutics."

10. See, e.g., Schulz, *Spruchquelle,* 94–114; further, Heinrichs, "Komposition der Weherede"; Beilner, *Christus und die Pharisäer,* 200–235; Schürmann, "Redekomposition." Cf. Kloppenborg, "*Nomos* and *Ethos.*" Kloppenborg makes it clear that concern in Q for the Torah emerged, if at all, only at the latest (tertiary) stage of its composition-history. For a critique of previous scholarship in this regard, see ibid., esp. pp. 35–37. Neusner ("'Israel'") demonstrates how volatile the notion of Israel was and remained within early Judaisms.

11. For a more down-to-earth portrait of the Pharisees, see M. Smith, "Palestinian Judaism"; idem, *Palestinian Parties and Politics;* Neusner, *From Politics to Piety;* Saldarini, *Pharisees, Scribes and Sadducees,* esp. chap. 12. It is amazing how little we actually know about the Pharisees in the first century c.e. See Mack, *Myth of Innocence,* 41–44.

12. Cf. Minear, "False Prophecy and Hypocrisy." At stake for Matthew is the question of who may rightfully sit on "the chair of Moses" (Matt 23:2). For this reason, only in Matthew (23:13, 14, 15) are the terms "hypocrite" and similar forms of personal abuse found in the context of the woes (*pace* Luke/Q [?] 11:40 — *aphrones*). Only in Matthew (23:8–12) is there an extended discussion of the use of social titles. Only in Matthew (23:13–22) is the subject of leadership of primary importance (thus in vv. 16–22, the credibility of the opponents' legal judgments is questioned; see, further, v. 23). Only in Matthew (23:24) does the discourse finally degenerate down to outright insult: "You blind guides, straining out a gnat and swallowing a camel."

13. Again, it is not because the Pharisees somehow officially represented

"Israel" that they are made the object of Q's woes. During the first century C.E., the Pharisees were but one of a number of groups in Palestine vying for the privilege of defining early "Judaism" and looking for wider recognition in this regard. As a religious/political party, they had perhaps six thousand members (thus, in any case, Str.-B. 4:335; see Josephus, *Ant.* 17.2–4). Instead of concern for the "conventional" or "convenanted" ethos, many scholars prefer to speak of "purity" regarding the Pharisees. From an anthropological point of view, these terms are essentially equivalent, insofar as they all equally have to do with the ratification of a particular way of life through sanctified strictures that are never "merely 'ritual,'" the mere keeping of certain rites as a formality" (see Neusner, "'First Cleanse the Inside,'" 494 n. 2; further, idem, *Idea of Purity*).

14. I neither wish to depict the Pharisees as ancient religious "fascists" nor to make of Q a "freedom-fighter's" document (both postures, in any case, typically amount to the same thing). It was rather the "totalizing" urge in the intellectual and spiritual program of the Pharisees that I suggest the "woes" in Q sought to upset. Insofar as the fundamental urge behind the Pharisees' approach to Jewish social life and identity was an ideal of complete "integrity" or "coherence" — the full elaboration of the Torah — the woes in Q would represent an "anarchist" or "antinomian" vision for which the successful achievement of total compliance with the law could only mean the triumph of tyranny and the orderly imposition of complete unhappiness.

15. Cf. Kloppenborg, "*Nomos* and *Ethos,*" 39: "While Q 11:39–41 acknowledges the Pharisaic distinction regarding cups, it immediately reduces this distinction to an absurd caricature and diverts the discussion onto an ethical plane by treating vessels as metaphors."

16. Cf. Downing, *Christ and the Cynics,* 64. The woe in 11:39–41 is said to be like other Cynic and Stoic texts that contrast inner reality with "mere" externals.

17. The cited parallels are not meant to be exhaustive. For rabbinic literature, see Neusner, "'First Cleanse the Inside'"; also Maccoby, "Washing of Cups." Jolliffe ("Woes on the Pharisees," 132) refers, in addition, to *Test. Mos.* 7.3–10; Epictetus, *diss.* 4.11; Diogenes Laertius 6.64.

18. See Diogenes Laertius 6.42.

19. See Julian, *or.* 6.196d.

20. See Diogenes Laertius 6.61.

21. See Diogenes Laertius 6.63.

22. See Diogenes Laertius 6.66.

23. See Diogenes Laertius 6.73.

24. See *P.Oxy.* 840.2; Kloppenborg, *Parallels,* 109. The rest of the saying (*P.Oxy.* 840.2) is a separate debate about the nature of true baptism, unrelated to the topic of 11:39–41.

25. See *GThom* 89; Layton, *Gnostic Scriptures,* 395 (slightly modified).

26. See ps-Phocylides 228; Charlesworth, *Old Testament Pseudepigrapha,* 2:582. For further discussion, see Kloppenborg, "*Nomos* and *Ethos,*" 40.

27. Julian equates a philosophical truism in antiquity, namely, that the mind was the divine part of the human being, with the distinctive wit and

repartee whereby the Cynics both defended themselves under attack and aggressively observed the multiple signs of incongruity in their contemporaries' thought and practice.

28. For a discussion of Cynic shamelessness, see Vaage, "Like Dogs Barking."

29. For the ancient Mediterranean world as an honor-shame culture, see Malina, *New Testament World*, 25–50; Crossan, *Historical Jesus*, 9–15: "I employ the category 'honor-shame' only in the most general sense, namely, as a term for human cultures in which social recognition and acknowledgment together with gender-specific roles are key to determining personal identity."

30. Cf. Foucault, *Use of Pleasure*, 54–57.

31. Cynic speech about living "in accordance with nature" should not be confused with the later (eighteenth- and nineteenth-century) Romantic opposition between Nature and Culture, insofar as *physis* for the Cynics meant simply everything not recognized by the ancient aristocratic male ethos as normative and good, a view thus capable of including many aspects of "ordinary" social experience as well.

32. Greek — "Western" — ethnography begins with the travels and writings of Herodotus (484–424 B.C.E.). For a brief discussion, see J. Z. Smith, "Adde Parvum," 244–49.

33. Cf. Mack, *Myth of Innocence*, 73–74.

34. The fact that water is used at all as a symbol of purification has some irony, given that it is also one of the best ways to communicate disease. This observation, however, lacks historical weight, to the degree that the knowledge of water as a means of bacteriological transmission is a recent discovery.

35. Cf. Miller, "The Inside Is (Not) the Outside." That Luke 11:40 does not preserve the original wording of Q, see below, appendix two.

36. At stake in both *GThom* 89 and Luke 11:40 is a different understanding of reality, one that rejects every system of purity in the name of a higher order. Thus, in *GThom* 89, the question is asked point-blank: "Why are you washing the outside of the cup?" Even though this is precisely the part of the vessel most likely to become contaminated. The point here is not the need to do a thorough job=Matt 23:26, but, rather: Why do it at all? In Luke 11:41, a program of moral uprightness is advocated, symbolized by giving "what is inside" as alms (or alms "internally"). In this way, any and all concerns about purity are taken care of: "and behold everything will be clean for you." The dismantling of the pure/impure mentality is less frontal in Luke 11:40–41 than in *GThom* 89, but the basic point remains the same.

37. Cf. Kloppenborg, "*Nomos* and *Ethos*," 39: "Q 11:39–41 indeed betrays knowledge of the Pharisaic view that in matters of purity, vessels are divided into inner and outer parts. Neusner ["First Cleanse the Inside"] has convincingly demonstrated that the Q saying can only be directed at the Shammaite opinion (which was dominant before 70 C.E.) that the inside and outside of cups function autonomously and that either or both might be clean or unclean." This perspective is not opposed to my interpretation. As both Kloppenborg and Neusner describe the saying, 11:39–41 would state that one cannot speak about distinct or autonomous zones of purity (versus Shammai)

as though the outside of a vessel were clean while the inside were not or vice versa. I simply go one step further in the same direction, arguing that 11:39–41 makes an even stronger claim that the very idea of the inner versus the outer parts of vessels is mistaken. 11:39–41 would thus disagree with the Pharisaic view in general, taking the Shammaite opinion as exemplary. For criticism of Neusner's view, see Jolliffe, "Woes on the Pharisees," 135 n. 154.

38. See Kloppenborg, "Nomos and Ethos," 42: like 11:39–41, 11:42 also engages "in rhetorical exaggeration and caricature. That it accurately reflects current tithing practice is most unlikely. Even a cursory glance at the Mishnaic discussions of tithing is sufficient to indicate that there was no unanimity in regard to the liability of any of the items of 11:42a." Indeed, rabbinical literature itself refers to the kind of behavior lampooned in 11:42 as the mark of a "stupid piety." See Str.-B. 4:336–37; further, Jolliffe, "Woes on the Pharisees," 119–25. Cf. Sir 35:9; Diogenes Laertius 6.48. At the same time, 11:42 does not oppose tithing as such. Registered is, therefore, not the opinion of the 'am-mei ha'aretz, who apparently repudiated the practice as such (see Str.-B. 4:335), perhaps because they experienced it (not incorrectly) as just another means of taxation.

39. See Diogenes Laertius 6.28.

40. See Diogenes Laertius 6.42.

41. See Diogenes Laertius 6.63.

42. See Diogenes Laertius 6.45.

43. See Diogenes Laertius 6.37.

44. See Diogenes Laertius 6.59.

45. See ps-Crates, ep. 5.

46. In the first saying (3.1) Diogenes claims to be motivated by the "[wish] to free her [the woman found in a compromising position at prayer] of superstition." The topic of superstition enjoyed a wide discussion in antiquity and was the pretext for many disputes about diverse "religious" practices. See, e.g., Wilken, Christians as the Romans Saw Them, 22, 48–54.

47. For the concept of rabbinic tradition as a "hedge around Torah," see m. Abot, 1.1.

48. Such distinctions are, of course, neither fair nor innocent. Governing perception here is the textual juxtaposition of 11:42 and ps-Crates, ep. 5. Both perspectives may finally be in error regarding the positions they opposed.

49. Cf. Kloppenborg, "Nomos and Ethos," 42: "Neither Q's criticism of the Pharisees nor its counterproposal is obviously nomocentric."

50. Kloppenborg ("Law and Salvation," 7) equates "the accusation that the Pharisees are 'unmarked graves'" with "corpse-uncleanness...employed as a metaphor for moral failing." He then continues: "Clearly, this woe takes for granted that Pharisees are concerned with purity. Otherwise it would have no rhetorical effect. The idea of purity remains important for Q, but it is redefined in exclusively ethical terms. It is even doubtful, in view of Q 9:59–60, that the traditional taboos associated with a corpse are given any importance. While Q knows of, and plays on, Pharisaic ideas of purity, there is no indication that it accepts them as valid."

51. For an interpretation of the burdens (*phortia*) referred to here as principally, though not exclusively, a matter of taxation (*phoros*), see Jolliffe, "Woes on the Pharisees," 77–83, esp. p. 78 n. 71.

52. See Diogenes Laertius 6.27–28.

53. See ps-Anacharsis, *ep.* 7 (to Tereus, the cruel despot of Thrace).

54. This is not a *vaticinium ex eventu*. The fate described here hardly anticipates the subsequent history of the Jews and Judaism. All I have done is try to express how the practice of leadership by the Pharisees might have looked to certain of their regional critics in the first century C.E. See, further, Jolliffe, "Woes on the Pharisees," 76–89.

55. Q 11:47–48 is yet another example of the importance of burial in the ancient world. Burial was an event that, because of its pervasive practice (everyone dies) and high estimation (defining one's final social status), could be referred to in a number of different ways in order to focus comment on a range of issues. Cf. Q 9:59–60; 2 Kgs 13:21; Sir 46:11–12; 48:13–14; 49:10; *GThom* 52.

56. Cf. Jeremias, *Heiligengräber;* further, idem, "Drei weitere Heiligengräber."

57. See Diogenes Laertius 6.78–79.

58. See ps-Aeschines, *ep.* 14 (to Xenophon).

59. See Teles VII.91f (O'Neil, 66).

60. For the quote, see Diogenes Laertius 6.69. Regarding Cynic shamelessness, see above, p. 175, n. 28.

61. Cf. Helgeland, "Civil Religion, Military Religion," 38: "Unlike any other war monument this one has become a cult, and it is in Washington, the sacred center"; also "Harper's Index," 15: "Number of walls the size of the Vietnam Memorial it would take to list all the Vietnamese who died in the war: 69."

62. See Jolliffe, "Woes on the Pharisees," 103–4.

63. See *GThom* 102.

64. See Diogenes Laertius 6.39.

65. See *GThom* 39. Additional parallels include 1 QH 4.11: "And they [the preachers of lies and seers of deceit] have withheld the draught of knowledge from the thirsty ones..." (Kloppenborg, *Formation,* 142 n. 176).

66. Kloppenborg (*Formation,* 142) opines: "the second part [of 11:52] implies that the scribes have deliberately and maliciously conspired to prevent entry into the kingdom." In a footnote (*Formation,* 142 n. 175) Kloppenborg goes on to say: "The agreement between Matt and Luke in the use of οὐκ εἰσέρχεσθε (εἰσήλθατε)...τοὺς εἰσερχομένους suggests that the original saying concerned entry into the kingdom. Luke may have altered 'kingdom' to 'knowledge' because of reluctance to attribute the kingdom to lawyers." This begs the question.

67. Cf. Jolliffe, "Woes on the Pharisees," 107.

Chapter Five
Memory: John and Jesus

1. I make no claim to be describing the "historical" John or Jesus, at least not as the term "historical" is usually understood in this regard. Nonetheless, I confess that I believe that the memory of Q's formative stratum is at least as reliable a source of information as any of the other early Christian textual traditions typically employed for the purposes of this distinctly modern (christological) undertaking. My main point, however, is simply that the way in which we currently remember significant figures of "our" past reveals much about the way in which we presently see ourselves here and now. At the level of social group formation, shared or repressed memory traditions are an integral part of the construction of a corporate identity. See, e.g., Davis, *Times and Identities*. For a brief discussion of what I mean by "peculiar," see Vaage, "Q¹ and the Historical Jesus," 161–63.

2. For the text of Q 7:31–35, see Cotter, "Parable of the Children," 293. For 7:33–34 as part of Q's formative stratum, see below, appendix one.

3. See Vaage, "Q¹ and the Historical Jesus," 163–64.

4. See, further, below, p. 183, n. 68.

5. Cf., however, John 7:20; 8:48, 49, 52; 10:20, 21. Q 7:33 is obviously not the only place in the synoptic tradition where demon-possession is discussed, but nowhere else is it referred to in this fashion.

6. See, e.g., Teles II.30ff (O'Neil, 8); II.114ff (O'Neil, 12); IVA.117–19 (O'Neil, 40); IVA.180ff (O'Neil, 44f); ps-Crates, *ep*. 14, 18; ps-Diogenes, *ep*. 26, 37, 44; Diogenes Laertius 6.104.

7. See Diogenes Laertius 6.54. The accusation of "insanity" is, of course, a common way of characterizing and thereby dismissing practices of social nonconformity and dissent.

8. I do not therefore assume, however, that the historical Jesus necessarily referred to himself as the "son of man." I merely mean that the formative stratum of Q had Jesus in mind when, in 7:34, the "son of man" is mentioned. Who else would it be, especially in contrast with John? This use of the term "son of man" is admittedly peculiar. See Hare, *Son of Man Tradition*, 247, 259–61; Vaage, "Son of Man Sayings," 121–23. Cf. Collins, "Origin." At the same time, repeated use of the same term "son of man" in Ezekiel, referring to the prophet himself, makes clear that the expression "son of man" need not inevitably have implied reference to a superhuman figure. Cf. Luria, "Quelle," 284 n. 1, who refers to an Egyptian text in Golenischchev, *Les papyrus hiératiques*, 7.

9. To my knowledge, no one questions that the two halves of 7:33–34 always formed a single unit. The differences between John and Jesus were not a problem for Q's formative stratum. Only at the level of the document's secondary redaction did it become important hierarchically to define the dynamic duo's relationship to one another as dissimilar predecessors.

10. In fact, the term *phagos* appears to be unknown before Q 7:34. See Liddell and Scott, *Greek-English Lexicon, ad loc.*; Arndt et al., *Greek-English Lexicon, ad loc.*; further, von Leutsch and Schneidewin, *Corpus Paroemiogra-*

phorum Graecorum, 26 ll. 4–5 (no. 73); Lentz, *Herodiani Technici Reliquiae,* 140 ll. 4–5; Schmidt, *Hesychii Alexandrini Lexicon,* 4:184; Eustathius, *Commentarii ad Homeri* 1630 (Stallbaum, 343 l. 17). The term *phagos* likely derives from the older longer word, *adēphagos,* which means essentially the same thing. See, e.g., Sophocles, *Philoctetes* 314; Kock, *Comicorum Atticorum Fragmenta,* 251 no. 84 (Hermippus); ibid., 761 no. 21 (Alcaeus); Callimachus, *Hymn to Artemis* 3.160.

11. On the other hand, both Luke and John speak frequently of friends. The theme was otherwise widely discussed.

12. See Kloppenborg, *Parallels,* 214, 231.

13. Cf. the slave in 12:45 who says in his heart, "My master is delayed," and begins to beat the other servants and to eat and drink and get drunk/with the drunkards: i.e., *oinopotēs* (7:34) and *meta tōn methyontōn/methyskesthai* (12:45). For 12:42–46 and 17:27 as part of Q's redaction, see below, appendix one. For the moral connotations of "eating and drinking" in antiquity, see Malherbe, *Paul and the Popular Philosophers,* 84–85. For a discussion of Jesus' indiscriminate "commensality," see Crossan, *Historical Jesus,* 341–44; also D. E. Smith, "Historical Jesus at Table," esp. pp. 477–85.

14. Cf. the Cynic "Cynulcus" in Athenaeus's *Deipnosophistae,* whose greater interest in eating than in observing the literate conventions of the depicted symposium earned him, among other names, the epithet "pot-bellied dog" (*gastros kyōn,* 4.160e). He was thus to be fed like other dogs with bones, bread, and scraps (3.96f–97a, 114a; 6.270d) and was disparaged by at least one detractor as being simply a voracious hound (13.611b–c). For further discussion, see Hock, "Dog in the Manger." Cf. also the description of the labors of dissociation later required in Syria in order to establish the reputation of a "holy man," in P. Brown, "Holy Man in Late Antiquity," esp. p. 131: the accomplished holy man's "attitude to food itself rejected all the ties of solidarity to kin and village that, in the peasant societies of the Near East, had always been expressed by the gesture of eating."

15. See D. E. Smith, "Historical Jesus at Table," 480–82, esp. p. 481: the terms "tax-collectors" and "sinners" functioned "from the outset" symbolically "as a term of slander" versus attesting "the existence of 'tax collectors' in the early Christian community." For the image of the tax-collector in Greco-Roman antiquity, see R. M. Grant, *Early Christianity,* 47. The Cynics, too, were upbraided for the low level of social company they kept. See, e.g., Diogenes Laertius 6.6; Dio Chrysostom, *or.* 32.9: *"apatōsi paidaria kai nautas kai toiouton ochlon."*

16. For the text of Q 9:57–58, see Moreland and Robinson, "Work Sessions 31 July–2 August, 20 November 1992," 503.

17. For the term "son of man" in this saying, see above, p. 178, n. 8. Cf. Luria, "Quelle," 282–84; Bultmann, *History,* 28; Fitzmyer, *Luke,* 1:835; Hare, *Son of Man Tradition,* 271–73. For 9:57–58 as part of Q's formative stratum, see below, appendix one.

18. The Cynics, too, for programmatic reasons, likewise lacked a place to lay their head. See, e.g., ps-Anacharsis, *ep.* 5: "The whole earth is my bed"; ps-Crates, *ep.* 18; Epictetus, *diss.* 4.8.31; Dio Chrysostom, *or.* 6.8; 8.30; 40.2; Julian, *or.* 6.195b (cf. Diogenes Laertius 6.38). According to Downing (*Christ*

and the Cynics, 43): "there seems to be no contemporary Jewish analogy for a wandering teacher inviting followers. Elijah provides a very partial model."

19. See, e.g., Manson, *Sayings,* 72–73.

20. This assumes, of course, that possession of a set spot to rest one's head was perceived in antiquity to be one of the signs of "civilized" human society. Cf. Plutarch, *T. Gracch.* 9.828c. See, further, Luria, "Quelle," 284–86. Cf. also P. Brown, "Holy Man in Late Antiquity," 112, and esp. pp. 131–32: "the holy man drew his powers from outside the human race: by going to live in the desert, in close identification with an animal kingdom that stood, in the imagination of contemporaries, for the opposite pole of all human society." For late Roman men and women, beasts and especially birds were ambivalent symbols of both the free and the demonic. Steinhauser (*Doppelbildworte,* 116–17) claims: "The choice of 'foxes' and 'birds' does not appear arbitrary.... A certain universality is intended with the selection of both types of animal." According to Diogenes Laertius (6.22) it was the example of a mouse running about "not looking for a place to lie down in" (*kai mēte koitēn epizētounta*) that inspired Diogenes to discover "the means of adapting himself to circumstances."

21. For the text of Q 9:59–60, see Moreland and Robinson, "Work Sessions 31 July–2 August, 20 November 1992," 503.

22. Linguistically, there is nothing distinctive about 9:59–60. For the saying as part of Q's formative stratum, see below, appendix one.

23. New Testament scholars typically refer to the "household" and the institution of the *paterfamilias* when describing the urban social culture of Pauline Christianity. See, e.g., Stambaugh and Balch, *Social Environment,* 84, 123; Meeks, *First Urban Christians,* 29–30. Cf. Malina, *Christian Origins,* 157–58; Elliott, "Temple versus Household." A different model is then used to depict life in so-called "rural" Galilee and Judea; not infrequently, it is the unclear image of a "peasant" society. This bifurcated terminology is misleading. First, it supports the erroneous distinction still too often made between Jesus' "Jewish" context and the "Hellenistic" world of Paul. The stark contrast between urban and rural is also questionable. See, e.g., MacMullen, *Roman Social Relations,* 28–56; D. R. Edwards, "Urban/Rural Relations"; Overman, "Urbanization in Galilee." In both the country and the city, moreover, the family unit with its patriarchal head remained the "normal" pattern of social organization. Cf. Batten, "Jesus and Family," 11–51.

24. See Hengel, *Charismatic Leader,* 8–15. The quotation is from p. 15.

25. See Hengel, *Charismatic Leader,* 12.

26. See Hengel, *Charismatic Leader,* 9–10.

27. For this reason, the Cynics likewise found the custom of burial an apt focus for their "shameless" assault on ancient moral and social conventions. See, e.g., Diogenes Laertius 6.52, 79; ps-Diogenes, *ep.* 25; Cicero, *Tusc. Disp.* 1.104; Lucian, *Dem.* 35, 66; Teles III.146ff (O'Neil, 28ff); further, above, p. 177, n. 55; Praechter, "Zur kynischen Polemik"; Daraki, "Les fils de la mort." According to Downing (*Christ and the Cynics,* 44): "There are no [sic] at all obvious Jewish parallels, only the contrast with 1 Kgs 19.20–21."

28. See Hengel, *Charismatic Leader,* 30: "what is missing [in every analogy to 9:59–60 cited by Hengel] is the concrete and personal summons issued by

the active God of history as he encounters men in his freedom, and which gives to the calling of the Jewish prophets and charismatics its unique stamp."

29. See Hengel, *Charismatic Leader,* 10 n. 24.

30. Cf. P. Brown, *Augustine of Hippo,* 32: "This was a public life, in which a man was committed, above all, to maintaining his reputation: to 'live forever in the mouths of the people' was the ambition of the successful [North] African." The internal quote is taken from the epitaph of a certain Vincentius the dancer. Inscriptions on other tombs underscore the same primacy of acquired praise among the aspirations and anxieties of ancient men.

31. See Hengel, *Charismatic Leader,* 12.

32. See Hengel, *Charismatic Leader,* 12–13.

33. See Hengel, *Charismatic Leader,* 29–30.

34. See Hengel, *Charismatic Leader,* 31.

35. Ibid.

36. Ibid.

37. For the text of Q 14:26, see Asgeirsson and Robinson, "Work Sessions 12–14 July, 22 November 1991," 507. Cf. Q 12:51–53; also *GThom* 55; 101a.

38. For 14:26–27 as part of Q's formative stratum, see below, appendix one.

39. See above, p. 90. The Cynics, too, opposed the standard relationship in antiquity between parent and child with its attendant sense of mutual and permanent obligation. See, e.g., ps-Diogenes, *ep.* 21: "One need not thank one's parents, either for the fact of being born, since it is by nature that what exists came into being; or for the quality of one's character, for it is the blending of the elements that is its cause." See, further, Epictetus, *diss.* 3.22.69; Diogenes Laertius 6.88, 96; Lucian, *fug.* 18. Cf. Philo, *de spec. leg.* 1.52; *de praem.* 17.

40. For the text of Q 14:27, see Asgeirsson and Robinson, "Work Sessions 12–14 July, 22 November 1991," 507.

41. For a discussion of "Jesus' Death in Q," see Seeley; also idem, "Blessings and Boundaries." Of course, Jesus was not the only person in antiquity to face the cross. See Hengel, *Crucifixion.*

42. Beyond the canonical passion narratives, the verb *stauroō* otherwise occurs only in Matt 20:19; 23:34; 26:2. In the first and third of these instances, in view is again plainly Jesus' crucifixion. The other passage (Matt 23:34) forms part of Matthew's redaction of the "Sophia oracle" from Q (11:49).

43. See Mack, *Myth of Innocence,* 340.

44. According to Downing (*Christ and the Cynics,* 79): "There seem to be no Jewish instances of 'cross' used to denote 'the cost of discipleship.'" Cf. Philo, *In Flacc.* 84; Josephus, *Ant.* 17.10; *J.W.* 2.241.

45. See Epictetus, *diss.* 2.2.20. Cf., further, ibid., 3.5, 7; 18.4; 22.12; 4.1.153–54; Dio Chrysostom, *or.* 8.16; Seneca, *ep. mor.* 4.24; *de beat. vit.* 19.3; Lucian, *Peregr.* 23.

46. In the history of scholarship, the differences between Antisthenes and Diogenes, and Diogenes and Crates, are sometimes "explained" by denying the status of "Cynic" to the former. Regarding Antisthenes, see, e.g., Rankin, *Sophists, Socratics and Cynics,* 227–28. Regarding both Antisthenes and Diogenes, see the unusual positions of Sayre, *Diogenes of Sinope;* idem, *Greek*

Cynics; Niehues-Pröbsting, *Kynismus des Diogenes,* 15–22. Cf. Schwartz, *Characterköpfe,* 116–35: "Diogenes der Hund und Krates der Kyniker," esp. pp. 128–29.

47. For the text of Q 7:26, see Robinson, "Work Session 17 November 1989," 500. For 7:24b–25, cf. Kloppenborg, *Parallels,* 54. For the whole unit (7:24b–26) as part of Q's formative stratum, see below, appendix one.

48. See, e.g., Fitzmyer, *Luke,* 1:673–74; Ernst, *Johannes der Täufer,* 62. In fact, I know of only two discussions specifically devoted to this text, namely, Krieger, "Mensch in weichen Kleidern"; Daniel, "Les Ésseniens." See also Schönle, *Johannes, Jesus und die Juden,* 64–66.

49. That 7:25 is crucial to the logic of 7:24b–26 is seen by Hoffmann, *Studien,* 217; Schönle, *Johannes, Jesus und die Juden,* 67.

50. Not every scholar agrees. See, e.g., Wink, *John the Baptist,* 5; Michaelis, *Matthäus,* 2:119: "one certainly would not be able to see such a reed in the desert, since no rush would grow there." But *erēmos,* often translated "desert," does not mean only desiccated wasteland, but also wilderness or uninhabited region, and thus could refer to the area beside the Jordan river, where some vegetation did grow. See Wellhausen, *Matthaei,* 52.

51. See Fitzmyer, *Luke,* 1:673–74, who adds "something frail and fickle," but this is plainly an overinterpretation. For a different reading, although not incompatible with mine, of the possible socio-political significance (*Lokalkolorit*) of the image of "Das 'schwankende Rohr,' " see Theissen.

52. See, e.g., Clement of Alexandria, *paed.* 2.109.3; Lisco, *Betrachtungen,* 232–35; J. Weiss, *Schriften,* 1:315; Wellhausen, *Matthaei,* 52; Manson, *Sayings,* 68; Michaelis, *Matthäus,* 2:119 (the reference to the reed means that John was "plagued with doubts"); Schlatter, *Matthäus,* 362; Schweizer, *Matthäus,* 169.

53. See Krieger, "Mensch in weichen Kleidern," 228. Indeed, Krieger ("Mensch in weichen Kleidern," 230) thinks that the rhetorical progression in 7:24b–26 reflects a certain chronology of events: "By his questioning, therefore, to a certain extent Jesus confronted John and the crowds chronologically, to be precise, *after, before,* and *as* they went out to him in the desert."

54. See Daniel, "Les Ésseniens."

55. Such readings typically say nothing about the fact that the reed is *in the desert* or that the persons dressed in soft apparel are to be found *in the royal palace.* Cf. Klostermann, *Matthäus,* 97; Hoffmann, *Studien,* 217; Schönle, *Johannes, Jesus und die Juden,* 67. Daniel ("Les Ésseniens") does suggest that there were Essenes at Herod's court.

56. The Greek particle *nai* is here not an affirmative response to the preceding question, but part of the emphatic introductory formula, *nai legō hymin,* giving emphasis to what follows. The same expression occurs as well in Luke 11:51; 12:5. Such a use of *nai* was not uncommon. See Berger, *Amen-Worte Jesu,* 9–12, esp. p. 10 n. 3; also J. Weiss, *Schriften,* 1:313–15.

57. For this sense of *idou,* see Fitzmyer's translation (*Luke,* 1:670): "you know."

58. See, e.g., Wellhausen, *Matthaei,* 52; Schulz, *Spruchquelle,* 231; Jacobson, "Wisdom Christology," 77; Fitzmyer, *Luke,* 1:674; Krieger, "Mensch in

weichen Kleidern," 230 n. 2 (reference is made to Klostermann and Kraeling). Krieger himself rightly notes that "really, however, no speaker would have been in a position casually to grab senseless questions of this sort out of the air."

59. Otherwise in the New Testament, *tryphē* occurs only in 2 Pet 2:13 with rather a different meaning.

60. In Matt 11:18, the expression, *en malakois,* is matched by the similar phrase, *ta malaka.*

61. See, further, Dio Chrysostom, *or.* 66.25; Lucian, *dial. mort.* 20.6, 8; Philo, *de som.* 2.9; *de mig. Ab.* 136.

62. Beyond pleasure and softness, Odysseus is also faulted because "he always succumbed to sleep [and] food." Cf. Philo, *de sac.* 21–23: "Pleasure comes languishing in the guise of a harlot or courtesan" and, among other things, offers "costly kinds of food and drink" and "softest sleep."

63. This theme is then elaborated in the rest of the epistle. Cf. Philo, *In Flacc.* 36–41, 179.

64. See Epictetus, *diss.* 1.24.7. Cf. Philo, *de som.* 1.125; 2.56.

65. See Julian, *or.* 6.200c. Cf. Philo, *vit. cont.* 69.

66. See ps-Lucian, *cyn.* 17. Softness is often listed among the vices that follow wealth. See, e.g., Lucian, *Tim.* 28; *de mer.* 25; *dial. mort.* 20.6.

67. See Dio Chrysostom, *or.* 77/78.41. Cf. Philo, *de vit. Mos.* 2.183–84; *de som.* 1.122–24; 2.9; *de mig. Ab.* 136.

68. Cf. Philo, *de vir.* 5–7. The reference to animal hides and woolly sheepskins as "allies" recalls the description in Mark 1:6; Matt 3:4 of John wearing clothes made out of "camel's hair and . . . a leather girdle around his waist." See, further, Windisch, "Notiz"; Ernst, *Johannes der Täufer,* 284–89. The Cynics often wore a coarse cloak called a *tribōn.*

69. See, e.g., Fitzmyer, *Luke,* 1:674; Wellhausen, *Matthaei,* 52; Schniewind, *Matthäus,* 142–43; Manson, *Sayings,* 68; Krieger, "Mensch in weichen Kleidern," 229, who claims that "the rough desert preacher [was] previously a man in soft clothes at the court of Antipas." Cf. Michaelis, *Matthäus,* 2:120; Lohmeyer, *Johannes der Täufer,* 165.

70. See Rawlinson, *Mark,* 82; further, Wink, *John the Baptist,* 10 n. 3. Cf. Theissen, "Legende."

71. See Lohmeyer, *Johannes der Täufer,* 17.

72. See Rawlinson, *Mark,* 81. Josephus (*Ant.* 18.5.2) characterizes John as "a good man" who "exhorted the Jews to lead righteous lives, to practice justice toward their fellows and piety toward God, and so doing to join in baptism." But "when others too joined the crowds about him, because they were aroused to the highest degree by his sermons, Herod became alarmed. Eloquence that had so great an effect on humankind might lead to some sort of sedition, for it looked as if they would be guided by John in everything that they did." The Slavonic version of Josephus, at the beginning of this passage, refers to John not as *agathos* (a good man) but as *agrios* (a wild man).

73. This is true, even recognizing that, in antiquity, a great variety of persons could be called "prophet," including the Cynics on at least one occasion. See ps-Diogenes, *ep.* 21: "As the prophet [*prophētēs*] of indifference I speak

these words plainly, which are opposed to the deluded life." Cf. Boring, " 'What Are We Looking For?' " 144. Though definitely in favor of the idea of early Christian prophecy, Boring takes no refuge in the term itself of "prophet," precisely due to "the immense variety of figures designated by PROFHTHS." See, further, Aune, *Prophecy.*

74. Cf. Hahn, *Hoheitstitel,* 375; Ernst, *Johannes der Täufer,* 62. In *Johannes und Jesus,* Becker entitles one chapter "Johannes als Prophet," contending that this description reflects "his most widespread broader personal characteristics" (p. 41). Becker then proceeds to explain how "John as prophet" was nonetheless unlike virtually every other ancient seer and inspired declaimer known to us. At one point, an exception is made by Becker for the Teacher of Righteousness at Qumran, although this person, too, is finally deemed to be incomparable with John in almost every respect (p. 18). Nevertheless, the two are somehow still supposed to represent together a special *Grundtyp* of prophet that simultaneously began and ended with them.

75. For the constitutive tension between Israel's canonical kings and prophets, see Hanson, *Diversity,* 14–36, esp. pp. 27–33.

76. Most scholars believe that 7:27 was secondarily added to 7:24b–26. 7:27 is also thought to interrupt the flow between 7:26 and 7:28. 7:27 was therefore most likely inserted at its present location after 7:28 had already been conjoined to 7:26. See, e.g., Bultmann, *History,* 165; Klostermann, *Matthäus,* 96; Lohmeyer, *Johannes der Täufer,* 19; Hirsch, *Frühgeschichte,* 93; Manson, *Sayings,* 69; Grundmann, *Matthäus,* 306; Hahn, *Hoheitstitel,* 374–76; Lührmann, *Redaktion,* 27 n. 4; Schweizer, *Matthäus,* 168; Hoffmann, *Studien,* 218; Schulz, *Spruchquelle,* 230; Polag, *Christologie,* 158–60; D. Zeller, "Redaktionsprozesse," 403; Kloppenborg, *Formation,* 110; further, below, appendix one. Codex Bezae has the following order of verses in Luke: 7:24–26, 7:28a, 7:27; likewise, *ps-Clem. recog.* 60 (Frankenberg, *Die syrischen Clementinen,* 65–66).

77. Cf. Kloppenborg, *Parallels,* 54.

78. For 7:28a as once an "independent" saying, see, e.g., Bultmann, *History,* 165; Dibelius, *Überlieferung,* 13–14; Klostermann, *Matthäus,* 96; Kraeling, *John the Baptist,* 138–40; Lührmann, *Redaktion,* 27; Wink, *John the Baptist,* 24; Hoffmann, *Studien,* 218; Jacobson, "Wisdom Christology," 78; further, Hahn, *Hoheitstitel,* 375–76; Robinson, *New Quest,* 117 n. 1; Codex Bezae (see above, n. 76); *ps.-Clem. recog.* 60. Schürmann (*Lukasevangelium,* 1:419) finds it impossible to believe that 7:28a was ever an independent saying: "since there will never likely have been such praise of the Baptist without further comment in Christian preaching." But this begs the question. See, further, D. Zeller, "Redaktionsprozesse," 403; Schönle, *Johannes, Jesus und die Juden,* 66: "taken as such, the verse itself seems to require some inevitable commentary"; also Lührmann, *Redaktion,* 27, esp. n. 3; Schulz, *Spruchquelle,* 230; Polag, *Christologie,* 158–60; Jacobson, "Wisdom Christology," 78–79; Wanke, "Kommentarworte," 215–16; Kloppenborg, *Formation,* 109 n. 30: "Schnackenburg (*God's Rule and Kingdom,* 133) argues that the parallelism between the two halves of the saying indicates an original unity. That [*GThom* 46] also presents both halves of the saying is perhaps a further indication of this."

79. Cf. J. Weiss, *Schriften*, 315; Lohmeyer, *Johannes der Täufer*, 19; Scobie, *John the Baptist*, 157.

80. See ps-Diogenes, *ep.* 33; further, Diogenes Laertius 6.32; Juvenal, *sat.* 14.311–14.

81. Cf. Horsley, *Sociology*, 69.

Conclusion: Galilean Upstarts

1. Although I have alluded in this book on more than one occasion to both the Cynics and the persons whom Q represents as "ascetic," it remains an open question, how exactly each might fit into a general history of "asceticism" in the ancient Mediterranean world.

2. For the concept of "social marginality," see above, pp. 13–14. There is no reason to believe that the "risks" of their way of life caught the Q people by surprise and unawares. See, e.g., Q 14:27.

3. See above, p. 69.

4. By "subversive wisdom," I mean to recall what I refer to in the title of my doctoral dissertation as an "itinerant intelligence." See, more recently, Vaage, "Q, Diogenes, and Jesus." The term "itinerant" was supposed to pick up and play off of Theissen's earliest proposal of "itinerant radicalism" (*Wanderradikalismus*) as the original *Sitz im Leben* of much of the traditional material in Q. Theissen's proposal has subsequently been subjected to a number of critiques, especially regarding the idea of "itinerants." I remain interested, nonetheless, in the possibility of describing Q's formative stratum as the discourse of an alternate "type" of "intelligence" characterized by its "itinerant" (or, in postmodern speak, disseminating) logic, comparable, e.g., to the account of *metis* or *Cunning Intelligence in Greek Culture and Society* by Détienne and Vernant.

Appendix One
The Formative Stratum of Q

1. See above, p. 7.

2. Only the status of 6:22–23 is questionable. In *Formation* (172–73, 178, 187, 190, 342; see, further, idem, "Social History," 101 n. 1) Kloppenborg concludes that the association in Q's inaugural discourse cum formative stratum of the admonition to love your enemies in 6:27–35 with the beatitudes in 6:20bff presupposes that 6:22–23b was already part of the latter group of sayings. This is hardly a necessary assumption (see Vaage, "Son of Man Sayings," 108). At the same time Kloppenborg observes that 6:23c fits poorly with the rest of the preceding beatitudes, shares the theological perspective dominant in the redactional stratum of the document, and is therefore likely an interpolation made from the perspective of that redaction. In "Blessing and Marginality" (45–46), following Colpe and others, the phrase "on account of the son of man" in 6:22c is also seen by Kloppenborg as a secondary addition from a tradition-historical

point of view (cf. *GThom* 68–69a) but not ascribed explicitly to Q redaction. In my opinion, the entire saying (6:22–23) was introduced into the document by Q's redaction. See Vaage, "Son of Man Sayings," 107–9.

3. I do not believe that Luke 9:61–62 ever was in Q. See Moreland and Robinson, "Work Sessions 31 July–2 August, 20 November 1992," 503. Cf. Kloppenborg, *Parallels*, 64.

4. See, further, Kloppenborg, "Social History," 101 n. 1: "To the instructional layer [of Q] I assign...probably also...15:4–7 (8–10?); 16:13, 18; 17:1–2, 3b–4, 6."

5. In *Formation* (246–62) only 4:1–13 is discussed by Kloppenborg as the work of a tertiary redaction. For 11:42d (cf. Kloppenborg, *Formation*, 140) and 16:17 as part of this final revision as well, see Kloppenborg, *"Nomos and Ethos,"* 42–43 (for additional literature, see ibid., 42 n. 33); idem, "Social History," 101 n. 1; further, Hoffmann, *Studien*, 59 n. 34; 170 n. 50; also Hoffmann's review of Schulz (*Spruchquelle*), where reference is made to a *Rejudaisierungstendenz* (p. 114).

6. But again, see above, n. 4. For discussion of 13:18–21 as well as 15:4–7 as part of Q's formative stratum, see Kloppenborg, "Parables of Jesus."

7. Cf. Cameron, " 'What Have You Come Out to See?' " Cameron's effort to describe the logic of the redactional composition of Q 7:18–35 as a chreia elaboration presupposes that the various sayings contained within this section are not all of the same tradition-historical provenance.

8. See Kloppenborg, *Formation*, 105 (regarding Q 3:7–9, 16–17).

9. The explicit reference to John in 7:24a is not due to the absence of any such reference in 7:24b–26. To whom else would the saying (7:24b–26) finally refer? (Cf. Cameron, " 'What Have You Come Out to See?' " 44: "It is Jesus who is the speaker [in *GThom* 78=Q 7:24b–25]; conceivably he or his followers are implicitly being characterized.") The reference to John in 7:24a is rather the result of the Q-redactor's desire to recall John as the narrative point of departure in 7:18–20, whence the discourse rapidly veered in 7:22–23 toward a characterization of Jesus; versus Kloppenborg, *Formation*, 116: "From a compositional point of view, 7:18–23 must be primary, not secondary. Q 7:24b–26, which contains no mention of John at all, depends upon 7:18–23 and upon the clearly redactional and transitional phrase Q 7:24a for its connection with John." Cf. Cameron, " 'What Have You Come Out to See?' " 44.

10. The insertion of 7:27 may be the work of Q's tertiary redaction (cf. above, n. 5). The principal reason for this suggestion, beyond the evident intrusiveness of the saying in its present literary context, is the saying's use of the citation formula, *gegraptai*, found otherwise in Q only in 4:4, 8, 10, along with the saying's explicit citation of the Septuagint — actually, a conflation of Mal 3:1 and Exod 23:20 — which again otherwise occurs in Q only in the temptation narrative. Cf. Cameron, " 'What Have You Come Out to See?' " 56–57.

11. See above, p. 88; further, Vaage, "Son of Man Sayings," 125.

12. For an analysis of the composition-history of 7:31–35, in which the twofold saying in 7:33–34 appears as the primary unit of tradition subsequently framed by the introductory and concluding pronouncements in 7:31–32 and

7:35 at the time of Q's redaction, see Vaage, "Son of Man Sayings," 109–13; further, Hare, *Son of Man Tradition,* 263–64.

13. Where 7:24b–26 and 7:33–34 originally appeared in Q's formative stratum can no longer be determined. It might seem better, therefore, simply to suggest that 7:24b–26, 33–34 have a different "tradition-historical" provenance from the rest of the sayings in Q regarding John. From my point of view, however, such an evaluation fails to explain adequately why the Q-redactor would have bothered with this material in the first place, given that these sayings otherwise hardly reflect the secondary stratum's own point of view. While it is always conceivable that the Q-redactor could simply have left anything out of Q's formative stratum with which he or she was not in full agreement or unable to reframe and thus was by no means obligated to include in the secondary stratum everything once found in the earlier document, it is easier to explain the evident "containment strategies" exercised upon the sayings in 7:24b–26, 33–34 as part of the secondary stratum's general effort to recast the previous version of Q than it is to imagine the Q-redactor self-consciously incorporating the same material into the document only, then, to rectify it immediately.

14. For 7:28a as once a separate saying, see above, p. 102, esp. nn. 78, 79. For the saying as part of Q's formative stratum, see the argument above, n. 13.

15. See Kloppenborg, *Formation,* 193.

16. See Kloppenborg, *Formation,* 194.

17. See Kloppenborg, *Formation,* 195.

18. See Kloppenborg, *Formation,* 196–97.

19. See Kloppenborg, *Formation,* 200.

20. See Kloppenborg, *Formation,* 202.

21. As Kloppenborg (*Formation,* 194–95) himself immediately recognizes: "Mark's version is somewhat less detailed and provides a slightly different instruction.... The Q version contains several elements not found in Mark: the greeting of peace [10:5], the command to greet no one on the road [10:4b], the proverb [in 10:7b]..., the command to 'eat whatever is placed before you' [10:7a — in my opinion, not originally in Q: see below, appendix two], and the references to healing and proclaiming that [the kingdom of God has arrived=10:9]." Comparison of Mark and Q thus reveals a "core" group of "mission" instructions rather like poorly made Swiss cheese, i.e., more full of holes than substance, limited only to the sayings in Q 10:4a, 6, 10–11. Given, moreover, the additional affirmations by Kloppenborg that "the Marcan account [of the equipment regulations] is [usually] viewed as a relaxation of the earlier, more stringent demands [in Q 10:4a]," and that "Dautzenberg rightly observes that in comparison with Mark, Q provides a much less abstract conception of the preaching of the kingdom and one which appears to be closer to the actual situation of preaching" or lived performance, it seems to me a fundamental error in procedure to take essentially what the "mission" instructions in both Mark and Q share in common as the primary point of departure for determining the "original" form of the speech in Q (10:2–16) — especially when the sayings in Q 10:3–6, 9–11, 16 otherwise betray, by Kloppenborg's own admission, a very high degree of internal coherence. Cf. Sellew, "Early Collections,"

59–162, who disagrees completely; also Uro, *Sheep among Wolves,* 98–110, whose approach is more eclectic.

22. For a description of the "aggregation" model of Q's composition-history, see Kloppenborg, "Literary and Stratigraphic Problems." I have criticized this view of Q's literary development in Vaage, "Son of Man Sayings," 104–6. See, also, idem, "Composition."

23. Reference is made to Jacobson, "Lc 10, 2–16," 421. See, further, Haupt, *Worte Jesu,* 27; Hoffmann, "Lk 10, 5–11," 51; Loisy, *Luc,* 293; D. Zeller, "Redaktionsprozesse," 404. A number of scholars especially note the difficult connection between 10:2 and 10:3. See, e.g., Haenchen, *Weg,* 224; Klostermann, *Lukas,* 114; Laufen, *Doppelüberlieferung,* 270; Manson, *Sayings,* 75; Schmid, "Matthäus und Lukas," 261; idem, *Matthäus,* 175; Wellhausen, *Lucae,* 48. Cf., further, Beare, "Mission," 7; F. C. Grant, "Mission," 304; Haenchen, *Weg,* 227; Hahn, *Mission,* 43; Lagrange, *Luc,* 293; Lührmann, *Redaktion,* 60; Polag, *Christologie,* 14; Schürmann, "Mt 10, 5b–6," 143 n. 24; Wernle, *Frage,* 66. As for 10:7b, its ascribed status, redactional or otherwise, is typically the result of "guilt by association" with 10:2. See, e.g., Haupt, *Worte Jesu,* 27; Hoffmann, "Lk 10, 5–11," 51; Jacobson, "Lc 10, 2–16," 421 (though he now appears to have changed his mind: see idem, *First Gospel,* 141–42); M'Neile, *Matthew,* 136; Schürmann, "Mt 10, 5b–6," 147 n. 39; Wiater, *Komposition,* 126; Zahn, *Lucas,* 413 n. 73; D. Zeller, "Redaktionsprozesse," 404. Other reasons are sometimes given. See, e.g., Hoffmann, *Studien,* 298: 10:7b "interrupts the connection" between 10:5–6 (or 10:7a) and 10:9 (cf. ibid., 296 n. 22); Klostermann, *Matthäus,* 87; Wiater, *Komposition,* 315 n. 13: both Klostermann and Wiater refer to the proverbial character of 10:7b, and the presence of the conjunctive particle, *gar;* Krauss, "Instruktion," 97: 10:7b is absent from the "older formulation" of the mission instructions in Mark 6:9.

24. See Kloppenborg, *Formation,* 193, 200. Actually, Jacobson ("Lc 10, 2–16," 421) says very little in this regard. Everything would depend upon what Jacobson means by: "conform the mission instructions to early Christian mission praxis." See, further, idem, *First Gospel,* 147–48. It is Lührmann (*Redaktion,* 60) following Bornkamm ("End-Expectation," 18) who has championed the view that the reference to "harvest" in 10:2 implies consciousness of the Gentile mission on the part of the Q community and, indeed, participation in their life together by the Gentiles. Against this interpretation, Kloppenborg's argument is rightly, but exclusively, directed. Left unconsidered by Kloppenborg is the degree to which the harvest imagery used in 10:2 develops the motif of judgment otherwise thought by Kloppenborg to be characteristic of Q's secondary stratum. Kloppenborg himself provides plenty of evidence that eschatological judgment was precisely the usual connotation of this trope. See Kloppenborg, *Formation,* 193 n. 93; further, Jacobson, *First Gospel,* 147 n. 57. No doubt exists that the harvest-imagery in Q 3:7–9, 16–17, esp. vv. 9 and 17, is employed as a metaphor for judgment, indeed, precisely the same kind of fiery fate that the towns of Chorazin, Bethsaida, and Capernaum are threatened with in 10:13–15. On the basis of stratigraphical coherence, 10:2 is certainly compatible with the rest of Q's redaction.

25. The fact that Jacobson's reasons for ascribing 10:2, 7b to a "late redac-

tion, i.e., *subsequent,* to the addition of 10:12, 13–15" leave undiscussed the question of the relation between these two groups of sayings does not mean that, therefore, no relationship exists. See above, p. 188, n. 24; below, n. 26.

26. The fact that both 10:2 and 10:7b occur elsewhere in early Christian tradition may also be a factor. For 10:2, see *GThom* 73; for 10:7b, see 1 Tim 5:18; *Did* 13:2; *Dial. Sav.* 53.

27. See Kloppenborg, "Social History," esp. pp. 94–96. The stark antagonism expressed in 10:13–15 vis-à-vis certain Galilean villages, thereby establishing the "external" face of the Q people's increasingly distinct social identity, is matched in 10:2, 7b by these sayings' more precise rendering of the group's developing "internal" self-consciousness. The Q people now see themselves essentially as the designated labor pool of an absent (heavenly) landlord, whose present (earthly) harvest requires a full complement of reapers, ideally more than a few good men, to gather in the sheaves. That nonetheless "the laborers are few" makes clear the group's growing awareness of the gap between what they thought ought to have been the case and what was in fact reality — precisely the same gap repeatedly remarked and denounced elsewhere by Q's redaction, for example, in 3:7–9, where those producing "fruit worthy of repentance" are apparently much fewer than those who still assume that being a child of Abraham is sufficient.

28. I would resist, however, any too "official" a description of the status of such "workers" at the level of Q's redaction (versus, e.g., Uro, *Sheep among Wolves,* 203–7; cf. Georgi, *Opponents,* 40; *Did* 13:2). It is not clear what these so-called "workers" actually would have done in order to acquire the particular recognition implied by the name and to enjoy its benefits (10:7b). Elsewhere in Q's redaction (13:27) the same term *ergatēs* (specifically, *ergatai adikias*=Luke) is used to characterize the opposition. See Kloppenborg, *Formation,* 235–36: "Percy draws attention to the similarity of Q 13:26–27 to the threat against Capharnaum in 10:15.... Q 13:26–27 reflects the general lack of success of those [Q] preachers [described in 10:4–10], and like 3:7–9; 10:13–15; 11:31–32; 12:8–9, pronounces judgment on those who fail to respond appropriately." Cf., further, Hoffmann, "πάντες ἐργάται ἀδικίας," 202–3.

29. Kloppenborg's reading of 11:14–52 is perhaps defensible as the perspective of Q's redaction, for which, then, the sayings in 11:29–32, 49–51 are obviously key. My point, however, is that by assuming such a point of view, the notable contrast in character between these two units (11:29–32, 49–51; plus 11:23) and the rest of the material in this section (11:14–20, 24–26, 33, 34–36, 39–48, 52) has been significantly muted.

30. See Kloppenborg, *Formation,* 121. The "structural argument" developed by Kloppenborg (*Formation,* 138–39, 147–48) for the redactional placement of 11:14–26, 29–36 in parallel sequences fails to convince, given that it depends wholly upon Kloppenborg's questionable characterization of the meaning of each of these various sayings for this arrangement to exist.

31. For 11:29–32, see Vaage, "Son of Man Sayings," 115–17. Cf. Kloppenborg, *Formation,* 128–34. For 11:49–51, see below, pp. 115–16; also, Vaage, "Woes in Q," 599–602.

32. See Kloppenborg, *Formation,* 148.

33. See Kloppenborg, *Formation*, 144.

34. See Kloppenborg, *Formation*, 147.

35. See Kloppenborg, *Formation*, 318–22. Cf. idem, "Social History," 83ff.

36. In *Formation*, Kloppenborg is plainly influenced by the type of form and composition-criticism propounded by Schürmann and followed by some of his students (Wanke, D. Zeller), which carries about as far as it can go the traditional German scholarly effort to discern behind the written text of the canonical gospels the complex antecedent process of the oral transmission and elaboration of this material, at the same time that the basic stages, particular social settings, and/or specific cultural mechanisms of the imagined "growth of the tradition" are simply taken for granted. It is to the implicit narrative logic of these unspoken but discursively operative assumptions that I refer when I speak of a tacit evolutionary myth of Christian origins. Cf. Bultmann, *History, vii.*

37. See Kloppenborg, *Formation*, 143, here quoting Schürmann ("Basileia-Verkündigung," 174–75), whose descriptive categories Kloppenborg does not otherwise seem to share (see, e.g., *"Nomos* and *Ethos"*), but whose schematic view of the development of early Christian tradition Kloppenborg nonetheless accepts, at least on this occasion.

38. Cf. R. Piper, *Wisdom.*

39. See Kloppenborg, *Formation*, 125.

40. Ibid.

41. For discussion of the status of Luke 11:21–22 par. vis-à-vis Q, see Kloppenborg, *Parallels*, 94. Cf. Moreland and Robinson, "Work Sessions 31 July–2 August, 20 November 1992," 504. Most scholars assume that the sequence of sayings in Luke 11:14–20, 23, 24–26 attests the original order of Q.

42. See above, pp. 60–61.

43. Kloppenborg (*Formation*, 126 n. 109) notes the "demonological" interpretations of 11:24–26 by Hull (*Hellenistic Magic*, 102) and Böcher (*Christus Exorcista*, 17) but claims, despite Kloppenborg's own affirmation of this line of interpretation as "perhaps rightly," that "In the context of Q, however, this is not its function" (see Kloppenborg, *Formation*, 126).

44. See Kloppenborg, *Formation*, 126–27.

45. See Kloppenborg, *Formation*, 126.

46. See Kloppenborg, *Formation*, 138.

47. See Kloppenborg, *Formation*, 138–39.

48. See, e.g., Dihle, "Vom sonnenhaften Auge," esp. p. 90; Elliott, "Fear of the Leer." Elliott's discussion (ibid., 60–62) of Matt 6:22–23 (versus Luke 11:34–36) is not, however, very satisfying.

49. Kloppenborg (*Formation*, 136) is aware of ancient theories of vision. But like Betz (*Essays*, 71–87), on whom Kloppenborg appears here to rely, Kloppenborg too quickly assumes that a theological critique of these conceptions was the main point of Q 11:34–36.

50. Kloppenborg (*Formation*, 138) tries to link interpretation of Q 11:33–36 with that of the preceding sayings in 11:31–32: "Q 11:33–36 should be seen as a continuation of the rhetoric." 11:33 supposedly "implies that the preaching of the kingdom is not something obscure or hidden, but universally and

openly manifest, so that all might respond." This is then followed by the first of the two quotations cited above (see p. 190, n. 44). Everything rides here on the proximity of the sayings (11:31–32 and 11:33, 34–36) to one another, for absolutely nothing in 11:33, 34–36 would otherwise suggest such a reading. Procedurally, this interpretation is quite consistent with Kloppenborg's stated methodological approach (see above, p. 114). At the same time, however, it prevents him from taking seriously the obvious discontinuity that exists between these two sets of utterances, as well as what conjoins 11:33, 34–36 to 11:14–20, 24–26.

51. See Kloppenborg, *Formation*, 92.

52. See Kloppenborg, *Formation*, 223 n. 214.

53. See Kloppenborg, *Formation*, 236.

54. See Kloppenborg, "Parables of Jesus."

Appendix Two
The Text of Q: Some Critical Problems

1. IQP materials may be obtained from the Institute for Antiquity and Christianity, 831 N. Dartmouth Ave., Claremont, CA 91711.

2. See R. Piper, *Wisdom,* 79=the main text of the citation; idem, "Q 6:27–36. Second Response," variant 6:27–28.1 = the same text, with variant wording indicated between square [ ] brackets; between pointed < > brackets is printed my additional clarification.

3. See R. Piper, "Q 6:27–36. Second Response," variant 6:27–28.1.

4. See R. Piper, *Wisdom,* 79 (emphasis mine); further, idem, "Q 6:27–36. Second Response," variant 6:27–28.1 (essentially equivalent to the text of the citation, with significant variant wording indicated between square [] brackets).

5. See Carruth, "Q 6:27–36. First Response," variant 6:29.1: "The ancient rhetorician Longinus suggests that an alternation between second person plural and second person singular is a way of gaining the attention of the individual hearer (*On the Sublime,* 26.3)." See, further, Arieti and Crossett, *Longinus,* 132–34.

6. See R. Piper, "Q 6:27–36. Second Response," variant 6:27–28.1.

7. See R. Piper, *Wisdom,* 79. Cf. idem, "Q 6:27–36. Second Response," variant 6:32.1.

8. See R. Piper, "Q 6:27–36. Second Response," variant 6:32.1.

9. See R. Piper, "Q 6:27–36. Second Response," variant 6:32.1.

10. See Kloppenborg, *Formation,* 180. Even in the Sermon on the Mount, i.e., Matthew's version of Q's inaugural discourse, the original connection between Q 6:36 (Matt 5:48) and 6:37ff (Matt 7:1ff) is still observable, insofar as everything that now occurs between these sayings in Matt 6:1–34 (plus Matt 7:6–12) is the work of Matthean redaction. See Bornkamm, "Aufbau der Bergpredigt."

11. See R. Piper, "Q 6:27–36. Second Response," variant 6:32.1.

12. See above, p. 45.

13. See, e.g., Uro, *Sheep among Wolves,* 68, and the authors referred to in n. 193; also ibid., 69 n. 195.

14. See, e.g., Laufen, *Doppelüberlieferung,* 219–20 (discussing, specifically, the "antithetical parallelism" of 10:8–9 and 10:10–11).

15. See Hoffmann, *Studien,* 278–80.

16. See Kloppenborg, *"Nomos and Ethos."*

17. It is furthermore always suspect, in my opinion, to argue that otherwise unparalleled material should be included in Q on the basis of our perception that without it the reconstructed text would make no or lesser sense. For such logic only tends to reveal what the Q "text-critic" already assumes to be the nature of the text he or she is supposedly "reconstructing" (versus willfully fabricating).

18. Only in Luke (10:7–8) are the same instructions essentially given back to back, namely, both to stay in one place (10:7aa, 7c) and to eat (and drink) whatever might be served (10:7ab, 8c). No version of the "mission" instructions in any of the other synoptic gospels has a similar reduplication of command. Prima facie, therefore, Luke is most likely responsible for this peculiarity of his text. Even if one were to assume that, say, 10:7aa and 10:7ab were once in Q, why, then, would Luke so quickly turn around and reiterate the very same instructions in 10:7c and 10:8b? Whatever reason might be given, the fact that, in this case, Luke can be imagined self-consciously and forthwith to have repeated what was just said in his source suggests that it is just as likely for Luke himself to say the same thing twice.

19. Versus Uro, *Sheep among Wolves,* 68.

20. Versus Uro, *Sheep among Wolves,* 69.

21. See, e.g., Luke 7:36–50; 11:37ff; 14:1ff; 15:1–2; 16:19–31; Acts 10:1ff.

22. Regarding the house, Matthew notably preserves the "good news, bad news" scenario of Q versus Mark (6:10), who only discusses "wherever you enter into a house." Had the same "yes-no" pattern also existed in Q regarding the city, why would Matthew now suddenly reverse his immediately preceding preference for Q and here essentially follow Mark (6:11)? (In fact, Matthew does not literally repeat Mark's reference to "any place [that] does not welcome you." Instead, there is a continuation of Matthew's own discussion of "whoever" is worthy [or does not welcome you]).

23. For the following, see Vaage, "Ethos and Ethics," 283–89.

24. See, again, Matt 10:40; Mark 9:37/Matt 18:5/Luke 9:48; John 13:20; also John 5:23; 12:44–45; 1 Thess 4:8; *Did* 11:4; Ign., *Eph.* 6.1.

25. See Hoffmann, *Studien,* 285–86; further, idem, "Lk 10, 5–11," 49.

26. See, e.g., Luke 5:1, 15; 6:18; 7:29; 8:18, 21; 10:38–41; 11:28; 15:1; 16:29ff; 19:48; 21:38.

27. See McLean, "Q 11:39b First Response," variant 11:39b.1.

28. See Robinson, "Q 11:40 Second Response," variant 11:40.1.

29. Ibid.

Bibliography

Abrams, Dominic, and Michael A. Hogg, eds. *Social Identity Theory: Constructive and Critical Advances.* New York: Harvester Wheatsheaf, 1990.

Arav, Ravi. *Hellenistic Palestine: Settlement Patterns and City Planning, 337–31 B.C.E.* Oxford: B.A.R., 1989.

Argyle, A. W. "Greek among the Jews of Palestine in New Testament Times." *NTS* 20 (1974): 87–89.

Arieti, James A., and John M. Crossett, trans. with commentary. *Longinus: On the Sublime.* New York and Toronto: Mellen, 1985.

Arndt, W. F., and F. W. Gingrich. *A Greek-English Lexicon of the New Testament and Other Early Christian Literature.* Revised and augmented by F. W. Gingrich and F. W. Danker. 2nd. ed. Chicago and London: University of Chicago Press, 1979.

Asgeirsson, Jon M., and James M. Robinson, "The International Q Project Work Session 16 November 1990." *JBL* 110 (1991): 494–98.

———. "The International Q Project Work Sessions 12–14 July, 22 November 1991." *JBL* 111 (1992): 500–508.

Auerbach, Erich. *Mimesis: The Representation of Reality in Western Literature.* Princeton: Princeton University Press, 1953.

Aune, David E. *Prophecy in Early Christianity and the Ancient Mediterranean World.* Grand Rapids, Mich.: Eerdmans, 1983.

Baltzer, Eduard. *Pythagoras, der Weise von Samos: ein Lebensbild.* Nordhausen: Fürsteman, 1868; repr. Walluf bei Wiesbaden: Sändig, 1973.

Bartsch, H. W. "Feldrede und Bergpredigt. Redaktionsarbeit in Luk. 6." *ThZ* 16 (1960): 5–18.

———. "Traditionsgeschichtliches zur 'goldenen Regel' und zum Apostel-dekret." *ZNW* 75 (1984): 128–32.

Batten, Alicia. "Jesus and Family: A Comparison of Luke 14:26 and the Parable of the Prodigal Son." M.A. thesis, University of St. Michael's College, 1992.

Bauer, Walter. *Aufsätze und kleine Schriften.* G. Strecker, ed. Tübingen: Mohr, 1967.

———. "Essener." Pp. 1–59 in idem, *Aufsätze und kleine Schriften.*

————. "Das Gebot der Feindesliebe und die alten Christen." Pp. 235–52 in idem, *Aufsätze und kleine Schriften.*

Beare, F. W. "The Mission of the Disciples and the Mission Charge: Matthew 10 and Parallels." *JBL* 89 (1970): 1–13.

Becker, J. *Johannes der Täufer und Jesus von Nazareth.* Neukirchen-Vluyn: Neukirchener Verlag, 1972.

Be Duhn, Jason David. "A Regimen for Salvation: Medical Models in Manichaean Asceticism." *Semeia* 58 (1992): 109–34.

Beilner, W. *Christus und die Pharisäer.* Vienna, 1959.

Bellinzoni, A. J. *The Two-Source Hypothesis: A Critical Appraisal.* Mercer, Ga.: Mercer University Press, 1985.

Berger, Klaus. *Die Amen-Worte Jesu.* Berlin: de Gruyter, 1970.

————. *Formgeschichte des Neuen Testaments.* Heidelberg: Quelle & Meyer, 1984.

Bernays, Jacob. *Lucian und die Kyniker.* Berlin: Hertz, 1879.

Betz, Hans Dieter. *Essays on the Sermon on the Mount.* L. L. Welborn, trans. Philadelphia: Fortress, 1985.

Billerbeck, Margarethe. *Epiktet: Vom Kynismus.* Leiden: Brill, 1978.

————, ed. *Die Kyniker in der modernen Forschung: Aufsätze mit Einführung und Bibliographie.* Amsterdam: Grüner, 1991.

Bleek, F. *Synoptische Erklärung der drei ersten Evangelien.* 2 vols. Leipzig: Engelmann, 1862.

Bloom, Alan D. *The Closing of the American Mind.* New York: Simon and Schuster, 1987.

Böcher, Otto. *Christus Exorcista: Dämonismus und Taufe im Neuen Testament.* Stuttgart: KBW, 1972.

Boff, Leonardo. *The Lord's Prayer.* Maryknoll, N.Y.: Orbis, 1983.

Bolton, Ralph, and Charlene Bolton. *Conflictos en la familia andina.* Cuzco, Peru: Centro de Estudios Andinos, 1975.

Borges, Jorge Luis, and María Esther Vázquez. *Literaturas germánicas medievales.* Buenos Aires: Falbo, 1966.

Boring, M. Eugene. " 'What Are We Looking For?' Toward a Definition of the Term, 'Christian Prophet.' " *SBLSP* 12 (1973): 2.142–54.

Bornkamm, Günther. "End-Expectation and Church." Pp. 15–51 in idem, Gerhard Barth, and Heinz Joachim Held, *Tradition and Interpretation in Matthew.* Percy Scott, trans. Philadelphia: Westminster, 1963.

————. "Der Aufbau der Bergpredigt." *NTS* 24 (1977–78): 419–32.

Bosold, Iris. *Pazifismus und prophetische Provokation.* Stuttgart: KBW, 1978.

Brancacci, A. "La filosofia de Pirrone e le sue relazioni con il cinismo." Pp. 211–42 in G. Giannantoni, ed., *Lo Scetticismo Antico.* Vol. 1. Naples: Bibliopolis, 1981.

Braun, H. *Qumran und das Neue Testament.* Vol. 1. Tübingen: Mohr, 1966.

Breech, James. *The Silence of Jesus: The Authentic Voice of the Historical Man.* Philadelphia: Fortress, 1983.

Bright, John. *The Kingdom of God: The Biblical Concept and Its Meaning for the Church.* New York: Abingdon, 1953.

Brown, Peter. *Augustine of Hippo: A Biography.* London and Boston: Faber and Faber, 1967.

———. "The Rise and Function of the Holy Man in Late Antiquity." Pp. 103–52 in *Society and the Holy in Late Antiquity.* Berkeley: University of California Press, 1982.

———. *The Body and Society: Men, Women, and Sexual Renunciation in Early Christianity.* New York: Columbia University Press, 1988.

Brown, Raymond E. "The Pater Noster as an Eschatological Prayer." Pp. 217–53 in *New Testament Essays.* Milwaukee: Bruce, 1965.

Bruner, Edward M., and Victor W. Turner. *The Anthropology of Experience.* Urbana: University of Illinois Press, 1986.

Bryant, H. E. "Matthew v. 38, 39." *ExpTim* 48 (1936–37): 236–37.

Bultmann, Rudolf. "The New Testament and Mythology: The Mythological Element in the Message of the New Testament and the Problem of its Reinterpretation." Pp. 1–44 in Hans Werner Bartsch, ed., *Kerygma and Myth.* Reginald Fuller, rev. and trans. New York: Harper & Row, 1961.

———. *The History of the Synoptic Tradition.* J. Marsh, trans. New York and Evanston: Harper & Row, 1963.

———. "The Problem of Hermeneutics." Pp. 234–61 in *Essays: Philosophical and Theological.* James C. G. Greig, trans. London: SCM, 1955.

Burkert, Walter. "Craft Versus Sect: The Problem of Orphics and Pythagoreans." Pp. 1–22 in Meyers and Sanders, *Self-Definition in the Greco-Roman World.*

Caizzi, F. Decleva. "Cinici." Pp. 503–11 in Francesco della Corte, ed., *Dizionario degli Scrittori Greci e Latini.* Vol. 1. Milan: Marzorati, 1987.

Cameron, Ron. " 'What Have You Come Out to See?' Characterizations of John and Jesus in the Gospels." *Semeia* 49 (1990): 35–69.

Camilleri, Carmel, ed. *Stratégies identitaires.* Paris: Presses Universitaires de France, 1990.

Camponovo, Odo. *Königtum, Königsherrschaft und Reich Gottes in den frühjüdischen Schriften.* Freiburg: Universitätsverlag, 1984.

Capelle, W. "Altgriechische Askese." *NJA* 13 (1910): 681–708.

Cappelletti, A. J. "Religiosidad e iconoclasía del cinismo." *Universidad* 52 (1962): 5–12.

Carmignac, Jean. *Recherches sur le "Nôtre Père."* Paris: Letonzey & Ané, 1969.

Carruth, Shawn. "Q 6:27–36. First Response." Claremont, Calif.: IQP, 1993.

Charlesworth, James H., ed. *The Old Testament Pseudepigrapha.* 2 vols. Garden City, N.Y.: Doubleday, 1985.

———. *Jesus within Judaism: New Light from Exciting Archaeological Discoveries.* Garden City, N.Y.: Doubleday, 1988.

Chilton, Bruce, ed. *The Kingdom of God.* Philadelphia: Fortress; London: SPCK, 1984.

Clifford, James. *The Predicament of Culture: Twentieth-Century Ethnography, Literature, and Art.* Cambridge, Mass., and London: Harvard University Press, 1988.

Collins, Adela Yarbo. "The Origin of the Designation of Jesus as 'Son of Man.' " *HTR* 80 (1987): 391–407.

Cotter, Wendy J. "The Parable of the Children in the Market-Place, Q (Lk) 7:31–35: An Examination of the Parable's Image and Significance." *NovT* 29 (1987): 289–304.

──────. "The Parables of the Mustard Seed and the Leaven: Their Function in the Earliest Stratum of Q." *TJT* 8 (1992): 38–51.

Couroyer, B. "Le 'doigt de Dieu' (Exode VIII, 15)." *RB* 63 (1956): 481–95.

Crossan, John Dominic. *In Parables: The Challenge of the Historical Jesus.* New York: Harper & Row, 1973.

──────. *The Historical Jesus: The Life of a Mediterranean Jewish Peasant.* San Francisco: HarperSanFrancisco, 1991.

Currie, S. D. "Matthew 5:39a — Resistance or Protest?" *HTR* 57 (1964): 140–45.

Dahl, Nils. "The Parables of Growth." *ST* 5 (1951): 132–66. Repr. as pp. 141–66 in *Jesus in the Memory of the Early Church.* Minneapolis: Augsburg, 1976.

Dalman, G. *Orte und Wege Jesu.* Gütersloh: Bertelsmann, 1924.

Daniel, C. "Les Ésseniens et 'ceux qui sont dans les maisons des rois.'" *RevQ* 6 (1967): 261–77.

Daraki, M. "Les fils de la mort: la necrophagie cynique et stoïcienne." Pp. 155–76 in *La mort, les morts dan les sociétés anciennes.* Cambridge: Cambridge University Press; Paris: Éditions de la Maison des Sciences de l'Homme, 1982.

Daube, David. "Matthew v. 38f." *JTS* 45 (1944): 177–87.

Davis, J. *Times and Identities.* Oxford: Clarendon, 1991.

Davison, W. H. "Note on Matthew v. 39." *ExpTim* 22 (1910–11): 231.

Degenhardt, H. J. *Lukas, Evangelist der Armen.* Stuttgart: KBW, 1965.

Deissmann, A. *Light from the Ancient East.* 2nd ed. London: Hodder & Stoughton; New York: Harper & Brothers, 1927.

──────. "Ἐπιούσιος." Pp. 115–19 in *Neutestamentliche Studien.* FS G. Heinrici. Leipzig: Hinrichs, 1914.

Delobel, Joël, ed., *Logia: Les Paroles de Jesus — The Sayings of Jesus.* Leuven: Uitgeverij Peeters/Leuven University Press, 1982.

Dentzer, Jean-Marie, and Winfried Orthmann, eds. *Archéologie et histoire de la Syrie.* Vol. 2. Saarbrücken: Saarbrücker Druckerei und Verlag, 1989.

De Sola Pool, David. *The Kaddish.* New York: Bloch, 1929.

Détienne, M. *Dionysos mis à mort.* Paris: Gallimard, 1977.

Détienne, M., and J. P. Vernant. *Les ruses de l'intelligence: la metis des Grecs.* Paris: Flammarion, 1974. ET: *Cunning Intelligence in Greek Culture and Society.* Chicago: University of Chicago Press, 1991.

Dibelius, Martin. *Die urchristliche Überlieferung von Johannes dem Täufer.* Göttingen, 1911.

Dihle, Albrecht. *Die Goldene Regel.* Göttingen: Vandenhoeck & Ruprecht, 1962.

──────. "Vom sonnenhaften Auge." Pp. 85–91 in H.-D. Blume and F. Mann, eds., *Platonismus und Christentum.* FS H. Dörrie. Münster: Aschendorff, 1983.

Dillon, Richard J. "Ravens, Lilies, and the Kingdom of God (Matthew 6:25–33/Luke 12:22–31)." *CBQ* 53 (1991): 605–27.

DiSante, Carmine. *Jewish Prayer: The Origins of Christian Liturgy.* M. J. O'Connell, trans. New York and Mahwah, N.J.: Paulist, 1991.

Dodd, C. H. *The Parables of the Kingdom.* London and Glasgow: Collins, 1961.

————. "The Beatitudes: A Form-critical Study." Pp. 1–10 in *More New Testament Studies.* Manchester: Manchester University, 1968.

Donzelli, G. Basta. "Un' ideologia 'contestataria' del secolo IV a.c." *SIFC* 42 (1970): 225–51.

Döring, K. "Die Kyniker, eine antike Protestbewegung." *AU* 28, no. 6 (1985): 19–38.

Douglas, R. Conrad. "Once Again 'Love Your Enemies': Rhetorical and Social Scientific Considerations of a Familiar Passage." Paper presented at the 1990 SBL meeting, New Orleans, La.

Downing, F. Gerald. "Contemporary Analogies to the Gospels and Acts: Genres or Motifs?" Pp. 51–65 in C. M. Tuckett, ed., *Synoptic Studies: The Ampleforth Conferences of 1982 and 1983.* Sheffield: JSOT, 1984.

————. "Cynics and Christians." *NTS* 30 (1984): 584–93.

————. "Ears to Hear." Pp. 97–121 in A. E. Harvey, ed., *Alternative Approaches to New Testament Study.* London: SPCK, 1985.

————. "The Social Contexts of Jesus the Teacher." *NTS* 33 (1987): 439–51.

————. "Quite Like 'Q': A Genre for 'Q,' the Lives of Cynic Philosophers." *Bib* 69 (1988): 196–225.

————. *Christ and the Cynics: Jesus and Other Radical Preachers in First-Century Tradition.* Sheffield: Sheffield University Press, 1988.

————. *Cynics and Christian Origins.* Edinburgh: T. & T. Clark, 1992.

Droge, Arthur J., and J. D. Tabor. *A Noble Death: Suicide and Martyrdom among Christians and Jews in Antiquity.* San Francisco: HarperSanFrancisco, 1992.

Dudley, D. *History of Cynicism from Diogenes to the 6th Century A.D.* London: Methuen, 1937.

Duhaime, J. "Early Christianity and the Social Sciences: A Bibliography." *Social Compass* 39 (1992): 275–90.

Easton, B. S. *The Gospel according to St. Luke.* New York: Scribner, 1926.

Edwards, Douglas R. "First Century Urban/Rural Relations in Lower Galilee: Exploring the Archaeological and Literary Evidence." *SBLSP* 27 (1988): 169–82.

Edwards, Richard A. *A Theology of Q.* Philadelphia: Fortress, 1976.

Elbogen, I. *Der jüdische Gottesdienst in seiner geschichtlichen Entwicklung.* Leipzig: Fock, 1913.

Elliott, John H. *A Home for the Homeless: A Sociological Exegesis of 1 Peter, Its Situation and Strategy.* Philadelphia: Fortress, 1981. 2nd ed. with a new introduction; Minneapolis: Fortress, 1990.

————. "The Fear of the Leer: The Evil Eye from the Bible to Li'l Abner." *Forum* 4, no. 4 (1988): 42–71.

————. "Temple versus Household in Luke-Acts: A Contrast in Social Institutions." Pp. 211–40 in Neyrey, *Social World of Luke-Acts.*

————, ed. *Social Scientific Criticism of the New Testament and Its Social World. Semeia 35.* Decatur, Ga.: Scholars, 1986.

Emaljanow, V. "A Note on the Cynic Short Cut to Virtue." *Mnemosyne* 18 (1965): 182–84.

Encyclopedia Judaica. 16 vols. Jerusalem: Keter, 1971.

Ernst, Josef. *Johannes der Täufer: Interpretation-Geschichte-Wirkungsgeschichte.* Berlin and New York: de Gruyter, 1989.

Ferrater Mora, J. "Cyniques et Stoïciens." *RMM* 62 (1957): 20–36.

Fischel, H. A. "Studies in Cynicism and the Ancient Near East: The Transformation of a Chreia." Pp. 372–411 in Jacob Neusner, ed., *Religions in Antiquity: Essays in Memory of Erwin Ramsdell Goodenough.* Leiden: Brill, 1968.

Fitzmyer, Joseph A. *The Gospel according to Luke.* 2 vols. Garden City, N.Y.: Doubleday, 1981–85.

Fleddermann, H. "The Mustard Seed and the Leaven in Q, the Synoptics and Thomas." *SBLSP* 28 (1989): 216–36.

Foner, Eric. "Restructuring Yesterday's News: The Russians Write a New History." *Harper's* (December 1990): 70–78.

Foucault, Michel. *The Birth of the Clinic: An Archeology of Medical Perception.* New York: Pantheon, 1973.

————. *The Use of Pleasure.* Vol. 2. *The History of Sexuality.* New York: Vintage Books, 1985.

Fox, Robin Lane. *Pagans and Christians.* San Francisco: Harper & Row, 1986.

Frankenberg, W. *Die syrischen Clementinen mit griechischem Paralleltext.* Leipzig: Hinrichs, 1937.

Frankenmölle, H. "Die Makarismen (Mt 5, 1–12; Lk 6, 20–23): Motive und Umfang der redaktionellen Komposition." *BZ* 15 (1971): 52–75.

Frei, Hans. *The Eclipse of Biblical Narrative: A Study in Eighteenth and Nineteenth-Century Hermeneutics.* New Haven: Yale University Press, 1974.

Freudenberg, J. "Die synoptische Weherufe: Tradition und Redaktion in Mt 23 par." Münster, 1972.

Freyne, Sean. *Galilee from Alexander the Great to Hadrian, 323 BCE to 135 CE: A Study of Second Temple Judaism.* Wilmington, Del.: Glazier, 1980.

————. *Galilee, Jesus, and the Gospels: Literary Approaches and Historical Investigations.* Philadelphia: Fortress, 1988.

Frye, Northrop. *The Secular Scripture: A Study of the Structure of Romance.* Cambridge, Mass., and London: Harvard University Press, 1976.

————. *The Great Code: The Bible and Literature.* Markham, Ont.: Penguin Books, 1990.

Fuchs, E. "Die Verkündigung Jesus: Der Spruch von den Raben." Pp. 385–88 in H. Ristow and K. Matthiae, eds., *Der historische Jesus und der kerygmatische Christus.* 3rd ed. Berlin: Evangelische Verlagsanstalt, 1964.

Furnish, Victor Paul. *The Love Command in the New Testament.* Nashville and New York: Abingdon, 1972.

Gächter, P. *Das Matthäusevangelium*. Innsbruck: Tyrolia, 1963.

Garland, David E. *The Intention of Matthew 23*. Leiden: Brill, 1979.

Geertz, Clifford. "Ideology as a Cultural System." Pp. 193–233 in *The Interpretation of Cultures*. New York: Basic Books, 1973.

George, A. "Note sur quelques traits lucaniens de l'expression 'Par le doigt de Dieu' (Luc XI, 20)." *ScEccl* 18 (1966): 461–66. Repr. as pp. 128–32 in *Études sur l'oeuvre de Luc*. Paris: Gabalda, 1978.

Georgi, Dieter. *Die Gegner des Paulus im 2. Korintherbrief*. Neukirchen-Vluyn: Neukirchener Verlag, 1964. ET: *The Opponents of Paul in Second Corinthians*. Edinburgh: T. & T. Clark, 1987.

Gerhard, G. A. *Phoinix von Kolophon*. Leipzig and Berlin: Teubner, 1909.

———. "Zur Legende vom Kyniker Diogenes." *ARW* 15 (1912): 388–408.

Golenischchev, Vladimir Semenovich. *Les papyrus hiératiques*. Catalogue general des antiquités égyptiennes du Musée de Caire, no. 58001–36 [n.d.].

Goulet-Cazé, Marie-Odile. "Les cyniques grecs." *RPh* 52 (1978): 112–20.

———. "Un syllogisme stoïcien sur la loi dans la doxographie de Diogène le Cynique. A propos de Diogène Laërce VI 72." *RM* 125 (1982): 214–40.

———. *L'ascèse cynique: un commentaire de Diogène Laërce VI 70–71*. Paris: Vrin, 1986.

———. "Le cynisme à l'époque impériale." *ANRW* II.36.4 (1990): 2720–2833.

Granata, Giovanni. "La 'sinapis' del vangelo: Nicotiana Glauca Graham o senape nera?" *B&O* 24, no. 133 (1982): 175–77.

———. "Some More Information about Mustard and the Gospel." *B&O* 25, no. 136 (1983): 105–6.

Grant, F. C. "The Mission of the Disciples: Mt 9:35–11:1 and Parallels." *JBL* 35 (1916): 293–314.

Grant, Robert M. *Early Christianity and Society*. San Francisco: Harper & Row, 1977.

Grundmann, Walter. *Das Evangelium nach Matthäus*. Berlin: Evangelische Verlagsanstalt, 1968.

———. *Das Evangelium nach Lukas*. 2nd ed. Berlin: Evangelische Verlagsanstalt, 1961.

———. *Das Evangelium nach Markus*. Berlin: Evangelischer Verlag, 1971.

Guenther, Heinz O. "Greek: The Home of Primitive Christianity." *TJT* 5 (1989): 247–79.

———. "The Sayings Gospel Q and the Quest for Aramaic Sources: Rethinking Christian Origins." *Semeia* 55 (1992): 41–75.

Güttgemanns, Erhardt. *Candid Questions concerning Gospel Form Criticism: A Methodological Sketch of the Fundamental Problematics of Form and Redaction Criticism*. W. G. Doty, trans. Pittsburgh: Pickwick, 1979.

Haas, H. *Idee und Ideal der Feindesliebe in der ausserchristlichen Welt*. Leipzig: Edelmann, 1927.

Haenchen, Ernst. "Matthäus 23." *ZTK* 48 (1951): 38–63.

———. *Der Weg Jesu: Eine Erklärung des Markus Evangeliums und der kanonischen Parallelen*. 2nd ed. Berlin: de Gruyter, 1968.

Hahn, Ferdinand. *Christologische Hoheitstitel*. Göttingen: Vandenhoeck & Ruprecht, 1963.

————. *Mission in the New Testament*. Frank Clarke, trans. London: SCM; Naperville, Ill.: Allenson, 1965.

Hanson, Paul D. *The Diversity of Scripture: A Theological Interpretation.* Philadelphia: Fortress, 1982.

Hare, Douglas R. A. *The Son of Man Tradition.* Minneapolis: Fortress, 1990.

Harnack, Adolf von. *The Sayings of Jesus.* J. R. Wilkinson, trans. New York: Putnam; London: Williams & Norgate, 1908.

"Harper's Index." *Harper's* 282/1691 (April 1991): 15.

Harpham, Geoffrey Galt. *The Ascetic Imperative in Culture and Criticism.* Chicago and London: University of Chicago Press, 1987.

Harrington, Daniel J. "Sociological Concepts and the Early Church: A Decade of Research." *TS* 41 (1980): 181–90.

Harris, B. F. "Stoic and Cynic Under Vespasian." *Prudentia* 9 (1977): 105–14.

Haupt, W. *Worte Jesu und Gemeindeüberlieferung.* Leipzig: Hinrichs, 1913.

Havener, Ivan. *Q: The Sayings of Jesus.* Wilmington, Del.: Glazier, 1987.

Hegel, Georg Wilhelm Friedrich. *Phaenomenologie des Geistes.* ET: *The Phenomenology of Mind.* J. B. Baillie, trans. with an introduction and notes. Introduction to Torchbook ed. by George Lichtheim. New York: Harper & Row, 1967.

Heichelheim, F. M. "Roman Syria." Pp. 121–257 in T. Frank, ed., *An Economic Survey of Ancient Rome.* Vol. 4. Paterson, N.J.: Pageant, 1959.

Heinemann, I. "Nochmals Matth 5, 42ff." *BZ* 24 (1938–39): 136–38.

Heinemann, Joseph. "Prayers of Beth Midrash Origin." *JSS* 5 (1960): 264–84.

Heinen, Heinz. "Göttliche Sitometrie: Beobachtungen zur Brotbitte des Vater-unsers." *TTZ* 99 (1990): 72–79.

Heinrichs, F. P. "Die Komposition der antipharisäischen und antirabbinischen Weherede bei den Synoptikern." Munich, 1950.

Helgeland, John. "Civil Religion, Military Religion: Roman and American." *Forum* 5, no. 1 (1989): 22–44.

Helm, R. "Kynismus." *RE* 12 (1924) 1:3–24.

Hengel, Martin. *Nachfolge und Charisma.* Berlin: de Gruyter, 1968. ET: *The Charismatic Leader and His Followers.* J. Greig, trans. New York: Crossroad, 1981.

————. *Crucifixion: In the ancient world and the folly of the message of the cross.* Philadelphia: Fortress, 1977.

Hennecke, Edgar, and Wilhelm Schneemelcher, eds. *New Testament Apocrypha.* 2 vols. R. McL. Wilson, trans. and ed. Philadelphia: Westminster, 1963–65.

Henrichs, A. "Zwei Fragmente über die Erziehung (Antisthenes)." *ZPE* 1 (1967): 45–53.

Hirsch, Emanuel. *Frühgeschichte des Evangeliums.* Vol. 2. *Vorlagen des Lukas und das Sondergut des Matthäus.* Tübingen: Mohr, 1941.

Hochkeppel, Willy. "Mit zynischem Lächeln: Die Kyniker als Hippies der Antike." Pp. 99–116 in *War Epikur ein Epikureer? Aktuelle Weisheitslehren der Antike.* Munich: Deutscher Taschenbuch Verlag, 1984.

Hock, Ronald F. "A Dog in the Manger: The Cynic Cynulcus among Athenaeus' Deipnosophists." Pp. 20–37 in David L. Balch, Wayne A.

Meeks, and Everett Ferguson, eds., *Greeks, Romans, and Christians: Essays in Honor of Abraham J. Malherbe.* Minneapolis: Fortress, 1990.

Hoffmann, Paul. "πάντες ἐργάται ἀδικίας: Redaktion und Tradition in Lk 13, 22–30." *ZNW* 58 (1967): 188–214.

———. "Lk 10, 5–11 in der Instruktionsrede der Logienquelle." Pp. 37–53 in *EKK-Vorarbeiten 3.* Zürich: Benzinger, 1971.

———. *Studien zur Theologie der Logienquelle.* 3rd ed. Aschendorff: Münster, 1982 (originally published 1972).

———. Review of "S. Schulz, *Q: Die Spruchquelle der Evangelisten.*" *BZ* ns 19 (1975): 104–15.

———. "Tradition und Situation: Zur 'Verbindlichkeit' des Gebots der Feindesliebe in der synoptischen Überlieferung und in der gegenwärtigen Friedensdiskussion." Pp. 50–118 in Karl Kertelge, ed., *Ethik im Neuen Testament.* Freiburg: Herder, 1984.

Hoïstad, Ragnar. *Cynic Hero and Cynic King: Studies in the Cynic Conception of Man.* Uppsala: Bloms, 1948.

———. "Cynicism." *DHI* (1968) 1:627–34.

Hommel, H. "Herrenworte im Lichte sokratischer Überlieferung." *ZNW* 57 (1966): 1–23.

hooks, bell. "Choosing the Margin as a Space of Radical Openness." Pp. 145–53 in *Yearning: race, gender, and cultural politics.* Boston: South End, 1990.

Horsley, Richard A. "Popular Messianic Movements around the Time of Jesus." *CBQ* 46 (1984): 471–95.

———. "Like One of the Prophets of Old: Two Types of Popular Prophets at the Time of Jesus." *CBQ* 47 (1985): 435–63.

———. "Popular Prophetic Movements at the Time of Jesus, Their Principal Features and Social Origins." *JSNT* 26 (1986): 3–27.

———. "Ethics and Exegesis: 'Love Your Enemies' and the Doctrine of Non-Violence." *JAAR* 54 (1986): 3–31.

———. *Jesus and the Spiral of Violence: Popular Jewish Resistance in Roman Palestine.* San Francisco: Harper & Row, 1987.

———. "Bandits, Messiahs, and Longshoremen: Popular Unrest in Galilee Around the Time of Jesus." *SBLSP* 27 (1988): 183–99.

———. *Sociology and the Jesus Movement.* New York: Crossroad, 1989.

———. "The Q People: Renovation, not Radicalism." *Continuum* 1, no. 3 (1991): 49–63.

Horsley, Richard A., and John S. Hanson. *Bandits, Prophets, and Messiahs: Popular Movements in the Time of Jesus.* Minneapolis: Winston, 1985.

Hull, John M. *Hellenistic Magic and the Synoptic Tradition.* Naperville, Ill.: Allenson, 1974.

L'identité: Séminaire interdisciplinaire dirigé par Claude Lévi-Strauss. Paris: Grasset, 1977.

Isenberg, S. R. "Millenarism in Greco-Roman Palestine." *Religion* 4 (1974): 26–46.

Jacobson, Arland D. "Wisdom Christology in Q." Ph.D. diss., The Claremont Graduate School, 1978.

———. "The Literary Unity of Q: Lc 10, 2–16 and Parallels as a Test Case." Pp. 419–23 in Delobel, *Logia.*

———. *The First Gospel: An Introduction to Q.* Sonoma, Calif.: Polebridge, 1992.

Jefford, Clayton N. *The Sayings of Jesus in the Teachings of the Twelve Apostles.* Leiden: Brill, 1989.

Jeremias, Joachim. *Heiligengräber in Jesu Umwelt (Mt. 23, 29; Lk. 11, 47): Eine Untersuchung zur Volksreligion der Zeit Jesu.* Göttingen: Vandenhoeck & Ruprecht, 1958.

———. "Drei weitere spätjüdische Heiligengräber." *ZNW* 52 (1961): 95–101.

———. "Vaterunser." *RRG* (1962) 6:1235–37.

———. *Abba.* Göttingen: Vandenhoeck & Ruprecht, 1966.

———. *The Prayers of Jesus.* London: SCM, 1967.

———. *The Parables of Jesus.* Rev. ed. London: SCM, 1972.

———. "The Lord's Prayer in Modern Research." Pp. 82–107 in *The Prayers of Jesus.*

———. *New Testament Theology.* Vol. 1. *The Proclamation of Jesus.* J. Bowden, trans. New York: Scribner, 1971.

Jolliffe, R. "The Woes on the Pharisees: A Critical Text and Commentary on Q 11:46, 43, 52, 42, 39–40, 47–48." Ph.D. diss., The Claremont Graduate School, 1990:

Jülicher, D. Adolf. *Die Gleichnisreden Jesu. Zweiter Teil. Auslegung der Gleichnisreden der drei ersten Evangelien.* Tübingen: Mohr, 1910.

Jüngel, Eberhard. *Paulus und Jesus.* 3rd ed. Tübingen: Mohr, 1967.

Kakridis, John Th. "A Cynic Homeromastix." Pp. 361–73 in John L. Heller, ed. with the assistance of J. K. Newman, *Serta Turyniana: Studies in Greek Literature and Palaeography in honor of Alexander Turyn.* Urbana, Chicago, and London: University of Illinois Press, 1974.

Kasher, A., G. Fuks, and U. Rappaport. *Greece and Rome in Eretz Israel: Collected Essays.* Jerusalem: Yad Ishak Ben-Zvi/Israel Exploration Society, 1990.

Kelber, W. *The Oral and the Written Gospel.* Philadelphia: Fortress, 1983.

Kim, M.-S. *Die Trägergruppe von Q: Sozialgeschichtliche Forschung zur Q-Überlieferung in den synoptischen Evangelien.* Ammersbek: Lottbek-Jensen, 1990.

Kindstrand, Jan Fredrik. *Bion of Borysthenes: A Collection of the Fragments with Introduction and Commentary.* Uppsala: Universitet, 1976.

Klassen, William. "Love Your Enemy: A Study of New Testament Teachings on Coping with an Enemy." Pp. 153–83 in Paul Peachey, ed., *Biblical Realism Confronts the Nation.* Scottdale, Pa.: Fellowship Publications, 1963.

———. *Love of Enemies: The Way to Peace.* Philadelphia: Fortress, 1984.

Kloppenborg, John S. "The Sayings of Jesus in the Didache." M.A. thesis, University of St. Michael's College, 1976.

———. "Tradition and Redaction in the Synoptic Sayings Source." *CBQ* 46 (1984): 34–62.

———. "Bibliography on Q." *SBLSP* 24 (1985): 103–26.

———. "Blessing and Marginality: The 'Persecution Beatitude' in Q, Thomas and Early Christianity." *Forum* 2, no. 3 (1986): 36–56.

———. *The Formation of Q: Trajectories in Ancient Wisdom Collections.* Philadelphia: Fortress, 1987.

———. *Q Parallels: Synopsis, Critical Notes and Concordance.* Sonoma, Calif.: Polebridge, 1988.

———. "Law and Salvation in Q." Paper presented at the 1986 CSBS meeting, Winnipeg, Man.

———. "*Nomos* and *Ethos* in Q." Pp. 35–48 in J. E. Goehring, J. T. Sanders, and C. W. Hedrick, in collaboration with H. D. Betz, eds., *Gospel Origins and Christian Beginnings: In Honor of James M. Robinson.* Sonoma, Calif.: Polebridge, 1990.

———. "Literary Convention, Self-Evidence and the Social History of the Q People." *Semeia* 55 (1992): 77–102.

———. "The Sayings Gospel Q: Literary and Stratigraphic Problems." Forthcoming in *ANRW* 25.6.

———. "Jesus and the Parables of Jesus in Q." Forthcoming in R. Piper, *Studies in Q.*

Klostermann, Erich. *Das Matthäusevangelium.* 2nd ed. Tübingen: Mohr, 1927.

———. *Das Lukasevangelium.* 2nd ed. Tübingen: Mohr, 1929.

Knox, W. L. *The Sources of the Synoptic Gospels.* Vol. 2. *St. Luke and St. Matthew.* Cambridge: University Press, 1957.

Kock, T. *Comicorum Atticorum Fragmenta.* 3 vols. Leipzig: Teubner, 1880–88.

Koester, Helmut. *Synoptische Überlieferungen bei den apostolischen Vätern.* Berlin: Akademie, 1957.

———. "Apocryphal and Canonical Gospels." *HTR* 73 (1980): 105–30.

———. "GNOMAI DIAPHOROI: The Origin and Nature of Diversification in the History of Early Christianity." Pp. 114–57 in idem and Robinson, *Trajectories through Early Christianity.*

———. "One Jesus and Four Primitive Gospels." Pp. 158–204 in idem and Robinson, *Trajectories through Early Christianity.*

Koester, Helmut and James M. Robinson. *Trajectories through Early Christianity.* Philadelphia: Fortress, 1971.

Kraeling, C. H. *John the Baptist.* New York: Scribner, 1951.

Kraft, H. *Die Entstehung des Christentums.* Darmstadt: Wissenschaftlicher Verlag, 1981.

Krauss, S. "Die Instruktion Jesu an die Apostel." *Angelos* 1 (1925): 96–102.

Kretschmar, Georg. "Ein Beitrag zur Frage nach dem Ursprung frühchristlicher Askese." *ZTK* 61 (1964): 27–67.

Krieger, Norman. "Ein Mensch in weichen Kleidern." *NovT* 1 (1956): 228–30.

Kruse, H. "Das Reich Satans." *Bib* 58 (1977): 29–61.

Kümmel, W. G. "Die Weherufe über die Schriftgelehrten und Pharisäer (Matthäus 23, 13–36)." Pp. 135–47 in W. P. Eckert, N. P. Levinson, and M. Stöhr, eds., *Antijüdisches im Neuen Testament? Exegetische und systematische Beiträge.* Munich: Kaiser, 1967.

Kuss, Otto. "Zum Sinngehalt des Doppelgleichnisses vom Senfkorn und Sauerteig." *Bib* 40 (1959): 641–53.

Labriolle, P. de. *La réaction païenne*. Paris: L'Artisan du Livre, 1948.

Lagrange, M. J. *Évangile selon Saint Marc*. Paris: Gabalda, 1929.

————. *L'évangile selon Saint Luc*. Paris: Gabalda, 1941.

Lang, B. "Grussverbot oder Besuchsverbot? Eine sozialgeschichtliche Deutung von Lukas 10, 4b." *BZ* 26 (1982): 75–79.

Laufen, Rudolf. *Die Doppelüberlieferung der Logienquelle und des Markusevangeliums*. Königstein: Hanstein, 1980.

Layton, Bentley. "The Sources, Date and Transmission of *Didache* 1.3b–2.1." *HTR* 61 (1968): 343–83.

————. *The Gnostic Scriptures: A New Translation with Annotations and Introductions*. Garden City, N.Y.: Doubleday, 1987.

————, ed. *Nag Hammadi Codex II, 2–7 together with XIII, 2*, Brit. Lib. Or. 4926(1), and P.Oxy. 1*. 2 vols. Nag Hammadi Studies, 20–21. Leiden: Brill, 1989.

Legrand, L. "Bare Foot Apostles? The Shoes of St. Mark (Mk. 6:8–9 and parallels)." *ITS* 16 (1979): 201–19.

Lentz, A. *Herodiani Technici Reliquiae*. 2 vols. Hildesheim: Olms, 1965.

Levine, Amy-Jill. "Feminist Food for Thought: The Leavening of the Q Community." Paper presented at the 1992 SBL meeting, San Francisco, Calif.

————. "Who's Catering the Q Affair?" *Semeia* 50 (1990): 145–61.

Lévi-Strauss, Claude. *The Savage Mind*. London: Weidenfeld & Nicolson, 1968.

Liddell, H. G., and R. Scott. *A Greek-English Lexicon*. Rev. and augmented by H. S. Jones with the assistance of R. McKenzie. Oxford: Clarendon, 1925.

Liechtenhan, R. *Die urchristliche Mission*. Zürich: Zwingli, 1946.

Lignée, H. "La Mission des Soixante-Douze: Lc 10, 1–12.17–20." *AssS* 45 (1974): 64–74.

Lisco, F. G. *Biblische Betrachtungen über Johannes den Täufer*. Berlin: Enslin, 1836.

Lohmeyer, Ernst. *Das Evangelium des Markus*. 17th ed. Göttingen: Vandenhoeck & Ruprecht, 1967.

Loisy, Alfred. *Les évangiles synoptiques*. Ceffonds: Loisy, 1907.

————. *L'évangile selon Luc*. Paris: Nourry, 1924.

Longstaff, Thomas Richmond Willis and Page A. Thomas, compilers and eds. *The Synoptic Problem: A Bibliography, 1716–1988*. Macon, Ga.: Mercer University Press, 1988.

Lovejoy, Arthur O., and George Boas. *Primitivism and Related Ideas in Antiquity*. With supplementary essays by W. F. Albright and P.-E. Dumont. Baltimore: Johns Hopkins University Press, 1935.

Lührmann, Dieter. *Die Redaktion der Logienquelle*. Neukirchen-Vluyn: Neukirchener Verlag, 1969.

————. "Liebet eure Feinde (Lk 6, 27–36/Mt 5, 39–48)." *ZTK* 69 (1972): 412–38.

Luria, S. "Zur Quelle von Mt 8:19." *ZNW* 25 (1926): 282–86.

Luz, M. "Salam, Meleager!" *SIFC* 6 (1988): 222–31.

————. "A Description of the Greek Cynic in the Jerusalem Talmud." *JSJ* 20 (1989): 49–60.

Maccoby, Hyam. "The Washing of Cups." *JSNT* 14 (1982): 3–15.

MacCunn, J. "The Cynics." *IJE* 14 (1904): 185–200.

Mack, Burton L. *A Myth of Innocence: Mark and Christian Origins*. Philadelphia: Fortress, 1988.

———. *The Lost Gospel: The Book of Q and Christian Origins*. San Francisco: HarperSanFrancisco, 1993.

MacMullen, Ramsay. *Roman Social Relations: 50 B.C. to A.D. 384*. New Haven, Conn., and London: Yale University Press, 1974.

Malherbe, Abraham J. " 'Gentle as a Nurse': The Cynic Background to 1 Thess ii." *NovT* 12 (1970): 203–17. Repr. as pp. 35–48 in idem, *Paul and the Popular Philosophers*.

———. "Cynics." *IDBSup* (1976): 201–3.

———. "Pseudo Heraclitus, Epistle 4: The Divinization of the Wise Man." *JAC* 21 (1978): 42–64.

———. "Self-Definition among Epicureans and Cynics." Pp. 46–54 in Meyer and Sanders, *Self-Definition in the Greco-Roman World*. Repr. as pp. 11–24 in Malherbe, *Paul and the Popular Philosophers*.

———. "In Season and Out of Season: 2 Timothy 4:2." *JBL* 103 (1984): 35–43. Repr. as pp. 137–45 in idem, *Paul and the Popular Philosophers*.

———. *Paul and the Popular Philosophers*. Minneapolis: Fortress, 1989.

———. " 'Pastoral Care' in the Thessalonian Church." *NTS* 36 (1990): 375–91.

———, ed. *The Cynic Epistles*. Missoula, Mont.: Scholars, 1977.

Malina, Bruce J. *The New Testament World: Insights from Cultural Anthropology*. Atlanta: Knox, 1981.

———. *The Gospel of John in Sociolinguistic Perspective: Protocol of the Forty-Eighth Colloquy, 11 March 1984*. Berkeley, Calif.: Center for Hermeneutical Studies in Hellenistic and Modern Culture, 1985.

———. *Christian Origins and Cultural Anthropology: Practical Models for Biblical Interpretation*. Atlanta: Knox, 1986.

Malina, Bruce J., and Jerome Neyrey. *Calling Jesus Names: The Social Value of Labels in Matthew*. Sonoma, Calif.: Polebridge, 1988.

Manns, Frédéric. *La prière d'Israël à l'heure de Jésus*. Jerusalem: Franciscan Printing Press, 1986.

Manson, Thomas W. *The Sayings of Jesus*. London: SCM, 1949.

Mansoor, M., trans. *The Thanksgiving Hymns*. Vol. 3. Leiden: Brill, 1961.

Marshall, H. "Palestinian and Hellenistic Christianity: Some Critical Comments." *NTS* 19 (1973): 271–87.

McArthur, Harvey K. "The Parable of the Mustard Seed." *CBQ* 33 (1971): 198–210.

McEleney, N. J. "The Beatitudes of the Sermon on the Mount/Plain." *CBQ* 43 (1981): 1–13.

McLean, Bradley. "Q 11:39b. First Response." Claremont, Calif.: IQP, 1991.

Meeks, Wayne. *The First Urban Christians: The Social World of the Apostle Paul*. New Haven, Conn., and London: Yale University Press, 1983.

Metzger, B. "How Many Times Does ἐπιούσιος Occur Outside the Lord's Prayer?" Pp. 64–66 in idem, *Historical and Literary Studies*. Leiden: Brill, 1968.

Metzger, M., ed. with an introduction, translation, and notes. *Les constitutions apostoliques*. Paris: Cerf, 1985.

Meyer, B. F., and E. P. Sanders, eds., *Jewish and Christian Self-Definition*. Vol. 3. *Self-Definition in the Greco-Roman World*. Philadelphia: Fortress, 1982.

Michaelis, W. *Das Evangelium nach Matthäus*. Vol. 2. Zürich: Zwingli, 1949.

Miller, Robert J. "The Inside Is (Not) the Outside: Q 11:39–41 and GThom 89." *Forum* 5, no. 1 (1989): 92–105.

Minear, Paul S. "False Prophecy and Hypocrisy in the Gospel of Matthew." Pp. 76–93 in J. Gnilka, ed., *Neues Testament und Kirche*. FS R. Schnackenburg. Freiburg: Herder & Herder, 1974.

———. *To Heal and to Reveal*. New York: Seabury, 1976.

Miralles, C. "Los cínicos, una contracultura en el mundo antiguo." *EClás* 14 (1970): 347–77.

M'Neile, A. H. *The Gospel According to St. Matthew*. London: MacMillan, 1915.

Moffatt, J. "Matthew v. 39." *Exp* (8th series) 7 (1914A): 89; 8 (1914B): 188–89.

Momigliano, Arnaldo. "Ancient History and the Antiquarian." Pp. 1–39 in idem, *Studies in Historiography*. London: Weidenfeld & Nicolson, 1966.

———. *Essays in Ancient and Modern Historiography*. Oxford: Blackwell, 1977.

———. *The Classical Foundations of Modern Historiography*. Foreword by Riccardo di Donato. Berkeley: University of California Press, 1990.

Montgomery, J. A. "Some Correspondences Between the Elephantine Papyri and the Gospels." *ExpTim* 24 (1912–13): 428–29.

Moreland, Milton C., and James M. Robinson. "The International Q Project Work Sessions 31 July–2 August, 20 November 1992." *JBL* 112 (1993): 500–506.

Moulder, J. "Who Are My Enemies? An Exploration of the Semantic Background of Christ's Command." *JTSA* 25 (1978): 41–49.

Mouzelis, Nicos P. *Back to Sociological Theory: The Construction of Social Orders*. Houndmills, Basingstoke, and Hampshire: MacMillan, 1991.

Mullins, T. Y. "Topos as a New Testament Form." *JBL* 99 (1980): 541–47.

Neirynck, Frans. "L'édition du texte de Q." *ETL* 55 (1979): 373–81.

———. "Recent Developments in the Study of Q." Pp. 29–75 in Delobel, *Logia*.

Neirynck, Frans, and F. van Segbroeck. "Q Bibliography." Pp. 561–86 in Delobel, *Logia*.

———. "Q Bibliography: Additional List 1981–1985." *ETL* 62 (1986): 157–65.

Neugebauer, Fritz. "Die dargebotene Wange und Jesu Gebot der Feindesliebe: Erwägungen zu Lk 6, 27–36/Mt 5, 38–48." *TLZ* 110, no. 12 (1985): 865–76.

Neusner, Jacob. *The Idea of Purity in Ancient Judaism: The Haskell Lectures for 1972–1973*. Leiden: Brill, 1973.

————. *From Politics to Piety: The Emergence of Pharisaic Judaism*. Englewood Cliffs, N.J.: Prentice-Hall, 1973.

————. "'First Cleanse the Inside': The 'Halakhic' Background of a Controversy-Saying." *NTS* 22 (1976): 486–95.

————. "'Israel': Judaism and its Social Metaphors." *JAAR* 55 (1987): 331–61.

Neyrey, Jerome. *An Ideology of Revolt: John's Christology in Social-Science Perspective*. Philadelphia: Fortress, 1988.

————. *Paul, In Other Words: A Cultural Reading of His Letters*. Louisville, Ky.: Westminster/John Knox, 1990.

————, ed. *The Social World of Luke-Acts: Models for Interpretation*. Peabody, Mass.: Hendrickson, 1991.

Niehues-Pröbsting, H. *Der Kynismus des Diogenes und der Begriff des Zynismus*. Munich: Fink, 1979; Frankfurt: Suhrkamp, 1988.

Oakman, Douglas E. *Jesus and the Economic Questions of His Day*. Lewiston, N.Y., and Queenston: Mellen, 1986.

O'Hagan, Angelo. "'Greet No One on the Way' (Lk 10, 4b)." *SBF* 16 (1965–66): 69–84.

O'Neil, Edward N., ed. and trans. *Teles [The Cynic Teacher]*. Missoula, Mont.: Scholars, 1977.

Onfray, M. *Cynismes: portrait du philosophe en chien*. Paris: Grasset, 1990.

Osiek, Carolyn. "The New Handmaid: The Bible and the Social Sciences." *TS* 50 (1989): 260–78.

Otto, Rudolf. "The Kingdom of God Expels the Kingdom of Satan." Pp. 27–35 in Chilton, *Kingdom of God*.

Overman, J. Andrew. "Who Were the First Urban Christians? Urbanization in Galilee in the First Century." *SBLSP* 27 (1988): 160–68.

Pace, Giuseppe. "La senapa del vangelo." *B&O* 22, no. 124 (1980): 119–23.

Paquet, L. *Les cyniques grecs: fragments et témoignages*. Ottawa: Éditions de l'Université d'Ottawa, 1975. 2nd ed., revue, corrigée et augmentée, 1988.

Perrin, Norman. *Jesus and the Language of the Kingdom: Symbol and Metaphor in New Testament Interpretation*. Philadelphia: Fortress, 1976.

————. *Rediscovering the Teaching of Jesus*. New York: Harper & Row, 1976.

Pesch, Wilhelm. "Theologische Aussagen der Redaktion von Matthäus 23." Pp. 286–99 in Paul Hoffmann, ed., *Orientierung an Jesus–Zur Theologie der Synoptiker: Für Josef Schmid*. Freiburg: Herder & Herder, 1973.

Petuchowski, Jakob J., and Clemens Thoma, eds. *Lexicon der jüdisch-christlichen Begegnung*. Freiburg, Basel, and Vienna: Herder, 1989.

Pilch, John J. "Sickness and Healing in Luke-Acts." Pp. 181–209 in Neyrey, *Social World of Luke-Acts*.

Piper, John. *"Love Your Enemies": Jesus' Love Command in the Synoptic Gospels and in the Early Christian Paraenesis*. Cambridge: Cambridge University Press, 1979.

Piper, Ronald A. *Wisdom in the Q Tradition*. Cambridge: Cambridge University Press, 1989.

————. "Q 6:27–36. Second Response." Claremont, Calif.: IQP, 1993.

————, ed. *Studies in Q*. Leiden: Brill (forthcoming).

Plummer, A. *The Gospel According to St. Luke.* 10th ed. New York: Scribner, 1914.

Polag, Athanasius. *Die Christologie der Logienquelle.* Neukirchen-Vluyn: Neukirchener Verlag, 1977.

———. *Fragmenta Q: Textheft zur Logienquelle.* Neukirchen-Vluyn: Neukirchener Verlag, 1979.

Posner, Raphael, Uri Kaploun, and Shalom Cohen, eds. *Jewish Liturgy: Prayer and Synagogue Service through the Ages.* Jerusalem: Keter, 1975.

Powell, J. U., ed. *Collectanea Alexandrina.* Oxford: Clarendon, 1925.

Praechter, Karl. "Zur kynischen Polemik gegen die Bräuche bei Totenbestattung und Totenklage." *Philologus* 57 (1898): 504–7.

Preisigke, Friedrich. *Sammelbuch griechischer Urkunden aus Ägypten.* Vol. 1. Strassburg, 1915.

Rankin, H. D. *Sophists, Socratics and Cynics.* London: Croom; Canberra: Helm, 1983.

Rathey, M. "Talion im NT? Zu Mt 5, 38–42." *ZNW* 83 (1991): 264–66.

Rausch, J. "The Principle of Nonresistance and Love of Enemy in Mt 5, 38–48." *CBQ* 28 (1966): 31–41.

Rawlinson, A. E. J. *St. Mark.* London: Methuen, 1925.

Rich, A. N. M. "The Cynic Conception of αὐτάρκεια." *Mnemosyne* 9 (1956): 23–29.

Ricoeur, Paul. *The Conflict of Interpretations.* D. Ihde, ed. Evanston, Ill.: Northwestern University Press, 1974.

———. "Nabert on Act and Sign." Pp. 211–22 in idem, *Conflict of Interpretations.*

———. "Preface to Bultmann." Pp. 381–401 in idem, *Conflict of Interpretations.*

———. "Explanation and Understanding: On Some Remarkable Connections among the Theory of the Text, Theory of Action, and Theory of History." Pp. 149–66 in Charles E. Reagan and David Stewart, eds., *The Philosophy of Paul Ricoeur: An Anthology of His Work.* Boston: Beacon, 1978. Repr. as pp. 125–43 in Ricoeur, *From Text to Action.*

———. "What Is a Text? Explanation and Understanding." Pp. 145–64 in John B. Thompson, ed. and trans., *Hermeneutics and the Human Sciences.* Cambridge: Cambridge University Press; Paris: Maison des sciences de l'homme, 1981. Repr. as pp. 105–24 in Ricoeur, *From Text to Action.*

———. *The Reality of the Historical Past.* Milwaukee: Marquette University Press, 1984.

———. *Time and Narrative.* 3 vols. Kathleen McLaughlin and David Pellauer, trans. Chicago and London: University of Chicago Press, 1984–88.

———. "The Golden Rule: Exegetical and Theological Perplexities," *NTS* 36 (1990): 392–97.

———. *From Text to Action: Essays in Hermeneutics, II.* Kathleen Blamey and John B. Thompson, trans. Evanston, Ill.: Northwestern University Press, 1991.

———. "The Hermeneutical Function of Distanciation." Pp. 75–88 in idem, *From Text to Action.*

———. "Science and Ideology." Pp. 246–69 in idem, *From Text to Action.*

———. "Hermeneutics and the Critique of Ideology." Pp. 270–307 in idem, *From Text to Action.*

———. "Ideology and Utopia." Pp. 308–24 in idem, *From Text to Action.*

———. *Oneself as Another.* Kathleen Blamey, trans. Chicago and London: University of Chicago Press, 1992.

Riesner, R. *Jesus als Lehrer.* Tübingen: Mohr, 1981.

Rist, John. "Cynicism and Stoicism." Pp. 54–80 in idem, *Stoic Philosophy.* Cambridge: Cambridge University Press, 1969.

Robbins, Vernon K. "Rhetorical Composition and the Beelzebul Controversy." Pp. 161–93 in Burton L. Mack and Vernon K. Robbins, *Patterns of Persuasion in the Gospels.* Sonoma, Calif.: Polebridge, 1989.

———. "Rhetoric and Culture: Exploring Types of Cultural Rhetoric in a Text." Forthcoming in S. E. Porter, ed. *Rhetorical Criticism of Biblical Documents.* FS W. Wuellner. Sheffield: Sheffield Academic Press.

Roberts, K. A. "Toward a Generic Concept of Counter-Culture." *SF* 11, no. 2 (1978): 111–26.

Robinson, James M. *A New Quest of the Historical Jesus.* Philadelphia: Fortress, 1983.

———. "LOGOI SOPHON: On the Gattung of Q." Pp. 71–113 in Koester and Robinson, *Trajectories through Early Christianity.*

———. "Sermon on the Mount/Plain: Work Sheets for the Reconstruction of Q." *SBLSP* 22 (1983): 451–54.

———. "The International Q Project Work Session 17 November 1989." *JBL* 109 (1990): 499–501.

———. "Q 11:40. Second Response." Claremont, Calif.: IQP, 1991.

———. "The International Q Project Work Session 16 November 1990." *JBL* 110 (1991): 494–98.

———. "The Q Trajectory: Between John and Matthew via Jesus." Pp. 173–94 in Birger A. Pearson, ed., in collaboration with A. Thomas Kraabel, George W. E. Nickelsburg, and Norman R. Petersen, *The Future of Early Christianity: Essays in Honor of Helmut Koester.* Minneapolis: Fortress, 1991.

———. "A Critical Text of the Sayings Gospel Q." *RHPR* 72 (1992): 15–22.

Rodier, G. "Morale d'Antisthène." *APhilos* 17 (1906): 33–38.

Rosaldo, Renato. *Culture and Truth: The Remaking of Social Analysis.* Boston: Beacon, 1989.

Saldarini, Anthony J. *Pharisees, Scribes and Sadducees in Palestinian Society: A Sociological Approach.* Wilmington, Del.: Glazier, 1988.

Sauer, Jürgen. "Traditionsgeschichtliche Erwägungen zu den synoptischen und paulinischen Aussagen über Feindesliebe und Wiedervergeltungsverzicht." *ZNW* 76 (1985): 5–14.

Sayre, Farrand. *Diogenes of Sinope: A Study of Greek Cynicism.* Baltimore: Furst, 1938.

———. "Greek Cynicism." *JHI* 6 (1945): 113–18.

———. *The Greek Cynics.* Baltimore: Furst, 1948.

Schenk, Wolfgang. *Synopse zur Redenquelle der Evangelien: Q Synopse und Rekonstruktion in deutscher Übersetzung mit kurzen Erläuterungen.* Düsseldorf: Patmos, 1981.

Schille, G. *Die urchristliche Kollegialmission.* Zürich: Zwingli, 1967.

Schlatter, Adolf. *Der Evangelist Matthäus.* Stuttgart: Calwer, 1957.

———. *Das Evangelium des Lukas.* Stuttgart: Calwer, 1960.

Schmid, Josef. *Matthäus und Lukas: Eine Untersuchung des Verhältnisses ihrer Evangelien.* Freiburg: Herder & Herder, 1930.

———. *Das Evangelium nach Matthäus.* 5th ed. Regensburg: Pustet, 1965.

Schmidt, M. *Hesychii Alexandrini Lexicon / Hesychius of Alexandria. Lexicon.* 5 vols. Jena, 1858–68; repr. Amsterdam: Hakkert, 1965.

Schnackenburg, R. *God's Rule and Kingdom.* New York: Herder & Herder, 1963.

Schneider, C. *Geistesgeschichte des antiken Christentums.* Munich: Beck, 1954.

Schniewind, J. *Das Evangelium nach Matthäus.* 4th ed. Göttingen: Vandenhoeck & Ruprecht, 1950.

Scholer, David. "Q Bibliography: 1981–1986." *SBLSP* 25 (1986): 27–36.

———. "Q Bibliography: 1981–1988." *SBLSP* 27 (1988): 483–95.

———. "Q Bibliography: 1981–1989." *SBLSP* 28 (1989): 23–37.

———. "Q Bibliography. Supplement I: 1990." *SBLSP* 29 (1990): 11–13.

———. "Q Bibliography. Supplement II: 1991." *SBLSP* 30 (1991): 1–7.

———. "Q Bibliography. Supplement III: 1992." *SBLSP* 31 (1992): 1–4.

———. "Q Bibliography. Supplement IV: 1993." *SBLSP* 32 (1993): 1–5.

Schönle, V. *Johannes, Jesus und die Juden: Die theologische Position des Matthäus und des Verfassers der Redenquelle im Lichte von Mt. 11.* Frankfurt am Main: Lang, 1982.

Schottroff, Luise. "Gewaltverzicht und Feindesliebe in der urchristlichen Jesustradition: Mt 5, 38–48; Lk 6, 27–36." Pp. 197–221 in G. Strecker, ed., *Jesus Christus in Historie und Geschichte.* FS H. Conzelmann. Tübingen: Mohr, 1975: ET: "Non-Violence and the Love of One's Enemies." Pp. 9–39 in *Essays on the Love Commandment.* R. H. and I. Fuller, trans. Philadelphia: Fortress, 1978.

———. "Itinerant Prophetesses: A Feminist Analysis of the Sayings Source Q." Occasional Papers, 21. Claremont, Calif.: Institute for Antiquity and Christianity, 1991. German: "Wanderprophetinnen: Eine feministische Analyse der Logienquelle." *EvT* 51 (1991): 332–44.

Schottroff, Luise and Wolfgang Stegemann. *Jesus von Nazareth–Hoffnung der Armen.* Stuttgart: Kohlhammer, 1978. ET: *Jesus and the Hope of the Poor.* M. J. O'Connell, trans. Maryknoll, N.Y.: Orbis, 1986.

Schulthess, F. "Zur Sprache der Evangelien." *ZNW* 21 (1922): 216–58.

Schulz, Siegfried. *Synopse der Q-Überlieferungen.* Zürich: Theologischer Verlag, 1972.

Schumacher, E. F. *Small Is Beautiful: A Study of Economics as if People Mattered.* London: Abacus, 1973.

Schürmann, Heinz. "Mt 10, 5b–6 und die Vorgeschichte des synoptischen Aussendungsberichtes." Pp. 137–49 in *Traditionsgeschichtliche Untersuchungen zu den synoptischen Evangelien.* Düsseldorf: Patmos, 1968.

———. *Das Lukasevangelium.* Vol. 1. Freiburg: Herder, 1969.

———. "Das Zeugnis der Redenquelle für die Basileia-Verkündigung Jesu." Pp. 121–200 in Delobel, *Logia.*

———. "Beobachtungen zum Menschensohn-Titel in der Redenquelle." Pp. 124–47 in *Jesus und der Menschensohn: Für Anton Vögtle.* Freiburg: Herder & Herder, 1975.

———. "Die Redekomposition wider 'dieses Geschlecht' und seine Führung in die Redenquelle (vgl. Mt 23, 1–39 par Lk 11, 37–54): Bestand–Akoluthie–Kompositionsformen." *SNTW* 11 (1986): 33–81.

———. *Q: Die Spruchquelle der Evangelisten.* Zürich: Theologischer Verlag, 1972.

Schwartz, E. *Characterköpfe aus der antiken Literatur.* Leipzig and Berlin, 1919.

Schwarz, G. "'Ihnen gehört das Himmelreich' (Matthäus V. 3)?" *NTS* 23 (1977): 341–43.

Schweitzer, Albert. *The Kingdom of God and Primitive Christianity.* London: A. & C. Black, 1968.

Schweizer, E. "Formgeschichtliches zu den Seligpreisungen Jesu." *NTS* 19 (1973): 121–26.

———. *Das Evangelium nach Matthäus.* Göttingen: Vandenhoeck & Ruprecht, 1973.

Scobie, C. H. H. *John the Baptist.* Philadelphia: Fortress, 1964.

Scott, Bernard Brandon. *Jesus, Symbol-Maker for the Kingdom.* Philadelphia: Fortress, 1981.

———. *Hear Then the Parable: A Commentary on the Parables of Jesus.* Minneapolis: Fortress, 1989.

Scroggs, Robin. "The Sociological Interpretation of the New Testament: The Present State of Research." *NTS* 26 (1979/80): 164–79.

Sedley, David. "Philosophical Allegiance in the Greco-Roman World." Pp. 97–119 in Miriam T. Griffin and Jonathan Barnes, eds., *Philosophia Togata: Essays on Philosophy and Roman Society.* Oxford: Clarendon; New York: Oxford University Press, 1989.

Seeley, David. "Blessings and Boundaries: Interpretations of Jesus' Death in Q." *Semeia* 55 (1992): 131–46.

———. "Jesus' Death in Q." *NTS* 38 (1992): 222–34.

Seitz, O. J. F. "Love Your Enemies: The Historical Setting of Matthew v. 43f.; Luke vi. 27f." *NTS* 16 (1969): 39–54.

Sellew, Philip H. "Early Collections of Jesus' Words: The Development of Dominical Discourses." Th.D. diss., Harvard Divinity School, 1985.

Shmueli, E. "Modern Hippies and Ancient Cynics: A Comparison of Philosophical and Political Developments and its Lessons." *CHM* 12 (1970): 490–514.

Sidebottom, E. M. "'Reward' in Matthew v. 46, etc." *ExpTim* 67 (1956): 219–20.

Sloterdijk, P. *Kritik der zynischen Vernunft.* 2 vols. Frankfurt am Main: Suhrkamp, 1983.

Smith, Dennis E. "The Historical Jesus at Table." *SBLSP* 28 (1989): 466–86.

Smith, Jonathan Z. "The Social Description of the New Testament," *RSRev* 1 (1975): 19–25.

———. *Map Is Not Territory: Studies in the History of Religions.* Leiden: Brill, 1978.

———. "When the Bough Breaks." Pp. 208–39 in idem, *Map Is Not Territory.*

———. "Adde Parvum Parvo Magnus Acervus Erit." Pp. 240–64 in idem, *Map Is Not Territory.*

———. *Imagining Religion: From Babylon to Jonestown.* Chicago and London: University of Chicago Press, 1982.

———. "In Comparison a Magic Dwells." Pp. 19–35 in idem, *Imagining Religion.*

———. "Sacred Persistence: Toward a Redescription of Canon." Pp. 36–52 in idem, *Imagining Religion.*

———. "The Devil in Mr. Jones." Pp. 102–20 in idem, *Imagining Religion.*

———. *To Take Place: Toward Theory in Ritual.* Chicago and London: University of Chicago Press, 1987.

———. *Drudgery Divine: On the Comparison of Early Christianities and the Religions of Late Antiquity.* Chicago and London: University of Chicago Press, 1990.

———. "Connections." *JAAR* 57 (1990): 1–15.

Smith, Morton. "Palestinian Judaism in the First Century." Pp. 67–81 in Moshe Davis, ed., *Israel: Its Role in Civilization.* New York: Jewish Theological Seminary of America/Harper & Brothers, 1956.

———. *Palestinian Parties and Politics that Shaped the Old Testament.* New York: Columbia University Press, 1971.

———. *Jesus the Magician.* San Francisco: Harper & Row, 1978.

Smith, Robert H. "The Southern Levant in the Hellenistic Period." *Levant* 22 (1990): 123–30.

Spitta, F. "Das Verbot von Schuhen und Stöcken für die Sendboten Jesu." *ZWT* 55 (1914): 39–45.

Sproule, John. "The Problem of the Mustard Seed." *GTJ* 1 (1980): 37–42.

Stallbaum, G., ed. *Eustathius. Commentarii ad Homeri.* 7 vols. Leipzig: Weigel, 1825–30.

Stambaugh, John E., and David L. Balch. *The New Testament in its Social Environment.* Philadelphia: Westminster, 1986.

Steck, Odil Hannes. *Israel und das gewaltsame Geschick der Propheten.* Neukirchen-Vluyn: Neukirchener Verlag, 1967.

Stegemann, Wolfgang. "Wanderradikalismus im Urchristentum? Historische und theologische Auseinandersetzung mit einer interessanten These." Pp. 94–120 in Willy Schottroff and Wolfgang Stegemann, *Der Gott der kleinen Leute.* Munich: Kaiser, 1979. ET: *God of the Lowly: Socio-Historical Interpretation of the Bible.* M. J. O'Connell, trans. Maryknoll, N.Y.: Orbis, 1984.

Steiner, G. "Diogenes' Mouse and the Royal Dog: Conformity in Non-Conformity." *CJ* 72 (1976): 36–46.

Steinhauser, Michael G. *Doppelbildworte in den synoptischen Evangelien.* Würzburg: Echter, 1981.

Sternbach, Leo, ed. *Gnomologium Vaticanum: E Codice Vaticano Graeco 743.* Berlin: de Gruyter, 1963.

Strecker, G. "Die Makarismen der Bergpredigt." *NTS* 17 (1971): 255–75.

———. "Die Antithesen der Bergpredigt (Mt 5:21–48 par)." *ZNW* 69 (1978): 36–72.

Sullivan, Lawrence E. *Icanchu's Drum: An Orientation to Meaning in South American Religions.* New York: Macmillan; London: Collier Macmillan, 1988.

Sutcliffe, E. " 'Not to Resist Evil': Matthew v, 39." *Scripture* 5 (1952): 33–35.

Tannehill, Robert. *The Sword of His Mouth.* Missoula, Mont.: Scholars, 1975.

Taussig, Michael. *Shamanism, Colonialism, and the Wild Man: A Study in Terror and Healing.* Chicago and London: University of Chicago Press, 1987.

———. *The Nervous System.* New York: Routledge, 1992.

———. *Mimesis and Alterity: A Particular History of the Senses.* New York: Routledge, 1993.

Taylor, Vincent. "The Order of Q." *JTS* ns 4 (1953): 27–31. Repr. as pp. 90–94 in idem, *New Testament Essays.* London: Epworth, 1970; Grand Rapids, Mich.: Eerdmans, 1972.

———. "The Original Order of Q." Pp. 246–69 in A. J. B. Higgins, ed., *New Testament Essays: Studies in Memory of T. W. Manson.* Manchester: Manchester University, 1959. Repr. as pp. 95–118 in Taylor, *New Testament Essays.* London: Epworth, 1970; Grand Rapids, Mich.: Eerdmans, 1972.

Theissen, Gerd. "Wanderradikalismus: Literatursoziologische Aspekte der Überlieferung von Worten Jesu im Urchristentum." *ZTK* 70 (1973): 245–71.

———. *Soziologie der Jesusbewegung: Ein Beitrag zur Entstehungsgeschichte des Urchristentums.* Munich: Kaiser, 1977. ET: *Sociology of Early Palestinian Christianity.* Philadelphia: Fortress, 1978.

———. *Studien zur Soziologie des Urchristentums.* Tübingen: Mohr, 1977.

———. "Zur formgeschichtlichen Einordnung der soziologischen Fragestellung." Pp. 3–34 in idem, *Studien zur Soziologie des Urchristentums.*

———. "Gewaltverzicht und Feindesliebe (Mt 5, 38–48; Lc 6, 27–36) und deren sozialgeschichtlicher Hintergrund." Pp. 160–97 in idem, *Studien zur Soziologie des Urchristentums.*

———. "Legitimation und Lebensunterhalt: Ein Beitrag zur Soziologie urchristlicher Missionare." Pp. 201–30 in idem, *Studien zur Soziologie des Urchristentums.*

———. *Social Reality and the Early Christians: Theology, Ethics, and the World of the New Testament.* M. Kohl, trans. Minneapolis: Fortress, 1992.

———. *Lokalkolorit und Zeitgeschichte in den Evangelien.* Freiburg: Universitätsverlag; Göttingen: Vandenhoeck & Ruprecht, 1989. ET: *The Gospels in Context: Social and Political History in the Synoptic Tradition.* Linda M. Maloney, trans. Minneapolis: Fortress, 1991.

———. "Das 'schwankende Rohr' (Mt 11, 7) und die Gründungsmünzen von Tiberias." Pp. 26–44 in idem, *Lokalkolorit und Zeitgeschichte.*

———. "Die Legende vom Tod des Täufers — eine Volksüberlieferung mit Nachbarschafts perspektive?" Pp. 85–102 in idem, *Lokalkolorit und Zeitgeschichte*.

Thilo, Georgius, ed. *Servii grammatici qui feruntur in Vergilii Bucolica et Georgica commentarii*. Hildesheim: Olms, 1961.

Townsend, John T. "Missionary Journeys in Acts and European Missionary Societies." *SBLSP* 24 (1985): 433–37.

Toynbee, A. J. *A Study of History*. London: Milford/Oxford University Press, 1939.

Tuckett, C. M. "A Cynic Q?" *Bib* 10 (1989): 349–76.

Turner, John C., Michael A. Hogg, Penelope J. Oakes, Stephen D. Reicher, and Margaret S. Wetherall. *Rediscovering the Social Group: A Self-Categorization Theory*. Oxford: Blackwell, 1987.

Ueberweg, F., and K. Praechter. *Grundriß der Geschichte der Philosophie des Altertums*. 12th ed. Berlin: Mittler, 1926.

Uro, Risto. *Sheep among the Wolves: A Study on the Mission Instructions of Q*. Helsinki: Suomalainen Tiedeakatemia, 1987.

Vaage, Leif E. "Q: Ethos and Ethics of an Itinerant Intelligence." Ph.D. diss. Claremont, Calif.: The Claremont Graduate School, 1987.

———. "An Archeological Approach to the Work of the Jesus Seminar." Paper presented to the 1988 Spring meeting of the Jesus Seminar, Sonoma, Calif.

———. "The Woes in Q (and Matthew and Luke): Deciphering the Rhetoric of Criticism." *SBLSP* 27 (1988): 582–607.

———. "Q[1] and the Historical Jesus: Some Peculiar Sayings (7:33–34; 9:57–58, 59–60; 14:26–27)." *Forum* 5, no. 2 (1989): 159–76.

———. "Composite Texts and Oral Myths: The Case of the 'Sermon' (6:20b–49)." *SBLSP* 28 (1989): 424–39.

———. "Cynic Epistles (Selections)." Pp. 117–28 in Wimbush, *Ascetic Behaviour*.

———. "The Composition of Q: A Response to Papers by Arland Jacobson, John S. Kloppenborg, and Dieter Lührmann." Paper presented at the 1991 Fall meeting of the Jesus Seminar, Edmonton, Alta.

———. "The Son of Man Sayings in Q: Stratigraphy and Significance." *Semeia* 55 (1992): 103–29.

———. "Like Dogs Barking: Cynic *parresia* and Shameless Asceticism." *Semeia* 57 (1992): 25–39.

———. "Monarchy, Community, Anarchy: The Kingdom of God in Paul and Q." *TJT* 8, no. 1 (1992): 52–69.

———. "Q, Diogenes, and the Historical Jesus: 'Money' and the Contradictions of Subversive Wisdom." Paper presented at the 1992 SBL meeting, San Francisco, Calif.

———. "Q and Cynicism: On Comparison and Social Identity." Forthcoming in R. Piper, *Studies in Q*.

van Unnik, W. C. "Die Motivierung der Feindesliebe in Lukas VI, 32–35." *NovT* 8 (1966): 284–300.

Vargas Llosa, Mario. *El hablador*. Barcelona: Seix Barral, 1987. ET: *The Storyteller*. Helen Lane, trans. New York: Farrar, Strauss, Giroux, 1989.

Vassiliadis, P. "The Original Order of Q: Some Residual Cases." Pp. 379–87 in Delobel, *Logia*.

Vollenweider, Samuel. *Freiheit als neue Schöpfung: Eine Untersuchung zur Eleutheria bei Paulus und in seiner Umwelt*. Göttingen: Vandenhoeck & Ruprecht, 1989.

von Fritz, Kurt. *Quellenuntersuchungen zu Leben und Philosophie des Diogenes von Sinope*. Leipzig, 1926.

von Leutsch, E. L., and F. G. Schneidewin, eds. *Corpus Paroemiographorum Graecorum*. 2 vols. Göttingen: Vandenhoeck und Ruprecht, 1839–51.

Waldmann, M. *Die Feindesliebe in der antiken Welt und im Christenthum*. Vienna: von Mayer, 1902.

Waller, Elizabeth. "The Parable of the Leaven: A Sectarian Teaching and the Inclusion of Women." *USQR* 35 (1979/80): 99–109.

Wanke, Joachim. "Kommentarworte: Älteste Kommentierungen von Herrenworte." *BZ* ns 24 (1980): 208–33.

———. *'Bezugs- und Kommentarworte' in den synoptischen Evangelien: Beobachtungen zur Interpretationsgeschichte der Herrenworte in der vorevangelischen Überlieferung*. Leipzig: St. Benno, 1981.

Weber, C. W. *Diogenes: Die Botschaft aus der Tonne*. Munich: Nymphenburger, 1987.

Wechssler, E. *Hellas im Evangelium*. Berlin: Metzner, 1936.

Weiss, Bernhard. *Das Matthäusevangelium und seine Lucas-Parallelen*. Halle: Waisenhaus, 1876.

———. *Das Matthäus-Evangelium*. Göttingen: Vandenhoeck und Ruprecht, 1898.

———. *Die Evangelien des Markus und Lukas*. Göttingen: Vandenhoeck und Ruprecht, 1901.

Weiss, Johannes. *Die Schriften des Neuen Testaments*. Vol. 1. 2nd ed. Göttingen: Vandenhoeck & Ruprecht, 1907.

Wellhausen, Julius. *Das Evangelium Lucae*. Berlin: Reimer, 1904.

———. *Das Evangelium Matthaei*. Berlin: Reimer, 1904.

Wernle, Paul. *Die synoptische Frage*. Freiburg: Mohr, 1899.

Wheelwright, Philip. *Metaphor and Reality*. Bloomington, Ind.: Indiana University Press, 1962.

White, Hayden. *Metahistory: The Historical Imagination in Nineteenth-Century Europe*. Baltimore: Johns Hopkins University Press, 1973.

Wiater, W. *Komposition als Mittel der Interpretation im lukanischen Doppelwerk*. Bonn: Rheinische Friedrich Wilhelms Universität, 1972.

Wilken, Robert L. *The Christians as the Romans Saw Them*. New Haven and London: Yale University Press, 1984.

Willis, Wendell, ed. *The Kingdom of God in 20th-Century Interpretation*. Peabody, Mass.: Hendrickson, 1987.

Wimbush, Vincent L., ed. *Ascetic Behaviour in Greco-Roman Antiquity: A Sourcebook*. Minneapolis: Fortress, 1990.

Windisch, Hans. "Die Notiz über Tracht und Speise des Täufers Johannes und ihre Entsprechungen in der Jesusüberlieferung." *ZNW* 32 (1933): 65–87.

Wink, Walter. *John the Baptist in the Gospel Tradition*. Cambridge: Cambridge University Press, 1968.

Wyschogrod, Edith. *Saints and Postmodernism: Revisioning Moral Philosophy*. Chicago and London: University of Chicago Press, 1990.

Yinger, J. M. "Contraculture and Subculture." *ASR* 25 (1960): 625–35.

———. *Countercultures: The Promise and the Peril of a World Turned Upside Down*. New York: The Free Press, 1982.

Zahn, T. *Das Evangelium des Lucas*. 4th ed. Leipzig: Deichert, 1920.

———. *Das Evangelium des Matthäus*. 4th ed. Leipzig: Deichert, 1922.

Zeller, Dieter. "Redaktionsprozesse und wechselnder 'Sitz im Leben' beim Q-Material." Pp. 395–409 in Delobel, *Logia*.

———. *Die weisheitliche Mahnsprüche bei den Synoptikern*. Würzburg: Echter Verlag, 1977.

———. *Kommentar zur Logienquelle*. Stuttgart: KBW, 1984.

Zeller, E. *Die Philosophie der Griechen in ihrer geschichtlichen Entwicklung*. 5th ed. Darmstadt: Wissenschaftliche Buchgesellschaft, 1963.

Index of Ancient Names

Index of Modern Names

Index of Ancient Sources

226